METAPHYSICS

METAPHYSICS
THE ELEMENTS

Bruce Aune

University of Minnesota Press, Minneapolis

Published by the University of Minnesota Press,
2037 University Avenue Southeast, Minneapolis MN 55414

Printed in the United States of America
Designed by Gale L. Houdek

Second printing, 1990

Library of Congress Cataloging in Publication Data

Aune, Bruce, 1933–
  Metaphysics: the Elements.
  Bibliography: p.
  Includes index.
  1. Metaphysics. I. Title.
  BD111.A96 1986   110   85–2540
  ISBN 0–8166–1412–1
  ISBN 0–8166–1414–8 (pbk.)

73109

To the memory of
Mary Shaw
and
Grover Maxwell

CONTENTS

PREFACE

IN HIS PREFACE to *Little Dorrit* Dickens wistfully remarked that, having devoted many working hours of two years to his story, he must have been very ill-employed if he could not leave its merits and demerits as a whole to the judgment of his readers. I, too, feel some embarrassment in including a preface—even though I know, from the many revisions I have had to make, that I was very ill-employed during a depressing number of hours that I spent on the manuscript. The difficulty I experienced in preparing the text prompts me to say something about the aims I had and the strategy I adopted.

I had two principal aims in writing this book. The first was somewhat personal: I wanted to work out my views on the main problems of metaphysics. Although I had thought about metaphysical issues for more than twenty years, taught a good many courses on the subject, and had a general idea of the position I wanted to defend, I knew that my views on metaphysical subjects were less determinate than I liked to admit. I felt the need, therefore, of clarifying my views in the only way possible for me—by sitting down at the typewriter, trying to formulate the basic issues as clearly as I could, and then working out solutions that I could defend in detail.

My other aim was pedagogical: I wanted to produce a systematic book on metaphysics that would be understandable by the general reader and that would be useful for students in the sort of middle-level course on metaphysics that I teach, from time to time, at the University of Massachusetts at Amherst. My concern with the general reader was prompted by my late friend and tennis partner Peter Farb, who wrote illuminating books for the general reader on anthropology and natural history, and who urged me to write a book on metaphysics that he could understand. It seemed to me that a book suitable for sophisticated nonphilosophers such as Peter could also be suitable for the students in my metaphysics course.

The students attending my course are advanced undergraduates and beginning graduate students, and I wanted to have available for them a text that deals with the basic issues of metaphysics in a systematic way and that prepares them for advanced work on specialized topics. A systematic text is important, in my view, because many subjects of general interest in metaphysics, such as the mind-body problem or the perplexities about freedom and determinism, can be adequately discussed only if various issues in basic ontology are already settled, or at least understood. Of course, careful thought about complex or derivative issues often requires one to back up and reconsider one's position on fundamentals. Still, an orderly presentation of issues is, as I see it, particularly desirable in a subject like metaphysics. The difficulty I had in writing the book is at least partly owing to the difficulty of presenting issues in an appropriate order.

Metaphysics is an ancient subject on which an enormous amount has been written. To make up one's mind about such subjects as the nature of particulars, the reality of attributes and facts, the possibility of alternative ontologies, and the nature of time, truth, and change (to name just a few), one should be familiar with the jungle of considerations that bear upon them. I have tried to help the reader gain this familiarity by discussing arguments and claims of numerous philosophers, past and present. Having lived through more than one "revolution" in philosophy, I am well aware of the attractions of finding some method that will sweep away all the problems. I now regard such methods as illusory, but the first step in applying them is, in any case, to discover what the problems are. I have done my best to describe these problems, and I offer my solutions for what they are worth.

Although I am far from doctrinaire on matters of philosophical method, I cannot deny that my approach to metaphysics belongs to the tradition of analytic philosophy. The reader will quickly see, for example, that my approach to ontology owes a great deal to Bertrand Russell, but I have tried to show that Russell's approach grows naturally out of Aristotle, the philosopher who wrote the first systematic treatise on metaphysics. Since analytic philosophers influenced by Russell have relied heavily on such technical devices as the so-called existential quantifier, I have made a special effort to come to terms with those devices early in my discussion. The elements of mathematical logic should be as familiar to undergraduates as high school algebra, but they are not—and I have therefore offered clear explanations of the few logical symbols that I introduce.

I have used the manuscript of this book as a text for courses at both the University of Massachusetts and Amherst College, and I have found that the material it contains is not too difficult for able undergraduates. Still, some chapters are harder than others, and instructors using the book in undergraduate courses might want to skip parts of chapters 4 and 7, which are more technical and perhaps less interesting to undergraduates than the others. Chapter 2, on existence, is also somewhat technical, but the material it contains is crucial for understanding the development of metaphysics in our century, and it should not, therefore, be skipped as well. Knowing that some undergraduates are easily confused or intimidated by the sight of a quantifier, I have taken special pains to make chapter 2 as simple and straightforward as humanly possible. I am convinced that, even without the help of a teacher, an undergraduate who is willing to *study* the chapter will find it comprehensible. I feel some regret that the relatively difficult material of chapter 2 had to appear in such an early chapter, but the concept of existence is so important to the principal subjects of metaphyics that I could not reserve it for a later discussion. Undergraduates who find the chapter daunting can perhaps be mollified by the promise that most subsequent chapters will be less technical and more dramatic.

There is one important subject traditionally assigned to metaphysics that I have not discussed: the existence and nature of a God or Supreme Being. I had several reasons for not discussing this subject, two of which are worth mentioning here. The first is that the existence of God is not generally covered in middle-level courses in metaphysics; usually, this topic is discussed in courses on the philosophy of religion, which I do not teach. The other reason is that theology is the part of metaphysics that, owing to my interests and temperament, I am least qualified to discuss. Fortunately, there is no shortage of books on natural theology, and the reader seriously interested in the subject will have no trouble finding books and articles that can be studied in conjunction with the matters I discuss here.

Since I am more interested in being right than in being original, I have taken what help I can from other writers. Although I am an omnivorous reader, I am, unfortunately, a careless taker of notes; consequently, it is often difficult for me to say if I have been influenced by this or that writer in this or that discussion. One philosopher whose influence on my thinking is not difficult to identify is Wilfrid Sellars, but I want to emphasize that, much as I admire his work, I do not share his views on all subjects and I am certainly not (as some people seem to suppose) an apologist for his views. Thus, while I am happy to acknowledge my intellectual debts to writers such as Sellars, I have done my best to think things through in my own way, and I want to be understood as always speaking for myself and not someone else.

I have been unusually fortunate in having friends comment on the manuscript of this book. Gareth Matthews, Cynthia Freeland, and Richard Gale wrote comments on parts of an early version; Murray Kiteley and Vere Chappell not only wrote comments but discussed the whole manuscript with me in an informal miniseminar that the three of us enjoyed in the summer of 1982. Hans Kamp made helpful remarks on the penultimate version of chapter 6, Jay Rosenberg put his finger on errors in chapters 2 and 7; and Ernie La Pore led me to change my views on central parts of chapter 7. The material in chapter 8 was drawn from a Chancellor's lecture that I gave at the University of Massachusetts; a large part of chapter 6 was read at Dartmouth College, the University of Rochester, the University of Sydney, and the annual meeting of the Australasian Philosophical Association; and chapters 2, 3, and 5 provided the basis for lectures I gave in Australia at the universities of La Trobe, NewCastle, New England, and Macquarie. My lectures in Australia resulted from my appointment as a Fulbright lecturer at La Trobe University, and I want to thank Professor Brian Ellis and his colleagues for their help and hospitality during my visit with them.

Except for a memorable year at UCLA when I studied logic with Rudolf Carnap, Donald Kalish, and Richard Montague, my formal education in philosophy took place at the University of Minnesota, and I am particularly pleased that this book is published by the University of Minnesota Press. The dear people to whose memory it is dedicated were teachers and friends at Minnesota.

Mary J. Shaw was my principal undergraduate teacher in philosophy and the director (with Alan Donagan) of my M.A. dissertation. Her annual course in the history of modern philosophy from Thales to Russell, which met five days a week for a full academic year, was an inspiration to me and to generations of students at Minnesota. Grover Maxwell was, in a way, a fellow graduate student, though, having already earned his doctorate in chemistry, he was learning a second academic trade as I learned my first one. I still think of him as my philosophical older brother, and he and Mary Shaw are two of the people who first come to mind when I think of the sonnet in which Shakespeare speaks of "precious friends hid in death's dateless night."

Amherst, Massachusetts

METAPHYSICS

Chapter 1
WHAT IS METAPHYSICS?

METAPHYSICS IS POSSIBLY the most basic but certainly the most controversial part of philosophy. It flourished in ancient Greece and in the universities of medieval Europe, but it lost favor in the Renaissance and, in spite of some lively growth in the late seventeenth century, was seen as more or less disreputable by the tough-minded philosophers of the Enlightenment. A scornful attitude towards metaphysics became particularly emphatic in the early years of our century, when logical positivists regarded the word "metaphysics" as synonymous with "philosophical nonsense" and insisted that metaphysical assertions are "cognitively vacuous."[1] At the present time there is a vigorous revival of interest in metaphysics, but owing to its long neglect, the subject is still badly misunderstood and doubts are still raised about its credentials.

Aristotle and the Origins of Metaphysics

To appreciate the basic issues traditionally included in metaphysics, we must go back to the ancient Greek philosophers who invented the subject. As it happens, the term "metaphysics" was first used to refer to a group of treatises written by Aristotle. Historians of philosophy tell us that the term represents the Greek phrase *ta meta ta physica*, which means "the [books] next after the *Physics*."[2] This phrase was not used by Aristotle himself but by ancient editors as a title for a group of treatises placed after the *Physics* in an early collection of Aristotle's works. Aristotle called the subject he was concerned with in his metaphysics "first philosophy," a subject that had gradually taken shape in the work of his predecessors—specifically, the so-called Presocratics, Socrates, and Plato.

Aristotle tried to impose some order on first philosophy, which had consisted largely of a nest of problems and rival solutions, by breaking it up into three related subjects or "sciences."[3] He called the first subject "the science of being *qua* being," saying that its aim is to investigate the general nature of anything insofar as it has some kind of being or *is* in some sense of the word. His second subject was concerned with the "highest kind of being," which he regarded as appropriate to divinity. His third subject was devoted to the "first principles" that are true of every existing thing and that lie at the basis of all proof or demonstration. Although Aristotle himself had no special names for

3

these three subjects, they eventually came to be known as ontology, theology, and universal science.

To understand why a philosopher as astute as Aristotle might undertake a study as peculiar as "the science of being *qua* being"—and to decide whether such a study really makes sense—we must first appreciate the wide variety of things that can be said to "be" in some sense or other. If these various "beings" are described in a sufficiently general way, we shall find that they can be arranged into fundamentally different kinds or categories and that they are sometimes so different from one another that we can reasonably wonder how they all fit together in the same world or universe. The wonder we might feel here will provide some basis, at least, for the sort of investigation Aristotle had in mind.

Perhaps the least problematic group of things that can be said to be (or exist) includes the familiar objects of everyday experience: people, animals, rocks, pieces of furniture. These things are made of various materials—flesh and blood, wood, granite—and these materials can be said to exist as well. Animals, plants, and rocks exist on the earth, a planet, which is a further, more inclusive object. Apart from planets, there are also moons, stars, comets, and other heavenly bodies. The planets of our solar system belong to our galaxy, the Milky Way; and millions of other galaxies exist in the universe.

A galaxy is an example of a group or aggregate of things. It is commonly said that the things composing an aggregate are more elementary than the aggregate itself. Since, according to current theories of matter, even physical bodies like trees and rocks are aggregates of more elementary things (in a descending order of molecules, atoms, protons, neutrons, and so forth), it is clear that many aggregates are made up of further aggregates. Many philosophers believe that an aggregate can be broken down, at least in thought, into progressively simpler objects and that this process of breaking down (or analyzing) an aggregate into simpler objects must have an end. Every aggregate, they say, is ultimately reducible to nonaggregates, though we may have extreme difficulty in telling, in particular cases, when a genuine nonaggregate is reached. The elementary objects of last year's physics are often found to be aggregates as well.

An aggregate must be distinguished from what mathematicians call a "class" or "set." Aggregates are made up of the more elementary things that constitute it, but classes or sets are said to have members. A striking feature of a class is that it may exist, as mathematicians say, even when it has no members at all. Thus, the class of unicorns exists—there is such a class—in spite of being empty. Since a class can exist without members and does not appear to have a location in space and time, a class is generally said to be an "abstract" entity. In sharp contrast to classes are the familiar objects of everyday experience— sticks, stones, people, and tractors. These familiar objects are commonly regarded as "concrete" entities.

Apart from classes, many sorts of objects are said to be abstract. Take the number three, for instance. This seems very different from anything concrete; it is certainly different from the numerals we use to name or denote it, such as the Arabic numeral "3" or the Roman numeral "III." Actually, there is a sense in which even numerals can be regarded as abstract. Consider the sequence: 5, 5, 2. How many numerals occur (or exist) here? According to one way of counting, there are three numerals in this sequence: two 5's and a 2. But according to another way of counting, there are only two: a 5, which occurs twice, and a 2. If we count the first way, some philosophers will say that we are counting the ''tokens'' occurring in the sequence; if we count the second way, they will say we are counting the ''types'' exemplified there.

As a particular mark on paper, a token would seem to be a concrete object, but a type is not. Some would say that a type such as 5 is a ''kind'' of symbol and that its tokens are ''instances'' of it. However this may be, words and sentences as well as numerals can be viewed as types having numerous tokens. Thus, the type ''the'' has at least two tokens in this very sentence. Quite apart from types, there are many *kinds* of object: there is, for example, the kind Whale, which has fewer instances now than it used to have. In fact, some kinds, such as the Dodo bird, have no instances at all.

According to many philosophers, a particular utterance or series of marks on paper, in addition to being a token of a linguistic type, also ''expresses'' something abstract. If I utter the words ''Snow is white,'' I not only produce a token of the type *Snow is white*, I also express a thought or proposition. If I say ''Snow is white'' and Jacques says ''La neige est blanche,' there is a sense in which we say the same thing about snow. In doing this we are expressing the same ''proposition'' about snow. This proposition is complex, having distinguishable parts, for I express by ''snow'' what Jacques expresses by ''la neige'' and by ''is white'' what he expresses by ''est blanche.'' Generally speaking, the things expressed by substantive parts of a sentence are usually called ''concepts.''

Another class of entities recognized by many philosophers includes attributes or, as they are sometimes called, universals. According to Aristotle, attributes are predicated of primary subjects or things. If we say that a ball is red, we are predicating a quality of the ball that might be called ''redness.'' If two things are red, they have this quality in common. The quality is called a universal because it may be exemplified all over the universe. In addition to qualities belonging to single things, universals include relations, which are exemplified by pairs, triples, and so forth of things. If New York is north of Atlanta and Edinburgh is north of London, both the pairs < New York, Atlanta > and < Edinburgh, London > exemplify the dyadic attribute or relation,—*is north of*—. And if Mary gives a book to John, the triple < Mary, the book, John > exemplifies the triadic relation, —*gives—to*—.

Although universals may be predicated of various subjects, not everything so predicable is happily called a universal. For example, we can say that a house has a particular location in space; but while a location seems abstract in the way that a geometrical point is abstract, it is also an individual thing. Similarly, we can predicate times and dates of various occurrences, and although times and dates are fairly tenuous entities, they are individual things—perhaps abstract individuals. According to Isaac Newton, locations in space are subregions of space, which is an infinitely large individual thing; and instants are points in time, which is another individual thing. Not all philosophers accept this view of space and time, but it is an important view that has to be taken seriously.

Another group of entities that, though singular, have a special status includes such things as smiles, handshakes, and serves. Consider the following assertions:

1. Mary's smile is enchanting.
2. Bill's handshake is limp and feeble.
3. Sarah's serve, in tennis, is powerful and tricky.

Since Mary may have an enchanting smile when she is not smiling, Bill may have a limp handshake when he is not shaking hands, and Sarah may have a tricky serve when she is not playing tennis, the objects ostensibly referred to by the three assertions seem to differ significantly from concrete "possessions" such as mouths, hands, or tennis racquets. Objects of an even more tenuous sort include imaginary and fictional things. If we contemplate a fictional character such as Mr Pickwick, a mythical being such as Pegasus, or even something like the Easter Bunny, we don't seem to be thinking of nothing: evidently, we are thinking of something, but not something that is real. If this is so, however, what we are thinking of must *be* something, and thus have some kind of being.

I have not, in the paragraphs above, described every important category of entity to which philosophers and others have attributed some special kind of being, but I have described a sufficient variety of such categories to add significance to Aristotle's "science" of being *qua* being. In fact, I have singled out a sufficiently varied group of alleged "beings" to make sense of all three subjects that Aristotle included in metaphysics.

Consider the first subject. If such a wide variety of entities as I have described can reasonably be said to *be* in some sense or other, there is no difficulty in understanding why Aristotle might want to speak of a general subject concerned with being as such. The obvious question one wants answered is: "By virtue of what may the various entities I have described be said to 'be,' and how are these beings related to one another?" This question seems perfectly significant and even important. We may not, on reflection, want to agree that everything on the list should be regarded as actually having some kind of being, or reality, but the question I raised nevertheless makes excellent sense. It is certainly not meaningless, as philosophers in our century have sometimes claimed.

As for the second subject, the science of the highest kind of being, we can at least say this. If there is to be a highest kind of being, some kinds of beings must be "higher" than others. This last idea—that some kinds of beings are higher than others—has appealed to many philosophers other than Aristotle. For example, Plato in his *Republic* described a great chain of being whose constituents were more or less real, with abstract objects called "Forms" having the greatest degree of reality and changing things having a lesser degree. But it is not necessary to appeal to the views of famous philosophers to support the levels-of-being idea. If we attend to the variety of "beings" I have already described, we can easily see why a reasonable person might want to say that some of them are higher in reality than others. 'Higher'' might not be the best word here, of course.

Consider the last group on the list of special-status entites, imaginary beings. If we allow that such things have a kind of being, so that when we are thinking of them we are not thinking of nothing, then we should no doubt want to say that their reality is more tenuous, less "perfect," than the reality of a living person or of the chair on which I am sitting. Similarly, if we consider aggregates, we shall probably want to say that the things making them up have a more fundamental kind of being than they do. We shall probably want to say this because, if we are asked "Are there both individual stones and piles of stones?" the obvious answer would be something like this: Well, piles of stones are just stones piled together; if we have taken account of all the individual stones there are and have noted their relations to one another, we shall not have to investigate some further objects of a special kind—namely, piles of stones. A pile of stones, we might add, is nothing over and above the individual stones involved. Although we can single out a pile of stones as a unitary "thing," the pile actually exists only in the sense that its constituent stones exist and are related to one another in an appropriate way.

As for the third subject, finally, we might say the following. If things of more than one of the kinds I have mentioned may truly be said to be, then a universal science of being would stand out as, at least, a possible subject for investigation. As we shall see, Aristotle himself did not believe that a universal science of being was actually possible without qualification, for he did not think that, as he put it, being is a proper genus having various species. Yet the possibility of such a science, or subject, does not seem objectionable in principle. As a matter of fact, later philosophers certainly thought that being is to some extent a genus and that different special sciences were concerned with different kinds of being. For example, Descartes said that the world we know in experience presents us with two irreducibly different kinds of being, mental being and physical being. Thus, even if, like Aristotle, one denies that there is really a single genus, Being or Existence, that includes *all* the things I have described, one might nevertheless reasonably contend that there is at least one genus of being with a few species of beings falling under it. Further, even if one is a materialist holding that there is only one fundamental kind of being, physical being, one might acknowledge that a universal science of this being is still possible. A first principle concerning this kind of being, one presupposed in all thought about it, might be a universal law of causation or, as Aristotle held, a law of contradiction.

Aristotle on Being

I pointed out that Aristotle did not think that there is one supreme genus of being of which the various "beings" I have described are species. To understand important developments in the history of metaphysics—and to have available a useful strategy for dealing with current metaphysical problems—it is important to see, at least in general outline, what Aristotle's approach to the nature of being amounted to.

Aristotle's approach is based on a distinction between senses of words and kinds of things. When we say that Fords and Chevrolets are different kinds of cars, we mean that they are cars in the same sense of the word. If, generally speaking, x and y are not K's in the same sense of the word "K"—as river banks and savings banks are not banks in the same sense of the word—then x and y are not species falling under the genus K. Although Aristotle granted that a good many of the kinds I have described may reasonably and truly be said to *be* (in the case of each we can say that *there is* such a thing), he denied that they can all be said to be in the same sense of the word. Consequently, he denied that they all fall under a common genus, Being. For him, they are not kinds-of-beings; they are beings in, generally speaking, different senses of the word.[4]

If the term "being" or "there is" has different senses, the question arises of how these different senses are related. Is one sense of "being" or "there is" more fundamental than the others? Aristotle's answer is yes. As he put it:[5]

> There are many different senses in which a thing may be said to *be*, but they are related to one central point, one definite kind of thing, and have not merely the epithet "being" in common.
>
> Some things are said to be because they are substances (concrete things), others because they are affections (features, qualities) of substances, others because they are a process toward substance, etc.

Aristotle attempted to clarify his view here by comparing "being" ("to be," "is," 'there are") with the term "healthy." We may speak of a healthy diet as well as of a healthy man or woman, and the term "healthy" does not have the same meaning in both cases. Nevertheless, these two uses of "healthy" are related in meaning, and one is more fundamental than the other. Roughly, to say that a diet is healthy (for a human being) is to say that it is the kind of diet that makes a human being healthy.

If we employ an analogous strategy in dealing with the variety of senses of "exists" (or "there is') we *might* say such things as this:

1. Marble exists $=df$ some substance exists that is made of marble.
2. The color red exists $=df$ some substance exists that is colored red.

Similarly, when we say that a pile of stones exists, we might explain our meaning by saying that certain particular stones exist together in a special spatial relationship. In these cases we should be explaining the meaning of "Marble exists," "The color red exists," and "A pile of stones exists" in relation to the more fundamental existence of certain primary substances.

By "primary substance" Aristotle meant, on the whole, a concrete thing such as a stone, tree, or animal. Such things are substances, Aristotle said, because they are fundamental objects of predication: we can predicate various things of them, but we cannot predicate them of anything else. Also, since they cannot be predicated of anything else, there is a sense, he thought, in which their being is not dependent on the being of something else.[6] Aristotle's metaphysical theory is complicated and not fully worked out, and we shall not explore it further here. Yet if the general strategy of his theory is correct, we should be able to define various senses of "being," "exists," or "there is" in relation to fundamental senses of these words that apply to substances or concrete things. The question whether it is really possible to do this is both interesting and important; if the answer is yes, a good many stubborn metaphysical problems can be resolved. In particular, if we know what we mean when we speak of the being or existence of concrete things, we shall know what we mean when we speak of the being or existence of the more exotic things I have described.

The theoretical advantages of Aristotle's approach can be seen more vividly if we look briefly at an alternative view of existence that has been highly influential in recent years. According to W. V. O. Quine, there is only one satisfactory or intelligible sense to "existence," the one that is expressed in his technical notation by the so-called existential quantifier, "$(\exists x)(\ldots x \ldots)$". The technical statement "$(\exists x)(x$ is red)" is the counterpart to the vernacular "Something is red" or to the semitechnical "There is at least one thing x that is red." If we use this quantifier to express our beliefs about what is or exists, we might say such things as:

$(\exists x)(x$ is human)
$(\exists x)(x$ is a prime number)
$(\exists x)(x$ is an empty set)
$(\exists Q)(Q$ is a quality and Quine has $Q)$.

Yet if all these claims affirm the existence of something in the same sense of the word, the questions immediately arise: "What does existence amount to?" "What exactly can existence be, if it is possessed by human beings, numbers, sets, and qualities?"

In his famous essay "On What There Is" Quine coined the slogan, "to be is to be the value of a variable." He explained the meaning of the slogan by saying this:

> In terms of the categories of traditional grammar, this amounts roughly to saying that to be is to be in the range of reference of a pronoun.[7]

But this explanation, which I shall examine in the next chapter, seems to raise more problems than it solves. We can certainly use pronouns to refer to Mr Pickwick or even to Zeus; yet if we believe that Mr Pickwick and Zeus are merely fictional or imaginary beings, we shall not want to say that their being amounts to "real existence." Many philosophers nowadays say that *there are* possible worlds, and they use the existential quantifier in speaking about them— but they do not suppose that such worlds are existent in the sense of being actual. In saying that "there are" such worlds they are ascribing some kind of being to them, though the sort of being they have in mind is none too clear.[8] An Aristotelian approach to their alleged being—one that relates it to the being of more fundamental realities—might remove the mystery and supply some very welcome clarification. I shall explore this possibility in the next chapter.

The Current Subject of Metaphysics

As I pointed out earlier, the part of metaphysics that is devoted to questions about the being (or existence) of things belonging to fundamentally different categories is known as ontology. I also pointed out that a related part of metaphysics—a part concerned with the so-called first principles applying to what exists—is sometimes called "universal science." Another part of metaphysics, at least as Aristotle described it, is devoted to the "highest" kind of being, which has often been taken to be the existence of some God or Supreme Being. Although these three subjects exhaust the field of metaphysics (or "first philosophy") as it was understood by Aristotle and his followers, other subjects have been pursued under the name of metaphysics since the Renaissance.

A fundamental distinction that has led to a great deal of metaphysical speculation is that between appearance and reality. Since reality is evidently not dependent on the appearance it presents, reality has the feature of "independent being" that Aristotle assigned to primary substance. Yet even opponents of Aristotle have usually considered the investigation of reality as opposed to appearance as a proper subject for metaphysics. This kind of investigation has sometimes resulted in notably bizarre theories of reality, such as Berkeley's theory that the world consists of minds and their ideas, or Schopenhauer's theory that the world is, in essence, pure blind "Will."[9] Such theories, which flourished in the eighteenth and nineteenth centuries, are largely responsible for giving metaphysics the bad name it still has: "baseless speculation."

Although (as I mentioned at the outset) logical positivists have insisted that metaphysical theories of reality are inherently meaningless because they are baseless, or "unverifiable," this extreme view is no longer in vogue. In the past few decades the trend has been to defend a scientific metaphysics, one according to which reality is substantially what the physical sciences say it is. This tendency, though widespread, has notable exceptions: Hilary Putnam and Richard Rorty have argued, in effect, that a metaphysical view based on a distinction between appearance and an underlying reality is seriously defective and that a purely "scientific" metaphysics is really no better than the wilder views of a hundred years ago.[10] The rule is not destroyed by its exceptions, however. Scientific metaphysics is still the prevailing view, at least in English-speaking countries.

Philosophers whose metaphysics is scientific or avowedly nonspeculative disagree, nevertheless, on important ontological issues. One concerns the "being" or existence of abstract entities. Thus, some scientific realists believe that the world consists entirely of particular things while others believe that it also contains universals (qualities and relations) as irreducible components. This ontological disagreement is accompanied by disputes about the reality of time and space, the status of mental events, and the categoreal nature of particular things. Philosophers in the Aristotelian tradition have no doubt that particular things are continuants—objects that persist in time—but others challenge this view, arguing that particulars are really momentary occurrences or "events." According to these other philosophers, the things we naturally regard as persisting in time are really complex systems of temporally related events. In opposition to both these views, some philosophers have held that so-called particulars are not ultimately real: they are actually "bundles" of attributes and thus have the derivative being of a herd or bunch.

A final group of metaphysical problems only loosely related to the distinction between appearance and reality concerns the freedom of the will, as it has traditionally been called. Every change that occurs in nature has, it is said, a cause or sufficient explanation. Since actions and volitions are changes in the world, they too must have some cause. Yet if an action is caused, it cannot be free. Thus, either no actions are free, or some changes do not have causes or sufficient explanations. Not every philosopher accepts this outcome, however. Some hold that freedom of the will (or free action) is possible even if everything has a cause. Philosophers holding this view are called "reconcilers"; those holding the first view are either fatalists or libertarians, depending on whether they admit freedom or not.

As it now exists, the subject of metaphysics can be described by a distinction that became standard in the seventeenth and eighteenth centuries.[11] According to this distinction, metaphysics has two principal divisions: general metaphysics and special metaphysics. General metaphysics includes ontology and most of what has been called universal science; it is concerned, on the whole, with the general nature of reality: with problems about abstract and concrete being, the nature of particulars, the distinction between appearance and reality, and the universal principles holding true of what has fundamental being. Special metaphysics is concerned with certain problems about particular kinds or aspects of being. These special problems are associated with the distinction between the mental and the physical, the possibility of human freedom, the nature of personal identity, the possibility of survival after death, and the existence of God. The traditional subject of what is real as opposed to what is mere appearance is treated in both general and special metaphysics, for some of the issues relevant to it are more general or fundamental than others.

In the chapters to follow I shall discuss in some detail the fundamental issues belonging to both these divisions of the subject. I shall begin with general issues involving the notion of existence or "being," then work my way though traditional problems about abstract and concrete entities, and eventually come to terms with the general conception of a world of objects. After discussion such subjects as time, space, and causation, I shall shift gears and introduce the topics of rival ontologies, metaphysical realism, truth, and meaning. My discussion of these topics will lead me to the subject of appearance and reality, where I shall consider the metaphysical issues that naturally arise from reflection on our knowlege of other minds and the external world. In my final chapter I shall come to terms with problems about the freedom of the will, or metaphysical freedom.

Chapter 2
EXISTENCE

A GOOD WAY TO APPROACH a basic philosophical issue is to consider what a great philosopher has said about it. I have already commented on Aristotle's suggestive strategy for resolving some of the oldest problems about existence (or being), but to understand current thought on the subject it is important to consider the views of a more up-to-date philosopher. The obvious choice here is Bertrand Russell, for contemporary views about existence are deeply indebted to his work. As we shall see, Russell's conception of existence is not entirely satisfactory; but its defects are not widely appreciated and they raise issues of great importance. At the end of the chapter I shall develop a conception of existence that improves upon Russell's conception and comes to terms with what I call "the new problem of existence."

Existence and Definite Descriptions

Some of Russell's most interesting remarks on existence can be found in his lectures on logical atomism, which he gave in 1918. One remark, which introduces a very important new idea, places him in the ontological tradition begun by Aristotle:

> There are no classes really in the physical world. The particulars are there, but not the classes. If you say "There is a universe," that meaning of "there is" will be quite different from the meaning in which you say "There is a particular," which means that the propositional function "x is a particular" is sometimes true.[1]

Russell's conception of a particular is not the same as Aristotle's conception of a primary substance, but his remark makes it clear that, like Aristotle, he assigned different meanings to various uses of "there is" and held that in one use (a primary one, as we shall see) these words apply to particular things that "are" *in the world.*

The chief respect in which Russell's approach to existence is historically novel is that it involves a special analysis of the primary use of "there is" applicable to particulars. As the quotation shows, this special analysis is based on the notion of a propositional function. Although the quotation does not indicate it, Russell related his special analysis of "there is" to a general strategy for dealing with ostensible "things" (numbers, classes) that do not exist in the primary sense. This general strategy is Aristotelian in spirit but technically advanced—and it has been as important for the development of metaphysics in our century as Russell's analysis of "there is." Both subjects are best understood, I believe, in relation to Russell's famous theory of definite descriptions, and I propose to begin my discussion of his views on existence by outlining the elements of this famous theory.

Russell's theory of descriptions was motivated, in part, by a semantical problem—one that concerns the proper interpretation of sentences containing descriptive phrases that apparently refer to nonexistent things.[2] Russell's favorite example of such a sentence was "The present king of France is bald." The problem with this sentence is that, although it makes perfectly good sense, it does not say anything true or false about its apparent subject, for that subject does not exist. According to the natural interpretation of subject-predicate sentences, such a sentence is true just when its predicate truly describes the thing denoted by its subject, and it is false just when the predicate falsely describes that subject. Yet if this were a correct account of such sentences, Russell's example could neither be true nor false. This is problematic because the law of the excluded middle (as Russell understood it) declares that every meaningful sentence is either true or false—and Russell's sentence is certainly meaningful. How, then, are we to understand it, if the natural interpretation of a subject-predicate sentence cannot apply to it?

Russell's answer was to say that the term "the present king of France" and others like it differ from truly referential expressions (such as proper names) in being "incomplete symbols': they have a significance in the context of a sentence, but their significance does not consist in standing for anything.[3] Their significance can be conveyed, Russell thought, by a *contextual definition*—by a definition, that is, of the sentences in which they occur. When we say that the present king of France is bald, we are really saying something both complex and general. In fact, we are tacitly saying three things. First, we are saying that at least one thing is a present king of France. Second, we are saying that at most one thing is a present king of France. Finally, we are saying that whatever is a king of France is bald. The complexity of our remark is owing to the fact that we are tacitly saying three things, and its generality is owing to the fact that no one of these things makes any reference to a particular individual.

Russell presented his analysis of definite descriptions, as he called them, in the technical notation of *Principia Mathematica*, a three-volume work that he wrote with A. N. Whitehead.[4] To clarify his treatment of definite descriptions in its full generality and to pave the way for a discussion of his views on existence, I must explain, in a provisional way, two of his special symbols: the so-called universal and existential quantifiers.

If we were discussing the basic laws of arithmetic, we might express the law of commutation for addition by saying this:

$$(a + b) = (b + a), \text{ for all } a \text{ and } b.$$

We should include the clause "for all a and b" to indicate that the formula "$(a + b) = (b + a)$" holds true for all numbers a and b: the formula is, as Russell said, "always true." Russell used the symbol "(a)" to say "for all a," and this symbol is known as a universal quantifier. Russell attached this symbol, moreover, to the beginning of the formula it quantifies; thus, he would have expressed the law above by a formula having two universal quantifiers:

$$(a)(b)((a + b) = (b + a))$$

Now consider another thing we might say in the context of discussing arithmetic: Every number has a successor. A slightly more explicit way of saying this would be to say that, for every number a, there is a number b that is the successor of a. Like Quine, whom I mentioned in the last chapter, Russell used the symbol "(Eb)" to say "There is a b"; he would therefore have expressed the statement that every number has a successor by the formula:

$$(a)(\text{if } a \text{ is a number, then } (\exists b)(b \text{ is a number and } b = \text{the successor of } a))$$

Russell called a formula containing an unquantified or "free" variable a "propositional function," and the formula "$y = $ the successor of 3" would be such a function. When Russell gave his lectures on logical atomism, he was in the habit of saying that the proposition "$(\exists y)(y = \text{the successor of } 3)$" means that the propositional function "$y = $ the successor of 3" is sometimes true, or true for at least one value of the variable "y."[5]

With this technical symbolism in hand, we can now return to Russell's theory of descriptions. According to that theory, the sentence "The present king of France is bald" has a meaning that can be expressed by the formula:

$$(\exists x)(x \text{ is a present king of France and } (y)(\text{if } y \text{ is a present king of France}$$
$$\text{then } y = x) \text{ and } x \text{ is bald}).$$

According to the explanation I have given, this formula means that at least one thing x is a present king of France and if, for any y, y is a present king of France, then $y = x$, and x is bald. Since, as we know, there is no present king of France, the formula above must be false, for it asserts, in part, that there is at least one thing that is a present king of France. Also, since Russell's example, "The present king of France is bald," is, by definition, *equivalent* to the formula given above, we can understand how Russell's example can be both meaningful and false even though there is no present king of France for it to be about or refer to.

It is important to realize that, strictly speaking, Russell's theory does not provide definitions for descriptive phrases such as "the present king of France." What it provides, or shows us how to provide, are definitions for *sentences* in which such phrases occur. Russell called such definitions "contextual definitions," for they give the meaning of a definite description as it occurs in the context of a sentence or formula. He said, not very happily, that such descriptions "have meaning" only in the context of a sentence or formula, but his considered view was that they should not be understood as denoting expressions that, taken by themselves, refer to some person or thing. They are, he said, "incomplete symbols" that contribute to the referential content of sentences in which they occur. The formula in the last paragraph refers not to the present king of France (there is no such person) but to the entire universe, as it were: It says that there is, in the universe, exactly one thing that is both a king of France and bald. If, unlike Russell, we think of so-called definite descriptions as denoting expressions when considered solely by themselves, we shall misunderstand the significance of many sentences in which they occur and be tempted to believe that the supposed referents of such expressions must, if they do not actually exist, have some kind of being anyway.[6]

I said that Russell's theory of descriptions does not provide a means of defining definite descriptions themselves but, rather, shows us how to define sentences in which definite descriptions occur. As it happens, Russell's theory is more complicated than I have thus far indicated, for I have merely shown how to define certain sentences—fairly simple ones—in which definite descriptions occur. In more complicated sentences the task of constructing the appropriate definitions is also more complicated, but the metaphysical significance of Russell's theory remains exactly the same.

As an example of a more complicated sentence, consider "It is false that the present king of France is bald." It is easy to see that this sentence is ambiguous. A moment's thought tells us that the sentence can mean either 1 or 2:

1. It is false that there is exactly one bald present king of France.
2. There is exactly one present king of France, and it is false that he is bald.

According to Russell's terminology, the description in 1 has primary occurrence whereas in 2 it has secondary occurrence.[7] However this may be, the sentences 1 and 2 are not equivalent; in fact, 1 is true and 2 is false.

For our purposes, the moral to draw from this last example is that Russell's theory cannot be automatically applied to sentences in the vernacular. When we are faced with a complex sentence containing a definite description, we must always consider how, in view of the context, the sentence is to be read or interpreted. If we understand the strategy of Russell's theory, we can find an appropriate interpretation by considering how the generality he associated with a definite description should be reflected in our interpretation. In doing this, we must pay careful attention to the conditions under which the sentence containing the definite description is reasonably considered true and false; we should not just consider the thing or things the speaker is ostensibly referring to.[8]

Logical Fictions and Logical Constructions

If we recall some of the supposed kinds of beings that philosophers have been tempted to accept as real, we can see right away that Russell's theory is highly illuminating, metaphysically. Instead of supposing that the present king of France must have some kind of being because, though "he" does not actually exist, a person who says or thinks "The present king of France is bald" is thinking about something rather than nothing, we can acknowledge that such a person is saying or thinking, falsely, that *there is* a certain king in the world. His speech or thought is about something rather than nothing, but the something is not a king with a tenuous kind of being; it is the world or the universe as a whole. A related approach can be taken to related problems that have been posed in jokes or in the history of philosophy. I shall describe one such joke and then consider a problem posed by Parmenides, an ancient Greek philosopher who concluded that reality is an indivisible, unchanging whole that has neither a beginning nor an end.

The joke is from Lewis Carroll's *Through the Looking-Glass*. The White King tells Alice that his two messengers have gone to town, and he asks her to look along the road to see if they are still there. Alice answers, "I see nobody on the road." To this the King replies:

> I only wish that *I* had such eyes. . . . To be able to see Nobody!
> And at that distance too! Why, it's as much as *I* can do to see real
> people, by this light.[9]

Here the King makes a mistake with the word "nobody" that is similar to the mistake some have made with terms like "the present king of France." If the term "nobody" has a reference or denotation, it is Nobody, whom Alice is supposed to see on the road. This Nobody is as hard to see as the present king of France; evidently, he has a shadowy kind of being. But, of course, when Alice says she sees nobody on the road, she is not using the term "nobody" to refer to something. She uses it as part of a sentence whose meaning is equivalent to "It's false that I see somebody on the road." We thus diagnose the White King's blunder by the same general strategy that Russell used to pinpoint the blunder of supposing that one who thinks that the present king of France is bald must be thinking of some mysterious king who, though he does not exist, has some kind of being anyway. The general strategy, to repeat, is that of finding a suitable interpretation (or "contextual definition") for the problematic word or phrase—an interpretation that does not refer to a nonexistent "being."

Unlike the White King, Parmenides was convinced that "whatever is, is; and whatever is not, is not." Since "nothing *is not*"—since there is no nothing—the word "nothing" does not refer to anything, and one who uses it, as in saying "There is nothing of that sort," does not, strictly speaking, make sense. According to Parmenides, "what is not can neither be said nor thought.[10] Parmenides's interpretation of such negative terms as "what is not" and "nothing" led him to assert that reality is, among other things, eternal and unchanging. To say that it changes would be to imply that it is one thing and then not that thing but something else. But to be *not a certain thing* is to be *not . . .* , and there is no not (or *nonbeing*) for a thing to be; in fact, to speak of a thing *not being . . .* is not to say anything significant. Consequently, saying that the world changes is saying something false or meaningless; we must accept the contrary view, which is hard to express in a meaningful way, that the world is "unchanging." For this true assertion to be meaningful, our word "unchanging" cannot mean "not changing"; it must mean something positive. Perhaps "static" will do.

Although Parmenides did not make the White King's mistake of supposing that nobody or, more generally, nothing might exist or, as philosophers would later say, have some kind of being, he did make the White King's mistake of supposing that "nobody" or "nothing" were denoting expressions. The truth is that these terms are what medieval philosophers called "syncategorematic expressions"; like Russell's definite descriptions, they contribute to the meaning of a sentence without standing for something themselves. To say that a changing thing must at one time be a certain way (brown, say) and not be that way at a later time is to affirm that it was that way at one time and to deny that it is that way at a later time. To deny something is implicitly to affirm that something is false, but affirming that something is false does not amount to referring to a mysterious nonbeing. One might say as a general matter that there is nothing in the significant use of negative terms that requires us to acknowledge the fundamental existence, or "being," of negative realities.

The solutions to the problems posed by the White King and Parmenides do not require Russell's theory of descriptions, but they do involve the general strategy involved in Russell's theory. According to Russell, many significant statements appear to refer to things of rather mysterious kinds, and the aim of his theory was to show how some of these statements—those containing definite descriptions—can be transformed into equivalent statements that do not refer to mysterious entities. By virtue of the logical transformations he described, he spoke of the mysterious (or at least problematic) entities supposedly referred to by descriptive phrases as "logical fictions." It does not sound natural to speak of the present king of France as a *logical* fiction,[11] but the epithet is appropriate for the supposed objects of many other descriptive phrases.

Consider the following assertion, which might actually be true:

The average American plumber has 2.5 children and an annual income of $20,000.00.

If "average" here means "typical," then the assertion is false, for a typical person may be an actual person, and no actual person could have 2.5 children. But remarks about average things of various sorts are generally understood in a different way. Specifically, the statement above is not used to refer to a real person, or to one having some shadowy kind of being. As one would normally use it, one would be saying something fairly complicated about American plumbers generally. One would be saying that the total number of children of American plumbers divided by the total number of American plumbers is 2.5 and that the total annual earnings of American plumbers divided by the total number of American plumbers equals $20,000.00. This complex assertion is not, therefore, about any individual plumber, whether abstract or concrete. It is a complex assertion about all American plumbers, all their children, and their total income.

Even though we know full well what the statement above actually means, we are sometimes willing to say that it is a statement "about" the average plumber. When we say this, we are not speaking strictly; we are speaking very loosely indeed. But, speaking loosely, we can reasonably say that the average plumber is a logical or, better, a mathematical fiction. Since Russell held, as we shall see, that mathematical statements are really logical statements, he would have urged that every mathematical fiction is a logical fiction. Another expression that Russell often used interchangeably with "logical fiction" is "logical construction."

When Russell wrote about logical constructions, he was generally concerned to show that significant statements apparently about a given subject matter are equivalent to, and can be replaced by, statements about (or apparently about) another subject matter. I added the qualification "apparently about" in my last clause because Russell sometimes proceeded to "reduce" the apparent subject matter of one class of assertions to another subject matter, and then "reduced" this second subject matter to a third one. For example, he argued in *Principia Mathematica* that statements about rational, real, and complex numbers are equivalent to, and can be replaced by, statements about the whole numbers—that is, 1, 2, 3, 4, and so on. He then argued that statements about the whole numbers are euqivalent to, and can be replaced by, statements about classes. As a final step, he argued that statements about classes are equivalent to statements about attributes.

In 1912, when he wrote his little classic *The Problems* of *Philosophy*,[12] he thought that the only things having ultimate reality are particulars and attributes, meaning by "attributes" qualities and relations. When, in 1918, he gave his lectures on logical atomism, he said that only "particulars" have fundamental existence. His ultimate reason for these reductive claims was that, in his opinion, statements apparently about entities of other kinds are contextually definable by statements about particulars and attributes, or about particulars only. Thus, in his considered opinion, the objects of all meaningful reference are, in the end, particulars and universals, or (as he held in 1918) just particulars. For him, all other objects of apparent reference are logical fictions or logical constructions.

Russell on Numbers and Classses

In this section I shall describe some of the details of Russell's attempt to reduce numbers to classes and then classes to attributes. My aim is not to dwell on technicalities but to give the reader a better sense of Russell's procedure in reducing one subject matter to another. For this reason, the only numbers I shall discuss are the so-called natural numbers, that is, 1, 2, 3, 4, . . .

If we have convinced ourselves, as we should, that numbers are different from the numerals we use to refer to them, such as the Arabic numeral "2" and the Roman numeral "II," we might naturally ask, "What can numbers possibly be?" A very elementary observation about numbers is that they are closely related to various classes of things. The number 2, for example, is closely related to all the couples that exist. Every couple is a twosome, and a twosome seems different from a threesome, or trio, by virtue of its special relation to the number 2. But how is this special relation to be understood? Plato evidently thought that the number 2 is an independently existing object in which all couples "participate": they are couples because of this participation. Unfortunately, Plato never could give a satisfactory account of what participation is, nor could he give a satisfactory explanation of how we could come to know about a number, or of what we could actually mean in saying that such a thing exists. Russell's strategy was to avoid such puzzling questions by arguing that we could, in effect, identify the number 2 with the class of all couples. Since the notion of a couple can be explained in purely logical terms without using any numerical notions—specifically, as a class having a member x and a member y not identical with x and having no other members—the definition of the number 2 as the class of all couples is not circular: we are not referring to the number in the very process of defining the class.

To show that all significant statements apparently about numbers are equivalent to statements about classes, Russell had to do more than merely identify numbers with corresponding classes of couples, triples, quadruples, and so on. He also had to show that what we regard as the relationships (or "relations") between numbers can be understood, roughly, as relations between classes. His demonstration of this matter is too technical to be considered here, but one point must be kept firmly in mind anyway: it is that in reducing numbers to classes, Russell was reducing one whole subject matter (arithmetic) to a more fundamental subject matter (the theory of classes). What he (along with Whitehead) showed in *Principia Mathematica* is that every mathematically significant statement about numbers is equivalent to a corresponding statement wholly about classes. As far as mathematics is concerned, he therefore felt justified in contending that mathematics may reasonably be viewed as a part of the metaphysically more fundamental theory of classes. The mathematical fact, for example, that the number 2 has a successor in the field of natural numbers can be interpreted, according to Russell, as the set-theoretical fact that the set of all couples is related in a certain way to another set with an appropriate structure.

Russell described the fine points of his reduction of mathematics to logic (or the theory of classes) in his *Introduction to Mathematical Philosophy*,[13] and I shall not try to relate them here. But I do want to say something about various nonmathematical facts about numbers, which Russell did not comment on. Actually, it is disputable whether there really are nonmathematical facts about numbers, but some would say that the following assertion expresses such a fact: "Hegel's favorite number was 3." If we allow that we really have a fact here, we might suppose that Russell's reductive strategy does nothing to show that this fact is really about Hegel and the class of triples rather than Hegel and an irreducible number 3. Yet Russell has an effective reply. However Hegel might have enjoyed a certain number, or taken pleasure in thinking about it, even he would have had to acknowledge that the nature of the number itself is very mysterious: at best, it seems to be merely an abstract "thing" with certain mathematical properties. But if these mathematical properties can reasonably be interpreted as properties of classes, the number Hegel enjoyed thinking about can reasonably be understood as a class itself—a very abstract class of classes, it is true, but a thing having an appropriate structure nevertheless.[14]

If, following Russell, we regard numbers as logical fictions in the sense that significant statements "about" them can reasonably be interpreted as statements about classes, then we can work out relatively satisfactory answers to metaphysical questions concerning numbers. Thus, if asked what it is for numbers to exist, or what it means to say that they exist, we can reply that statements affirming them to exist are really shorthand for corresponding statements affirming certain classes to exist. These answers will be *relatively* satisfactory because they will be satisfactory *if* we know what we are talking about when we speak of classes and affirm their existence.

It seemed clear to Russell, however, that if classes are viewed as irreducible entities, we cannot really claim to know what we are talking about when we speak of their existence and relations to other things. Many philosophers and mathematicians have urged that there is nothing problematic about classes, but they seem to mistake clarity about some features of classes with clarity about their ontological status. As far as the latter is concerned, even present-day logicians seem clear on just two fundamental points. One concerns the so-called identity conditions for classes: we can say that a class A is identical with a class B just when the members of A are the same as the members of B. The other point concerns what might be called the construction of new classes out of old ones. If we assume the existence of certain basic classes, we can appeal to widely accepted and well-understood axioms that justify us in speaking of certain additional classes. Thus, if A and B are classes, we can say that the class that is the union of A and B also exists, that the intersection of A and B exists, that the set of subsets in A and B also exists, and so on. But none of this information, which belongs to the mathematical theory of classes, tells us anything about what it means to say that a class exists in the first place.

To avoid basic metaphysical unclarity about classes, Russell proceeded to reduce them to attributes, that is, to properties and relations. Since he was convinced that we are directly "acquainted" with attributes, he had no doubt that they are real—in fact, the "particulars" he regarded as basic realities in 1918 were nothing more, as we shall see, than attribute-instances (such as *the redness here*) or bundles of such instances. Since he developed a method of translating statements ostensibly about classes into statements about attributes, he thought that Ockham's Razor—the maxim requiring us not to multiply entities beyond necessity in constructing our theories—went a long way toward justifying a reduction of the theory of classes to the theory of attributes.

As in his theory of descriptions, the translations Russell offered were based on contextual definitions. To achieve the proper results, these definitions had to be constructed with due attention to details. The simplest sentences in which an apparent reference to a class occurs are of the form:

y is a member of the class of F's.

An example of such a sentence is "John is a member of the class of animals." Although Russell offered (for technical reasons) a general rule according to which this sentence should be translated as

> John has some attribute *G* that is possessed by all and only those things that have the attribute of being an animal,

it is possible to adopt the simpler translation, "John is an animal"; Russell's more complicated translation is not actually necessary.[15]

An example of a more complicated statement concerning classes is this:

1. The class of *F*'s is included in the class of *G*'s.

In the theory of classes the statement 1 is an abbreviation of the longer statement:

2. For any *y*, *y* is a member of the class of *F*'s only if *y* is a member of the class of *G*'s.)

Since the simple formula "*y* is a member of the class of *F*'s" can be rewritten as "*y* is an *F*," the statement 2 can be rewritten without reference to classes as follows:

3. For all *y*, *y* is an *F* only if *y* is a *G*.

Put in familiar language, the statement about classes "The class of men is included in the class of animals" can be transformed into the equivalent statement "Anything that is a man is also an animal." Russell would interpret this last statement as meaning "A thing has the attribute of being a man only if it has the attribute of being an animal."

Although the statements about classes that one might encounter in a book on mathematics may have a very complicated structure, they can all be expressed, Russell said, in a form that allows us to find an equivalent statement composed of expressions that refer only to particulars and attributes. For this reason we can say, according to Russell, that classes are really logical fictions: statements apparently referring to them can be interpreted as, or explicitly translated into, statements about particulars and attributes.

Ontological Reductionism

In holding that all categories of being are reducible to universals and particulars—or, as in his lectures on logical atomism, to "particulars" only—Russell was a paradigm instance of a philosophical reductionist. Reductionism now has something of a bad name in philosophy, and its prevalence in our century is often deplored. Since I shall be defending a reductionist metaphysics in this book, I want to offer some general remarks about the subject.

As I see it, the current distrust of reductionism is a natural response to some of the extreme and implausible reductionist theories that were fashionable just a few decades ago. As the result, partly, of Russell's and Whitehead's apparent success in reducing mathematics to logic, many philosophers attempted to rule out, as mere logical fictions, all sorts of things whose fundamental reality seems undeniable. Two striking examples of their misguided efforts are phenomenalism and analytical behaviorism. These theories were motivated by a common epistemological difficulty, which I shall discuss fully in chapter 8: the difficulty of understanding how, given accepted principles of inductive (or experimental) inference, we could possibly verify the existence of entities that are, in principle, unobservable. Phenomenalists held that the only objects we can directly experience are "sense data"—these being, roughly, objects of subjective experience. Finding in such objects no rational basis for inferring an external cause and wishing to avoid a skeptical view of the external world, phenomenalists attempted to reduce true statements ostensibly about external objects such as trees and flowers to statements about actual and possible sense data. Analytical behaviorists, on the other hand, convinced that we do have observational knowledge of such external objects, did not see how we could possibly have knowledge of the alleged subjective experiences or mental states of others. They therefore attempted to reduce true statements ostensibly about such experiences to statements about observable behavior.

The failure of these reductionist programs, which were as extreme as they were implausible, does not, of course, demonstrate the error of every reductionist theory. In particular, it does not demonstrate the error of the ontological reductionism that I see in Russell and have traced back to Aristotle. The aim of this sort of reductionism is, in fact, very different from the aim of the phenomenalist and the analytical behaviorist. As I have explained, phenomenalism and analytical behaviorism were developed in the effort to avoid a problem about verification—to show how statements ostensibly about unobservable entities could possibly be known to be true. But the aim of ontological reductionism is significantly different: it is to show what we can *mean* in saying that entities of certain categories exist or have being. Tacitly adopting the classical strategy of Aristotle, the ontological reductionist is concerned to distinguish ultimate or fundamental existents from derivative ones and to argue that the "existence" or being of the latter is to be understood in relation to the fundamental existence of the former.

A fresh example may be helpful here. Consider corporations. Obviously, *there are* such things; they exist in some sense or other. But what sense is this? If we investigate the conditions under which a corporation can truly be said to exist, we shall find that they "exist" just when (a) certain legal actions have taken place and (b) certain other legal actions have not taken place. Actions of the first sort can be described as "actions of forming a corporation"; they consist in drawing up and recording certain documents. Actions of the second sort can be described as "actions of dissolving a corporation." Generally speaking, a corporation can be said to exist just when it has been formed but not dissolved. Given this, we might say that a corporation exists only in the sense that certain legal actions have, and others have not, been performed. If this is right, the existence of a corporation, though perfectly genuine in its way, is derivative: it is based on, or understandable in relation to, the more fundamental existence of human beings and their legal institutions—the latter also having a derivative existence understandable in relation to the existence of human beings who, as Jean Jacques Rousseau put it, express their general will in various ways.

Corporations are legal persons and, thus, legal or logical fictions. But to call them fictions is not to say that they do not exist in any sense at all. They do exist—derivatively, as we have seen. The fact that their existence is derivative does not mean that they are imaginary, unimportant, or not worth thinking about. They simply do not exist in the fundamental sense in which people exist.

The ontological reductionist, such as Aristotle and, as I have interpreted him, Russell, argues that the existence of entities of a certain category (or of a small number of categories) is fundamental and that the being of other ostensible entities is derivative or, technically speaking, reducible to entities of the fundamental sort. Russell, I must admit, was not as clear about the aims of his reductionism as one could wish: he often wrote as if he thought that only fundamental entities had any being (or reality) at all. But this attitude does not represent Russell's best thinking on ontological matters. In less reckless moments he would never have denied that, in some sense, *there are* herds of cattle, gaggles of geese, or pairs of twins—nor would he have denied that, in some sense, *there are* prime numbers. He would have insisted, however, that these "entities" are not fundamentally real: in his considered opinion fundamental existents are invariably "particulars" or, as he held in his *Problems of Philosophy*, particulars and universals.

As we shall see in chapter 4, some contemporary philosophers, on grounds other than a wholesale rejection of reductionism, will argue that Russell's ontology is not entirely, or even largely, satisfactory. Their arguments concern specific categories of entities such as possibilities, states of affairs, and even numbers. Although I shall examine such arguments in due course, I want to emphasize here that only specific arguments supporting the fundamental existence of various objects should be taken seriously in sober discussions of ontology. Wholesale rejections of reductionism may accord with some philosophical trend or fashion, but they have no place in any careful treatment of the problems of ontology.[16]

Russell on Fundamental Existence

Having explained Russell's treatment of derivative objects, I can now consider his account of existence in the primary sense. As I mentioned at the beginning of the chapter, Russell claimed that such existence is really "a property of propositional functions," not a property of such things as you or I. This way of stating his view sounds odd or paradoxical, but his basic idea is now very widely accepted. The key point is that statements affirming the existence of something are best expressed by the use of quantifiers and propositional functions, not by the use of the predicate "exists."

In ordinary life we often say such things as "Homer actually existed" and "Lions exist," but the meaning of what we say is really different, Russell thought, from what we might initially suppose. Take "Lions exist," for example. According to Russell, this means that there is at least one lion, an idea expressed in his logical symbolism by "$(\exists x)(x$ is a lion)." If we expressed "Lions exist" by "All lions exist," we should be saying something strictly hypothetical—namely, "If something is a lion, it exists." This hypothetical statement would be true, in Russell's opinion, but it would be necessarily true and not a mere matter of fact, as it should be. The parallel statement "Unicorns exist" is clearly false, but if it were interpreted hypothetically as "If something is a unicorn, it exists," we should have to count it as true. When we say that unicorns exist, we mean that there are unicorns; and this statement, which Russell would express by "$(\exists x)(x$ is a unicorn)," is clearly false.

As a general matter, then, when we say something of the form "*K*'s exist" (where "*K*" is a general term like "lions" or "unicorns") we are saying something that has the sense of "$(\exists x)(x$ is a *K*)." Since the quantifier, "$(\exists x)$," expresses existence, and since this quantifier is conjoined to a propositional function, "*x* is a *K*," Russell thought it appropriate to say that our statement affirms the existence of a propositional function. This is a confusing way of speaking, but Russell's idea is perfectly clear: to say "Lions exist" is to convey the information that *there is* at least one lion. Russell's technical way of saying this is to say "$(\exists x)(x$ is a lion)."

Now consider the statement "Homer existed." If someone who asserts this means by "Homer" (or regards the name as equivalent to) "the blind epic poet who composed the *Iliad* and the *Odyssey*," he is using "Homer" as a disguised definite description. As I have emphasized, Russell thought that definite descriptions are incomplete symbols that have a determinate meaning only in the context of a sentence. According to him, the sentence "The author of the *Iliad* and the *Odyssey* existed" is, by definition, equivalent to the general statement, "There was exactly one author of the *Iliad* and the *Odyssey*." If we ignore the complications required by the past tense, we can formulate this general statement in Russell's technical language by an assertion beginning with an existential quantifier:

$(\exists x)(x$ is an author of the *Iliad* and the *Odyssey* & (y)(if y is an author of the *Iliad* and the *Odyssey*, then $y = x$)).

Thus, the vernacular existence statement "Homer existed" actually has the sense, if "Homer" is a disguised definite description, of an existentially quantified statement. In this respect it is like "Lions exist." An ordinary existence statement is again equivalent to one beginning with an existential quantifier.

Suppose, however, that "Homer" is not used as a disguised definite description, but as a true proper name. Wouldn't the sentence "Homer existed" then be a true existence statement attributing the property of past existence to the man Homer? Russell's answer was no.[17] According to him, a genuine proper name has significance only in the sense of standing for a certain thing. If "Homer" were such a name, and if the predicate "existed" stood for the property of existence, then the statement "Homer did not exist" would be a "contradiction" and thus would not provide a significant contrast to "Homer existed." But every significant sentence must have a significant contrast.[18] Consequently,

"Homer exists" (or "Homer existed," since we are disregarding the complications introduced by the past tense) would not be significant under this reading. As far as Russell was concerned, therefore, the predicate "exists" makes genuine logical sense only when it is joined to a general term such as "lions" or a definite description such as "the author of the *Odyssey*." When it is joined to a true proper name, the result, for him, is logical nonsense. If we want to affirm the existence of something denoted by a genuinely proper name, we must either describe it in some way, so that we can obtain an appropriate existentially quantified statement, or perhaps say (as Russell sometimes did) that it, or its proper name, is a value of the variable "x" in the propositional function "x is a particular." In either case we are dealing with a propositional function rather than a sentence containing the predicate "exists."

These considerations give the basis for Russell's claim that "existence is a property of a propositional function"—a claim better expressed by saying that significant existence statements are equivalent to formulas bound by an existential quantifier. Russell had interesting things to say about the meaning of such formulas, but before considering his remarks on this subject, I want to mention two important criticisms of his view as I have developed it in this section. Both criticisms are concerned with his claims about proper names.

According to Russell, almost every proper name one can think of is not a genuine or, as he preferred to say, a "logically proper" name. In his view only certain uses of "this" and "that" are logically proper names because only certain uses of these words denote objects of one's immediate attention.[19] A name like "Ronald Reagan" or even "Bertrand Russell" is really a disguised description of some kind. This idea has been vigorously criticized in recent years, but in defense of Russell we should say that his view of what actually counts as a proper name is based very largely on his conception of what we can directly experience—and this conception is separable from his basic interpretation of existence statements. For reasons that we shall discuss in a later chapter, Russell thought that only momentary sense data are presented to our consciousness and that ordinary objects such as trees and animals must be regarded as highly complex entities—strictly speaking, logical constructions. But we do not have to accept this view to appreciate, or even accept, Russell's principal contributions to ontology. If we think that we are actually aware of animals, trees, and human beings, we can insist that the names we give them are genuine or logically proper names and not disguised descriptions. The decision we make on this matter is irrelevant to our assessment of Russell's basic interpretation of existence statements.

The second criticism I wish to discuss concerns Russell's view that a statement such as "Homer exists" is actually meaningless if "Homer" is a logically proper name. The criticism purports to demonstrate an error in Russell's argument for this view. I think the criticism is sound. The criticism is that even if "Homer does not exist" were contradictory (where "Homer" is a true proper name), it would not follow that "Homer exists" is other than a perfectly meaningful statement. The denials of every theorem of logic, every logical truth, are contradictory, but it is absurd to suppose that they do not make sense. In fact, the assumption that they are true is frequently used in proving that they are false, when the proof proceeds by *reductio ad absurdum*. If we allow that "exists" does denote the property of existence, then the statement "*A* exists" (in which "*A*" is a logically proper name) *must* be true and the statement "*A* does not exist" *must* be false—just as the statement "2 + 2 = 4" must be true and its denial must be false. None of this casts any doubt on the idea that the predicate "exists" may denote or connote the property of existence. Of course, if there is such a property, only existing things have it. But to say this is not to be committed to the absurd view that nonexistent things have a corresponding property of nonexistence. Since nonexistent things do not exist, "they' cannot have any properties at all.

In defense of Russell someone might argue that, even if "Homer" is a logically proper name, the statement "Homer exists" cannot be necessarily (or logically) true because it is clearly a contingent fact that any person exists at all. Thus, Homer's nonexistence must be a logical possibility. The obvious reply to this is that "Homer exists" is necessarily true only in the sense that, if "Homer" is a proper name and thus names something, the statement is self-verifying in the way that "I am speaking" is self-verifying when someone utters it. "Homer exists" is nevertheless contingent in the sense that the person named by "Homer" need not have existed. Yet *if* that person now bears the name "Homer," the statement "Homer exists" is bound to be true.

If, in view of these last considerations, we reject Russell's view of existence statements containing logically proper names, we need not thereby reject the rest of his views on existence. We can maintain, in other words, that other existence statements—those containing general terms such as "lions" or definite descriptions such as "the author of the *Iliad*"—can be understood as Russell interpreted them. Of course, if we allow that "exists" is an acceptable predicate in such statements as "Homer exists," we shall have to explain what is reasonably meant (or what we mean) by it. But perhaps we can get an idea of how to do this when we have a better understanding of Russell's analysis of existentially quantified statements—the statements that, in his view, are the preferred means of affirming the existence of things in the fundamental sense of the word.

Russell on Existential Quantification

Although some contemporary philosophers evidently believe that an existentially quantified formula owes its meaning to such words as "there is" or "there exists" (which may used to translate it), Russell held a contrary view. According to him, the existential quantifier is a technical device that helps us understand the logical content of standard utterances of "there is" or "there exists": ordinary utterances are to be illuminated by reference to his logical symbolism, and not the other way around. This is a very important point for current debates in ontology. If our ordinary talk about existence is to be clarified, or interpreted, by reference to the existential quantifier, the latter must have a meaning that can be understood independently of ordinary talk about what is or exists. Without this independent meaning, the existential quantifier would provide no genuine enlightenment, or clarification, of basic ontological issues. It would merely provide a new or technically fancy way of saying the same old things—the things that have to be clarified if standard ontological problems are to be resolved.

Russell explicitly analyzed existentially quantified statements in relation to the logical notions of truth and propositional functions. Let "*x* is human" be a propositional function. According to Russell, a propositional function may be always true (or "necessary"), sometimes true (or "possible"), or never true (or "impossible"). If the function is always true, we can assert that everything is human or, in symbols, that $(x)(x$ is human). If it is sometimes true (as it actually is in this case) we can assert that something is human or, in symbols, that $(\exists x)(x$ is human). If, finally, the function is never true, we can assert that nothing is human or, in symbols, that $(x) \sim (x$ is human), where the tilde sign "$\sim$" is to be read as "It is not the case (it is false) that. . . . " Russell pointed out that just one of the ideas—always true, sometimes true, and never true—may be taken as basic, for the others can be defined in terms of any one of them. For example, "sometimes true" means "not always not true," and "never true" means "always not true." If we take "sometimes true" as our basic idea, we can say that the existentially quantified formula "$(\exists x)(x$ is human)" is true when and only when the propositional function "*x* is human" is sometimes true.[20]

If we are to clarify the primary notion of existence that we have been concerned with in this chapter, we cannot leave the matter here. At the very least, we must ask a further question: "Can anything illuminating be said about the meaning of 'sometimes true' as it applies to propositional functions?" As it happens, Russell said two things that are relevant here. He said that a propositional function is sometimes true when it is "true in at least one instance"; and he also said that it is sometimes true when it is "satisfied" by at least one thing.[21] Unfortunately, Russell's meaning was vague when he said these things, for he did not clearly explain what an instance of a propositional function is supposed to be, or how an object or thing can "satisfy" a propositional function. As matters stand, he could have meant two very different things by these two remarks. It is very important to consider these two possibilities, because each suggests a different interpretation of the "existential' quantifier, and both interpretations have their defenders today.

One thing Russell might have meant can be explained as follows. An "instance" of a propositional function containing a variable "*x*" is an actual proposition, a sentence with a fixed interpretation, that differs from the propositional function in having a proper name in place of "*x*". On this view, "Tom is a man" might count as an instance of the propositional function "x is a man." If "Tom" is a logically proper name, there is something that it names; if it names a man, the quantified statement "$(\exists x)(x$ is a man)" will then be true. Viewed this way, the truth of an existentially quantified statement will depend on the truth of a nonquantified statement that, by virtue of containing a logically proper name, picks out some particular thing and, by virtue of the predicate, characterizes or describes that thing correctly. This interpretation of the existential quantifier has come to be known as "the substitution interpretation," for it characterizes an existentially quantified statement as true just when there is at least one true "substitution instance" of the relevant propositional function.

When Russell spoke of a propositional function being "satisfied" by some thing, he may alternatively have meant that the function is *true of* some non-linguistic object. For example, if Tom is a man, then the propositional function "*x* is a man" could be true of Tom in the sense that Tom is correctly described by the part of the propositional function that does not include the variable "*x*." Essentially this interpretation of the ∃-quantifier has come to be known as "the range interpretation'. According to this interpretation variables are associated with a range of objects (a "domain" or "universe of discourse"), and an existentially quantified statement is true with respect to a domain D (or a "model" that includes D[22]) just when at least one object in D is correctly described by the statement's predicate.

Since Russell made remarks that are compatible with both interpretations, it is not clear which he would have favored. On the other hand, both involve difficulties from his point of view. The difficulty with the first interpretation is that not everything has a name. Suppose a is a particular object having 105 peculiar stripes. The statement "(∃x)(x has 105 peculiar stripes)" may then be true even though, owing to the fact that a has never been named, the propositional function "*x* has 105 peculiar stripes" has no true substitution instances. This difficulty might be avoided, however, if one argued that, although every particular does not actually have a name, every particular *could* be named. If, in line with this, we consider every conceivable enlargment of our stock of names, we might modify the substitution interpretation and say that a statement "(∃x)(x is F)" is true just when there is a name n in our actual vocabulary or *some enlargement of it* such that the statement (substitution instance) "*n* is *F*" is true.[23]

Although the second interpretation is more popular today than the first one, it too raises difficulties for Russell. The key difficulty concerns the domain of objects associated with the variables of quantification. Since Russell was concerned with reality and not fictions, not any domain will serve his purpose. For example, the domain of mythical beings, which "contains" centaurs and hippogriffs, is plainly out of the question. How, then, is the appropriate domain to be identified? If Russell had argued that the appropriate domain is the class of things that really exist, then his attempt to clarify the notion of existence or the logic of existence statements by reference to existential quantification would have been patently circular, and could have provided no enlightenment at all. Of course, given his view that "exists" is not a logically satisfactory predicate—that existence is not a property of things or objects—Russell could not have resorted to speaking of the class of existing things (or things that exist) at all.

A New Problem about Existence

As I explained in the last section, Russell's attempt to clarify the meaning of existentially quantified statements by reference to truth and propositional functions did not go far enough to resolve problems of current interest and debate. Also, his offhand remarks about "instances" and "values" of a propositional function were extremely vague and suggested two different interpretations of the existential quantifier. If, consequently, we are to achieve the clarification we want about existence, we shall have to go beyond Russell and consider matters that he did not explicitly discuss.

At the present time the most widely accepted interpretation of the ∃-quantifier is the so-called range interpretation. This is the interpretation assumed by Quine when he said that "to be is to be the value of a variable." For Quine, though not for Russell,[24] the value of a variable is an object or thing—a member of the domain over which variables "range." If Tom is a value satisfying the propositional function "x is a man," then the existence statement "$(\exists x)(x$ is a man)" is true, and we may then say, using the vernacular, that there is (or exists) at least one man. Quine's idea is that existence statements, in technical language, are existentially quantified formulas; and when we assert, for example, that $(\exists x)(x$ is a man), we are, in effect, claiming that there is at least one value of the variable satisfying the function "x is a man."

Most philosophers who adopt this approach to existence statements assume that the relevant values of the variables are existing things. The reason is this. Suppose that I am speaking of Greek gods and say, "$(\exists x)(x$ is the wife of Zeus)." Is my assertion true with respect to the domain of Greeks gods? Well, if we allow that this domain of mythical beings has Hera as a member, we shall have to admit that my assertion is true with respect to that domain. But, of course, Hera does not exist—there is no such goddess. Thus, either we maintain that nonexistent or mythical things are not members of domains—that domains contain only existent things—or we must admit that ∃-quantified statements that are true with respect to domains of nonexistent things are not existence statements in the intended sense.

I speak of the "intended" sense here for the following reason. Some contemporary philosophers who adopt the range interpretation draw a distinction between "actual" and "merely possible" beings, and say that *there are* non-actual possibilities.[25] These philosophers are willing to permit quantification over domains of nonexistent or "nonactual" beings. If D is a domain of mythical beings, some are prepared to say that "$(\exists x)(x$ is the wife of Zeus)" is true with respect to D. It is obvious that on this interpretation the ∃-quantifier does not have the meaning intended by such writers as Quine. If Hera and Zeus are mythical beings, they do not really exist; and if we allow that "$(\exists x)(x = Zeus)$" is true with respect to the domain of mythical beings, we may say that, in a sense, *there is* such a thing as Zeus—but this sense of "there is" does not imply that Zeus exists in the sense intended by Quine.

If the range interpretation can be stretched to allow quantification over mythical or merely possible objects, it does not, at least by itself, provide a satisfactory clarification of "exists." In fact, if the ∃-quantifier is to be the primary means of making existence claims (as Russell thought) the relevant domain of quantification must consist of existing (or "actual") things. But this leaves us with the task of explaining what an existing (or "actual") thing is. As far as ontology is concerned, we are apparently back where we started. By itself, the ∃-quantifier does not provide the clarification we are looking for.

The other interpretation of the ∃-quantifier—the substitution interpretation—might seem helpful at this point. This interpretation is suggested by the following quotation from Russell:

> A form of words containing a . . . variable—for instance, "*x* is a man"—is called a "propositional function" if, when a value is assigned to the variable, the form of words becomes a proposition. Thus, "*x* is a man" is neither true nor false, but if for "*x*" I put "Mr. Jones" I get a true proposition, and if I put "Mrs. Jones" I get a false one.[26]

If "Mr. Jones" is the proper name of a man, then at least one man exists and we are entitled to say "$(\exists x)(x$ is a man)." Here our basis for an existence claim is our confidence that a certain man has been picked out by a name.

Quine, who was particularly influential in espousing the range interpretation of quantifiers, has at one time or another pointed out certain difficulties with this substitution approach.[27] One is that certain names are not attached to existing things: "Pegasus" and "Zeus" are examples. This difficulty is not decisive, however. Since nonexistent or nonactual things are never present in our experience, we cannot name them in the normal or standard way. We may associate such names with descriptions or the assumed "objects" of mythical stories—as in saying that Pegasus is the winged horse ridden by Bellerophon—but this does not render them "logically proper' names, which are attached to their bearers by some causal or ostensive gesture.[28] Thus, if we insist that the relevant substitution instances for propositional functions are logically proper names, we can avoid this first difficulty.

Another difficulty mentioned by Quine is that not every existing thing has a name—in fact, some existing things (he said) cannot possibly be named. If names are verbal symbols that we can attach to objects, our vocabulary of names is finite or, at least, denumerable—no larger than the set of natural numbers 1, 2, 3, 4, and so on. But the set of real numbers (or points on a line) is larger than this. Thus, some existing things—some real numbers—could not possibly be named. This objection is, again, not decisive. For one thing, it is not obvious that real numbers exist in the primary sense we are concerned with: they are natural candidates for logical (or mathematical) fictions. Still, there are no doubt plenty of things that, though clearly existent, will never actually be named: "full many a flower is born to blush unseen, and waste its sweetness on the desert air." The strategy mentioned in the last section—of specifying substitution instances in relation to possible extensions of our vocabulary—may help us here, but it is not very promising if we have no prior idea of what an existing thing is. If a logically proper name must have an existing bearer, our conception of such a name seems to presuppose some conception of a thing that exists in the primary sense.

Although Russell argued that the predicate "exists" is not a logically satisfactory predicate, his arguments were not, as we have seen, satisfactory. In fact, the considerations developed above imply that "exists" must be understood if the existential quantifier (interpreted in either of the ways common today) is to serve as an acceptable device for making existence claims. If we think of the ∃-quantifier as interpreted by reference to a domain of objects, those objects must exist if the quantifier is to express existence claims; if it is interpreted substitutionally, the required substituends must be logically proper names, that is, names of existing things. Thus, the new problem of existence reduces to the problem of clarifying the meaning of a primary existence predicate.

Existence and the World

One way of clarifying the notion of an existing thing is to say that existing things collectively constitute the world. As Kant observed in his *Inaugural Dissertation*, a world can be characterized by three basic concepts: matter, form, and totality.[29] The matter of a world consists of the fundamental objects composing it; the form is the manner in which the basic objects are interrelated; and the concept of totality enters the picture because the world is the totality of objects that are held together by a formal, world-forming relation.

The matter of the world consists of fundamental objects because complexes of objects, such as piles of stones or herds of goats, belong to the world only in the derivative sense that their elements belong to the world and are related to one another in an appropriate way. Thus, existing objects, in the primary sense, are those objects or things that comprise the substance of the world. The form of the world, or at least the form of our world, is the space-time-causal network in which primary objects are located. We are in direct experiential contact with some objects, which we may take to be fundamental, and the other objects of our world are related to these experienced objects in ways that make them all belong to a common spatio-temporal-causal system.

I have described our world by reference to objects of experience for a reason that should at least be mentioned here. If we had a God's-eye view of the world, we might be able to describe it in unique general terms—that is, in general terms that would not truly describe any merely possible world. But we are limited beings with limited knowledge, and our conception of the world is inescapably egocentric: it applies to a system of objects that "radiates out," as Russell once put it, from those nameable objects at the center of our attention. When I say that a certain thing exists, I mean that it exists now, now being the time of my utterance. As we shall see in chapter 6, our conception of the past and future also radiates out, in a sense, from what we now experience. If I think that something did exist, I think of that thing as having been part of the causally related system of objects of which I am now aware. And if, realizing that I am a merely contingent being, I entertain the possibility that I might not have existed, I imagine that the system of objects that, as it happens, includes me and the objects of my attention, has included, and continues to include, some glaring gaps—or has some intruders in their place.

According to the empiricist tradition, the fundamental objects making up our world are all possible objects of experience. In the eighteenth century George Berkeley argued that *esse est percipi*—that to be is to be perceived—but later empiricists, believing that a thing could exist when it is not actually perceived, insisted that an existing thing is merely one that *could* be perceived or *would* be perceived by a suitably placed observer. Russell's commitment to this point of view, at least when he composed his lectures on logical atomism, stands out in his remarks about "metaphysical objects, . . . which are supposed to be part of the ultimate constituents of the world, but not the kind of thing that is ever empirically given."[30] If something could not be "empirically given," not just because the observer is too far away to experience it but because it is the kind of thing that is strictly imperceptible, then it is a "metaphysical entity" whose existence Russell would not have acknowledged.

Although the point can be securely established only by an adequate theory of knowledge, this empiricist view of an existent object is far too narrow. At least, it is far too narrow to be believable at the present time. We commonly assume that there are countless things—germs, molecules, even electrons—that unquestionably exist but cannot be perceived. Someone is bound to object that microscopic things can be perceived with the aid of instruments; yet when such instruments are used, certain objects must serve as a medium of perception, and these objects are not perceived themselves—and some cannot be perceived. As an example, consider the electron microscope, which might be used to "perceive" viruses and medium-sized molecules. When we use this device, we use electrons as a medium for producing an image of the perceived object: the electrons penetrate the object and interact with the mechanism in which the image is produced. It is theoretically possible, I suppose, that entities of a single kind could be used as an ultimate means of instrumental perception, but if so, these entities would have to exist (since they causally interact with perceived existents) without being perceivable themselves. Thus, if we accept even the main lines of current theories of matter, we shall have to acknowledge the existence of some things that cannot possibly be perceived.

If, on broadly scientific grounds, we reject the view that an existent object is a possible object of experience, we need not reject the spirit of empiricism. Empiricists have invariably held that the world of existing things is a space-time-causal system, and we can accept this idea if we allow that the world includes *more* than merely experienceable objects. Allowing this is not only reasonable, but it permits us to agree with the empiricist that the world is a system to which we have direct experiential access. When Hume identified the fundamental form of reasoning appropriate to "matters of fact and existence" as that of causal inference,[31] he was well within the spirit of this revised conception. As an eighteenth-century empiricist, he may have conceived of basic existents as experienceable objects (impressions and ideas), but this conception is not something that we have to share. If we are confident that the world includes shoes and sealing wax as well as purely theoretical objects such as mesons or quarks, we can allow that such things exist, too.

Most things in philosophy are subject to dispute, and no doubt some philosophers will want to quarrel with the conception of fundamental existence that I have just outlined. It is important to realize, therefore, that although that conception is more liberal than what an eighteenth-century empiricist would accept, it is very close to being philosophically orthodox. I have noted that Aristotle attributed fundamental existence to substances or concrete things, these being the objects that he regarded as making up the space-time-causal system. Before him, Plato eventually proposed as "a sufficient mark of real things the presence . . . of the power of being acted upon or of acting in relation to however insignificant a thing"—and this causing can take place only in some kind of causal system.[32] I mentioned that my conception accords with the spirit, at least, of the more restrictive conceptions of Berkeley and Hume; and it also, of course, accords with the ideas expressed by Kant in his *Inaugural Dissertation*. In his later *Critique of Pure Reason* Kant defined an actual (or existing) thing as "that which is bound up with the material conditions of experience' and, as regards anything of which we can have knowledge, as in "thoroughgoing interaction" with other possible objects of experience.[33] Finally, C. S. Peirce, one of the most learned and acute metaphysicians in the history of the subject, asserted that "whatever exists *ex-sists*, that is, really acts on other existents . . . and is definitely individual."[34]

Historical precedent is not by itself sufficient to render a conception of existence acceptable, but any conception that accords so well with the considered views of the philosophical luminaries I have mentioned certainly deserves careful consideration. Since I know of no other conception that is anywhere nearly as plausible as the one I have outlined, I shall assume that it is provisionally acceptable. To develop its implications fully, I shall have to devote further attention to the notions of space, time, and causation. I shall do this in chapter 6.

Two final points. First, some readers might want to object that my conception of existence cannot be acceptable because it arbitrarily rules out the very possibility of God's existence. The objection is naive. For one thing, it is by no means obvious that if God is the creator of the universe, God is not causally related to the objects he has created. People who believe in a Divine Creator may thus conceive of the totality of existence as including a supernatural realm that, together with the natural realm, makes up a larger causal system. But there is another possibility—one more consonant with the history of theology. As medieval theologians argued, God's attributes can be conceived of only inadequately and analogically by finite creatures. Those who say that God is wise or intelligent or merciful do not mean that he has the attributes of a wise, intelligent, or merciful human being; they mean that he has attributes in some way analogous to those of such a being. A similar view can be taken of God's existence: whatever Divine Existence may be, we can conceive of it only as something analogous to human existence. We may use the word "existence" in our attempts to refer to it, but we cannot maintain that we are thus using the word with its ordinary meaning.

My last point is that my conception of existence provides an obvious means of defining the predicate "exists." We can simply say:

a exists $=df$ *a* belongs to the space-time-causal system that is our world.

Our world is, again, that system of (roughly) causally related objects with which we are, and anyone who is alert enough to understand us is, in direct experiential contact. It is abstractly conceivable that just one of us is the only person in existence, but if you exist as well as I, we shall both (if we are awake and alert) be objects that belong to the same causal system: those objects will be related to one another in an appropriate spatio-temporal-causal way.

With this definition of the predicate "exists" in hand, we can proceed to elaborate upon the interpretations of the ∃-quantifier that were suggested earlier. That is, we can specify our basic universe of discourse as the domain of existing things, and we can, alternatively, describe the proper substituends for our variables as names that denote existing things. Having done this, we can use the ∃-quantifier (interpreted in either way) as a technical means of expressing existence claims.

Chapter 3
UNIVERSALS AND PARTICULARS

THE OBJECT OF this chapter is to consider what sorts of things, very generally speaking, belong to our space-time-causal system. Although most philosophers agree that the system contains particulars, they often disagree about the nature of particulars, some holding that they are events, and others holding that they are continuants—things that, like plants and animals, persist in time and undergo change. In addition to allowing that our world contains particulars of one sort or another, many philosophers insist that it contains universals as irreducible objects. I shall begin by assuming that the world contains continuants and consider whether, in addition to particulars so understood, there is good reason to believe that it also contains irreducible universals. I shall discuss the fundamental reality of continuants in chapters 5 and 6.

Traditional Arguments for Universals

The earliest philosophical writings in which arguments for the fundamental reality of universals can be found are by Plato (427-347 B.C.). In his early dialogues Plato presented conversations in which Socrates, whom we can take as speaking for him, defends a theory of Ideas or Forms. Although Plato's Forms have historically been called universals, they are by no means the same as the entities (or supposed entities) to which later philosophers have applied the name. However this may be, traditional thought about universals began with Plato, and I shall begin with him as well.

According to Plato, Socrates regarded Forms as the sole objects of genuine knowledge. In his view things in the world of experience are in a state of constant change, and we can understand their nature only by reference to the Forms they imitate or participate in. By studying geometry, we can attain knowledge of objects such as triangularity and squareness, but objects in the world of experience are only approximately triangular or square, and we can conceive of them only as approximations to these more perfect objects. The same holds true for the objects of moral and aesthetic knowledge. With proper training, at least, we can achieve genuine knowledge of beauty and of virtues such as courage, but nothing in the world is perfectly beautiful or perfectly virtuous—and we can recognize various approximations of beauty and virtue only because we can comprehend, perhaps only dimly, their more perfect exemplars.

The claim that we can, at least in principle, have knowledge of perfect triangularity or perfect squareness does not really imply that perfect objects must actually exist. On the contrary, we can interpret such knowledge as being tacitly hypothetical—as concerning, not perfect objects, but hypothetical propositions of the kind: "If an object *were* perfectly triangular, the sum of its interior angles would be exactly 180 degrees." Yet Socrates, or at any rate Plato, had independent reasons for believing in the reality of Forms, and these reasons have been highly influential in subsequent discussion of universals. The most important of them make up what is known as the One Over Many argument.

The argument can be developed as follows. If a number of different things can truly be described by the same predicate, they must be the same in some way: they must have a common feature by virtue of which the same description is applicable to them. Thus, if the paper on which I am writing, the typewriter I am using, and one of the books on the shelf in front of me are all truly described by the predicate "white," they must share a common feature that justifies this description. Without a common feature a common description could hardly be applicable to them all. If we ask what this common feature is, the obvious answer is "the color white, or whiteness." Anything having this feature can be truly desribed as white, and for that reason the color can be called a universal: it is at least potentially present all over the universe. If, as Plato suggests, we were born with a knowledge of this color, we could know what whiteness is—and know what a thing would be like if it were white—even if we had never actually perceived a white object.

Similar considerations apply to countless other qualities and even to relations between things. Thus, if it is true both that New York is north of Miami and that Edinburgh is north of London, then the pairs of cities < New York, Miami > and < Edinburgh, London > are both truly describable by the relational predicate "is north of"; and if this is so, both pairs must share an abstract feature, *being north of*, which justifies the common description. This abstract feature is also a universal, since it could be exemplified by countless pairs of things. In contrast to qualities or qualitative attributes, this kind of universal may be called a "relation."

Like Leibniz after him, Plato was troubled by relations, for they seem to have a leg, as Leibniz put it, in the things they relate.[1] As I have pointed out, Plato denied that Forms were actually in particular things. Different white things are distinguishable in their whiteness: some are grayish white, some are creamy white, and some have a bluish tinge. To Plato this suggested that particular white things are more or less white: they "participate in" or "partake of" whiteness in different degrees, or they more or less successfully "imitate" it. As far as we know, Plato never arrived at a fully satisfactory conception of the relation between particulars and Forms; in his dialogue *The Parmenides* he himself criticized the descriptions he was accustomed to using. But whatever exactly the true relations between Forms and particulars may be, Plato seems to have held fast to the view that Forms exist apart from particulars. The obvious reason for maintaining this view is that universal qualities are not perfectly exemplified by particulars: particulars are never perfectly round, perfectly white, or perfectly beautiful.

Aristotle rejected Plato's view of universals as transcendent objects. Aristotle's criticism of Plato's view is complicated and his own alternative is difficult to describe, but it is easy to develop a plausible objection to Plato without Aristotle's help. The objection arises naturally from the One Over Many argument. If things truly describable by the same predicates must have some common feature that justifies the description, then, even if particulars do not fully exemplify some transcendent Form, they must possess "within" them some feature, however imperfect, that justifies the description. To put it in another way, they must themselves have some intrinsic character or feature by virtue of which they exemplify, to the extent that they do, a supposed Platonic Form. The paper I am writing on right now may not be perfectly white, but it has a quality to it, a whiteness of sorts, by virtue of which it is correctly describable as white and by virtue of which, if Platonic Forms exist, it "partakes" of Platonic whiteness to the extent that it does. Yet if, in addition to partaking of a supposed Platonic Form, a white thing must actually possess a quality of whiteness itself, then the One Over Many argument does not really support Plato's theory of transcendent universals. In fact, on the basis of that argument we may go on to insist that there is no need to postulate Plato's Forms at all. The ideal whiteness by reference to which we classify particular objects as whites on observing the whitenesses they possess may be viewed as a mere idea we have or, perhaps more realistically, as a standard that we ourselves have constructed.

The force of this last point is best seen by an example. While waiting for a haircut one afternoon, I read a magazine that contained a drawing of the perfect English bulldog. We may grant, with Plato, that no actual English bulldog will ever be an absolutely perfect specimen of the breed, no matter how much time and effort bulldog fanciers may expend in attempting to realize their ideal. But this does not mean that an ideal English bulldog exists in some transcendent realm. Human beings have invented the standards for perfection here; we have built up our own idea of bulldog perfection. Actual bulldogs have wholly immanent features of bowleggedness, tenacity, strength, and flat-faceness on the basis of which we may classify them as English bulldogs. There is absolutely no reason to suppose that the ideal standard for the breed which we may picture to ourselves or express in words amounts to a transcendent entity to which actual bulldogs are somehow related.

In analogy with these remarks about the ideal English bulldog we could say that the ideal of whiteness by reference to which we can estimate the extent to which particular things are white need not be viewed as a transcendent existent. We could say that this ideal is at most an idea that we have, or a standard that we develop ourselves. The actual feature by virtue of which a particular thing is correctly describable as white may thus belong to the thing in the sense of being some sort of component of it. Perfect whiteness—and, more generally, perfect courage, perfect beauty, and perfect triangularity—may be just as imaginary and unreal as the perfect English bulldog.

These observations about the need for postulating perfect exemplars can be related to a celebated remark that Ludwig Wittgenstein made about the One Over Many argument.[2] Wittgenstein said that we should not simply assume that if a number of things fall under a common description they must actually possess a common feature. What we should do, he said, is look to see if they have such a feature. When we do so, we shall find in most instances a complex network of similarities among the things in question—a "family resemblance" that does not invariably involve any common feature at all. He asked us to consider the example of various games. There are important similarities between football and baseball that do not hold between football and tennis; and tennis and ping-pong are similar in ways that tennis and chess are not. Wittgenstein's point is that we classify things together on the basis, often, of complicated similarities between them and that, if we survey these similarities, we shall not always find a feature that is common to everything we assign to the same class.

A diagram may be helpful here. Consider the following:

ABCD   BCDE   CDEF   DEFG   EFGH

Assume that each sequence of letters represents a particular thing, each letter representing a determinate feature of that thing. The first thing is naturally classified together with the second thing, for they differ only in one feature. The second thing is equally similar to the third, and they, too, are naturally classified together—and so on for the others. Thus, each of the five things is put in the same class because each is strikingly similar to one of the others. Nevertheless, the first thing has no determinate feature in common with the last thing. This may be taken as an abstract illustration of the fact that things classified together on the basis of similarities among them might have no common determinate feature.

In describing Wittgenstein's illustration I have used the term "determinate feature." This is a very useful term, but it requires an explanation. Think of the color red, for example. There are many shades of this color: crimson, vermilion, barn red, and so on. These shades may be called *determinate* forms of red, and the color red may be called a *determinable* having these determinate forms. The relation between a determinable and its associated determinates is actually a relative one. If not every object correctly called scarlet is indistinguishable in color from other scarlet things, then scarlet is itself a determinable relative to more determinate forms of scarlet. It is reasonable to suppose that, in any quality dimension, there are absolutely determinate forms—the most determinate qualities belonging to that dimension.

If we are reminded of the distinction between fundamental and derivative modes of existence, we might ask whether it is necessary to admit both determinates and determinables as fundamental realities. The answer, I believe, is no. Determinables (at least) can be regarded as logical fictions. When we say that a thing has a certain determinable quality, we can be understood as meaning that it has some determinate feature that belongs to an appropriate family of determinates. If, for example, there are just two determinate forms of scarlet, scarlet

A and scarlet *B*, then a thing having one of these features may be described as scarlet and, more generally, as red and, even more generally, as colored—all by virtue of possessing one of these determinate features. In the strict sense, therefore, we do not have to acknowledge that determinables are fundamentally real; the assertion that a thing has some determinable quality can be understood as short for the ontologically more strict assertion that the thing has some absolutely determinate quality that is classifiable in an appropriately generic way.

The remark by Wittgenstein that I mentioned a moment ago is sometimes taken to undermine the theory of universals. But this is a mistake. What Wittgenstein's remark shows, if it is sound, is that a group of objects may fall under a common description without having any determinate feature in common. But this could be true, if my claim in the last paragraph is sound, even for the class of red objects. As a matter of fact, some red objects do seem to share a determinate form of redness, but this need not be so; it is certainly not a logical consequence of the fact that those objects are red. If there are determinate qualities, then even if no two objects have one of them in common, they are still universals because they *could* perfectly well be possessed by more than one object. What Wittgenstein's remark requires us to recognize is that the One Over Many argument needs qualification to be seriously tempting. It is not that, to be correctly describable by a common predicate, a group of objects must actually share some attribute in the strict sense of "sharing an attribute." If the argument is to be plausible, the objects must be understood, rather, as having some determinate attributes or other by virtue of which they fall under the common description.

It is worth observing that things may fall under common descriptions for a wide variety of reasons. Take the term "jetsam," for example. Something is an example of jetsam, not by virtue of having some universal component, but by virtue of having been jettisoned from some boat or ship. This latter feature is commonly called a "relational property," for to be jettisoned from a ship is to be related to a ship in a certain way. As in the case of determinables, however, it is not necessary to acknowledge the irreducible being of relational properties. When, speaking loosely, we say that a thing has a relational property, we can mean that, in the strict sense, the thing is related to something else in an appropriate way. If we accept the theory of immanent (or nontranscendent) universals, we shall acknowledge that determinate forms of relations are real, but we need not accept generic relations or relational properties.

We can now return to the One Over Many argument. According to the argument in its revised form, if several things fall under a common description, they must possess some absolutely determinate features by virtue of which the description is correctly applied to them. These ultimately determinate features, if they are not relations, are in some sense "present in" the relevant objects, for it is by virtue of possessing them that *the objects* (and not something else) merit the appropriate descriptions. It is substantially in this form that the One Over Many argument retains its philosophical interest.

To understand the implications of the One Over Many argument in this revised form, we might consider one standard objection to it. The objection is this. Even though certain objects in my study are correctly describable as white, there is no need to assume that they merit this description by virtue of each possessing a determinate (but still abstract) quality of whiteness. It is enough to say that they are all white, and that to be white is, roughly, to look white to normal observers when viewed under good light. If we want to isolate something "by virtue of which" the predicate "white" is applicable to the objects, we can point to the fact that each is such as to look white to normal observers viewing them in such light. There is no need to point to some determinate "whiteness" that each of them somehow possesses.

The argument is instructive because it misses the point of the One Over Many argument. According to that argument, a thing can fall under a description only by virtue of having *an* appropriate determinate feature. Yet if the predicate "white" is understood in the dispositional sense of "looks white to normal observers in standard conditions," the appropriate determinate feature will not be a form of white but, perhaps, some microphysical feature describable in the language of physics. It is only if we understand the predicate in an ordinary, "naive" sense that we shall want to identify the determinate feature as a form of whiteness. From a scientific perspective, we may conceive of a white object as one that merely presents a certain appearance to normal observers, but then we must acknowledge that the object will present this appearance only because it has some determinate surface structure (certain determinate features) that reflects light in an appropriate way. Thus, when we begin to view the world from a scientific perspective, we shall have to identify its determinate features by reference to our scientific theories. Scientific considerations cannot undermine our metaphysical belief in determinate features; at best, they can only change our conception of what those features are. So claims the proponent of the revised One Over Many argument.[3]

Problems with the Theory of Universals

It is obvious, on reflection, that the One Over Many argument is fundamentally based on a certain conception of predication. When one says something having the subject-predicate form of "That paper is white," one predicates something of a subject; and if one's statement is true, the subject must (according to the argument) have some determinate feature or features by virtue of which the predicate truly applies to it. This last assumption is very plausible, which is no doubt why so many philosophers have accepted it; yet it generates such serious difficulties for the theory of universals that the theory deserves, ultimately, to be rejected.

A good name for one fundamental difficulty with the theory is "the Chinese Boxes absurdity." According to the assumption just stated, if a predicate truly applies to a subject, the subject must possess or perhaps "contain" some determinate feature, or features, by virtue of which the predicate truly applies to it. But if the assumed determinate features can successfully account for such a thing, they cannot themselves be characterless: they must have some positive features of their own. The point here is obvious: if the presence of F in a thing

x can account for the fact that x is truly described by the predicate "white," then F must differ from the feature that accounts for the fact that another thing y is truly described by the predicate "black." Furthermore, if two determinate features differ, they must differ in this or that respect; they cannot be indiscernible. Thus, one feature must have a higher-order feature that the other lacks, and vice versa.

Suppose, then, that F is a determinate feature by virtue of which a predicate P is applicable to an object x. Since F differs from other features, it has a positive character of its own, which means that it is truly describable by some higher-order predicate $P*$ that is not applicable to every other feature. But by the assumption on which the One Over Many argument is based, the feature F must then possess (or "contain") some higher-order feature $F*$ by virtue of which the predicate $P*$ is truly applied to F. If, as before, $F*$ can account for the fact that the predicate $P*$ is applicable to $F*$, $F*$ must also have some positive character of its own, which is to say some further feature $F**$. But there is no end to this. Since we are supposed to assume that the features by virtue of which a predicate is applicable to a subject are "present in" that subject, we are led to the amazing result that every particular is like an infinitely complicated Chinese box: an infinite system of boxes within boxes. This outcome is incredible.

If we look closely at the One Over Many argument, we can quickly see what has gone wrong. The argument purports to provide an ultimate explanation of why a predicate (any predicate) is applicable to a subject (any subject), but the "explanation" it offers simply introduces a new subject of further (and unknown) predicates. The explanation is bogus because it tacitly assumes what it purports to explain. The presence of U in a subject S could explain why S is truly describable in one way rather than another only if U is different (or describable differently) from other objects. But for U to be thus describable, it must be truly describable in one way rather than another. The ultimate "explanation" of true predication thus reduces to the claim that a thing is truly describable in a certain way because something else is truly describable in a certain way. As an explanation, this claim is utterly useless. If we didn't already understand why, in general, a description (or predicate) is truly applicable to a thing, we could not even understand what we are being told.

The difficulty can be put in another way. I describe a piece of paper as white, but I am told that the predicate I use is applicable to the paper not because the paper is white but because the paper possesses a special component—a determinate universal—that is peculiar to white objects. Although the nature of the special component is not described by proponents of the One Over Many argument, any description of it would have to be justified (if the argument is sound) by components of a further sort. The trouble is, no thing is ever sufficient, in and of itself, to account for the correct application of any predicates applied to it. Consequently, no object is ever reached that can provide an ultimate explanation of true predication—and this is exactly what the argument claims to provide.

A true believer in universals might try to avoid this line of criticism by arguing that, although a predicate is truly applied to a particular only because that particular somehow contains a universal, the universal it contains can have a determinate character (a definite nature) without thereby having to contain some higher-order universal. The claim would be that a statement *"u is F"* could be true even though the universal denoted by *"u"* does not have any component by virtue of which the predicate *"F"* truly applies to it. This move would defeat the criticism I have made, but it would effectively undermine the grounds for the belief in universals as well. One could just as well insist that a statement *"p is G"* could be true even though the particular *p* contains no universal component by virtue of which the predicate *"G"* applies to it. To insist on this point is to deny that there is any need, so far as predication is concerned, to postulate universal components at all.

Since the One Over Many argument has been so stubbornly defended, I want to round out my criticism with a few additional remarks. Proponents of the One Over Many argument insist on raising the question "By virtue of what is that paper truly described as white?" They disallow the answer "It is truly described as white because it is white" and offer instead "It is truly described as white because it possesses a determinate whiteness, which is peculiar to white things." Yet in giving this answer they simply apply a further, more complicated predicate to the very same subject—namely, "possesses a determinate whiteness. . . . " This answer allows us to raise the same sort of question that we were induced to raise in the first place: "By virtue of what is the predicate 'possesses a determinate whiteness' applicable to the paper?" Proponents of the theory would like to answer this question by saying "The paper is truly described by this predicate because the paper does possess the determinate whiteness." But this answer tacitly allows us to reply to the question "By virtue of what does the predicate '*F*' apply to the object *o*?" by saying "Object *o* is truly described by '*F*' because it is *F*." Parity of reasoning would then allow us to answer our original question by saying "The paper is truly described as 'white' because it is white." A simple answer of this kind would not lead us to a theory of universals, however.

If we consider relations rather than qualities, we get an outcome analogous to the Chinese Boxes absurdity; it is known as Bradley's Regress, after the British philosopher F. H. Bradley. This regress is not the same as the one involved in the Chinese Boxes absurdity, for relations are not said to be "present in" the objects they relate. Yet if, when *A* is next to *B*, there is an abstract third thing, a relation, which is somehow associated with *A* and *B*, then this third thing must bear some relation to *A* and *B*. But if bearing a relation to a thing involves another thing, a relation, we have four things that must somehow be related to a fifth thing, and then a sixth thing, and then a seventh thing, and so on to infinity. But this outcome is as absurd as the Chinese Boxes outcome: it introduces infinite complexity into a simple case of predication, and it makes a mystery out of how two things are actually related to one another.

Philosophers who believe in relations, or accept the theory of universals we have been considering, are aware of Bradley's Regress, and they attempt to meet it by arguing that, though relations are genuine things, they are not related to the things they relate. But this contention is extremely puzzling and unclear. If a is related to b by a third thing R, it is hard to see how R could possibly fail to be related to a and b. The claim that a's being next to b does not involve a and b's being related to *next to* seems to be a way of denying that three genuine things have being when a is next to b. How a genuine third thing can relate things without somehow being related to them remains an utter mystery.

The general nature of the connection between particulars and universals has been acknowledged to be problematic ever since Plato discussed it in his *Parmenides*. As I pointed out earlier, Plato described this connection with words that we translate as "imitation," 'participation," or "partakes of." In his *Parmenides* Plato made it clear that particulars could not be related to Forms in these ways, and none is appropriate, obviously, for the connection between particulars and universals as the latter are conceived of by the theory we have been considering. Recent believers in universals generally use the expression "exemplification" to describe the connection, and although they never successfully explain what exemplification is, they contend that it has the merit, at least, of not being metaphorical.[4]

This last contention does not stand up to criticism, however. According to my desk dictionary, the literal meaning of "exemplifies" is "to show or illustrate by example" or "to furnish, or serve as, an example." But, obviously, a white thing does not serve as an example of whiteness, though it is said, by believers in universals, to exemplify it. If anything could serve as an example of whiteness, it would no doubt be the whiteness of a particular white thing—but this latter whiteness is a determinate universal, not a particular at all. As far as a white individual thing is concerned—a polar bear, say—the sort of thing of which it could serve as an example is, say, an arctic animal.

The obscurity of the notion of exemplification as used to describe the relation, connection, or whatever between universals and particulars is merely a symptom of the thoroughgoing obscurity of the entire theory. This point stands out sharply if we turn to the supposed nature or character of universals themselves. As we have seen, Plato thought at the time of his early dialogues that Forms were perfect exemplars, like the perfect English bulldog. Contemporary believers in universals not only deny that universals are perfect objects aping the features particulars ideally possess, but they have little if anything to say themselves about what universals are supposed to be like. Of course, coupled with the view of predication implicit in the One Over Many argument, the idea that universals have any features at all leads to the Chinese Boxes absurdity. Yet it is clear that, if universals do not have some positive character of their own, they cannot serve to explain anything about why certain predicates are applicable to certain particulars.

It is sometimes said that the nature of universals is in no way mysterious, for they are entirely open to view. If you look at a creamy-white object, you can *see* its creamy whiteness, and you will therefore know what creamy whiteness is like. It is hard to take this view seriously. Does creamy whiteness have a surface, so that it can reflect light? Can it possess a square shape and have black letters typed upon it? Obviously not: one who expounds such a view of creamy whiteness is confusing an alleged universal with something else—in this case the surface of a piece of paper. We can easily see the surface of a piece of paper and observe that the surface is square in shape and has, perhaps, some words typed on it. In such a case we are seeing a creamy-white surface, not some abstract component. The surface is open to view and, though it may cover a yellowish core, it can be seen for what it is: a creamy-white thing. But creamy whiteness is not supposed to be white. What, then, is it like? The answer remains a mystery.

Problems about Particulars

A classic difficulty with the theory of universals is that it threatens to make a mystery of particulars as well as universals. The classic difficulty here does not result from the line of thought leading to the Chinese Boxes absurdity; it results from the mere idea that a particular is an ultimate subject of predication. According to John Locke, a particular is merely something in which universal qualities "inhere." Considered in itself, a particular is, Locke said, "a thing I know not what"—a mere "support" for qualities.[5] This might be called "the pincushion conception" of particulars, for it describes particulars as mysterious x's, or "substrata," that support qualities somewhat as a pincushion supports pins.

The pincushion theory has seemed plausible to many philosophers who accept both particulars and universals as irreducibly real. It also makes it easy to offer a philosophical interpretation of the doctrine of transubstantiation as set forth in the Council of Trent (1545):

> If any one shall say that in the Holy Sacrament of the Eucharist there remains together with the Body and Blood of Our Lord Jesus Christ the substance of the bread and wine, and shall deny the wonderful and singular change of the whole substance of the bread into [his] Body and of the wine into [his] Blood, the appearances alone of the bread and wine remaining . . . , let him be anathema.[6]

According to the philosophical interpretation of this dogma proposed by the pincushion theory, the substrata x and y that are bread and wine miraculously change into the z and w that are Christ's Body and Blood, though the original qualities of bread and wine persist throughout the change. The dogma of transubstantiation does not, of course, have to be interpreted according to the pincushion theory. But however that may be, the pincushion theory seems to be a clear-cut example of a philosophical absurdity—one that makes an utter mystery out of a familiar object such as a piece of bread or chalk.

David Armstrong, a recent supporter of immanent universals, has attempted to avoid the pincushion theory by drawing a distinction between a thick and thin conception of particulars. Suppose that Tom is a red particular. Instead of thinking of Tom as a mysterious x in which redness inheres, we can conceive of Tom "thickly," Armstrong says, as Tom-as-red or Tom-being-red. So conceived, thick-Tom is not a bare x but (as Armstrong puts it) a "state of affairs," something that includes redness within it.[7] Yet if Tom-being-red is a genuine object that includes redness, it must also include a component that might be called "thin-Tom." This latter component is the referent of the ingredient "Tom" in the complex expression "Tom-being-red." Armstrong allows this inference and says, in effect, that thin-Tom is the total spatio-temporal position occupied by the thick Tom-as-red that includes redness or some more basic determinate feature.[8] There are, however, crucial difficulties with both these thin and thick conceptions of a particular.

To begin with the thick conception, it seems obvious that a state of affairs is a very odd sort of entity to regard as actually belonging to nature—particularly since states of affairs do not always "obtain" and thus are sometimes mere possibilities. According to standard philosophical jargon, states of affairs that obtain are called "actual"; but even actual states of affairs do not seem to be objects in the world. To say that John's loving Mary obtains is to say nothing more than "John loves Mary"; and if this latter statement is true, the only objects that must then exist are John and Mary. He may love her, but this does not require us to acknowledge the existence of a peculiar entity called "John-as-loving-Mary."

Suppose that Tom has just two determinate qualities, P and Q. We can then say that thick-Tom is identical with thin-Tom-having-S, where S is the conjunction of P and Q. Since S includes all Tom's qualities, we cannot identify thick-Tom with Tom ordinarily understood, for thick-Tom appears to have none of ordinary Tom's qualities: thick-Tom does not have the quality P, for example; thin-Tom has it. Since thin-Tom has S, it looks as if ordinary Tom is thin-Tom. Yet thin-Tom, Armstrong says, is a total spatio-temporal position. This is bizarre. Ordinary Tom may occupy, throughout his life, a certain total position, but the position he occupies could not have the property of being red-haired, if P were that property. Armstrong might, of course, object that there is no property of being red-haired, for genuine properties (or qualities) are, for him, absolutely determinate. But the point does hold good for those properties, whatever they are, that justify our applying the predicate "has red hair" to ordinary Tom: those alleged properties belong to him, not to the total space-time position that he occupies.

Armstrong tells us that thin-Tom is ordinary Tom "taken in abstraction from all [his] properties"; it is only thus "taken" that thin-Tom is a total position.[9] But now we can ask, "How do these thin-particulars differ from one another? Or are they perhaps Lockian substrata?" Since Armstrong explicitly rejects substrata, he should certainly reject the idea that thin-particulars are such things. Since he says that thin-particulars are total positions, he might want to say that thin-particulars differ in spatio-temporal ways and thus have spatio-temporal properties. But what could these spatio-temporal properties possibly be? Could they be the spatio-temporal properties of ordinary Tom? However we answer this last question, we are in trouble, for if a total position has any properties at all, we can distinguish them from their ultimate subject—and thus draw a distinction between a thick and a thin total position. It seems obvious that, if there is an end to this multiplication of particulars, we must at some stage admit substrata. Thus, Armstrong's attempt to avoid substrata by his distinction between thick and thin particulars ultimately breaks down.

Philosophers accepting the theory of immanent universals but not wanting to render particulars fundamentally mysterious objects generally follow Bertrand Russell and say that particulars are really "bundles" of universals. According to Russell, a bundle of universals is bound together by a relation that may be called "compresence."[10] If I see a flash and at the same time hear a bang, my visual and auditory experiences will be compresent with one another. In Russell's view the experiences I have (or the universals I am aware of) when I experience an event comprise a group having two distinctive features:

1. All the members of the group are compresent.
2. Nothing outside the group is compresent with every member of the group.

Russell called such a group a "complete complex of compresence." He argued that such a complex has the formal properties of an event and that what we ordinarily regard as a particular—a piece of chalk, say—may be understood as a complex system of such events. Roughly speaking, the events making up the system of complexes that Russell was prepared to call a piece of chalk might alternatively be described as momentary stages in the history of that chalk.

As I have described it, Russell's view of an ordinary particular has two parts: the view that ordinary particulars such as dogs or pieces of chalk can be interpreted as systems of events or temporal stages; and the view that the events entering into the system, which are also particulars of sorts, can be interpreted as bundles or complete complexes of compresent universals. These two subviews are interdependent on Russell's view, but we can render them independent of one another if we conceive of compresence more broadly than Russell did. To consider how this might be done, we must first call to mind some general facts about particulars such as pieces of chalk.

A piece of chalk, as we ordinarily conceive of it, is a continuant—something that persists through time and undergoes change. So conceived, a piece of chalk has a history. It was no doubt made in a certain factory, perhaps bought by a certain person, and used on a number of occasions to write on a blackboard. As the result of being used as a writing implement, the chalk becomes worn down and smaller in size. Eventually, it becomes too small to be useful and is thrown away. At the last stage of its existence, the chalk is qualitatively different from what it was when it was new. It has changed during the course of its existence.

If we wish to regard a piece of chalk as a bundle of compresent qualities, we cannot view it as a bundle of qualities compresent at a particular moment. As a continuant, it exists for too long a time. We therefore must make a choice: Either we may say, as Russell did, that the chalk is constituted by a series of momentary events, each of which is a complete complex of compresent qualities, or we may deny that the chalk itself (as opposed to its history) is a series of such events and say that the relation of compresence is not exemplified merely at a particular moment but holds numerous qualities together over an extended period of time, different qualities at different moments. There is no doubt, I think, that Russell's way of viewing the matter has certain theoretical advantages, but the alternative view makes sense and is worth describing because the considerations favoring a reduction of continuants to events are, as I shall argue, independent of the problem of universals.

A fundamental difficulty with any version of the bundle theory is that it cannot, without inconsistency, guarantee the uniqueness of every bundle. This guarantee must be possible if the theory is sound, because any bundle that could be duplicated would be a universal and not, as the theory requires, a particular. Since two different particulars could, like two apples, be equally red, round, sweet, and juicy, each bundle must have some quality that makes duplication impossible. What kind of quality could this be? The answer Russell gave is "a spatio-temporal quality." However similar two apples may be, if one is here and the other is there, they must be different because of their different spatio-temporal qualities.

This view is not satisfactory, however. Objects of our immediate attention may have the properties of being here and of being there, but as Russell himself had to admit, such properties are implicitly relational and involve "emphatic particulars." Here and there, like now and then, are not themselves universals: they are either emphatic particulars proper or logical fictions that can be understood only in relation to such particulars. The latter alternative would be acceptable if by "is here" we mean "is close to *this*," this being an object of our attention, and by "occurs now" we mean "coincides temporally with *this* occurrence," this occurrence again being an object of our attention. In either case we should be making an ultimate reference to some kind of irreducible particular that is not just a bundle of universals. This violates the requirements of the bundle theory.

Another, perhaps more fundamental difficulty with the bundle theory is that the considerations favoring a bundle theory of particulars equally favor a bundle theory of universals. If universals are not to be understood as characterless abstractions that are indistinguishable from one another, they too must have attributes. But if things having attributes are to be understood as bundles, universals must also be regarded as bundles—bundles of further bundles, which are themselves bundles, and so on without end. Particulars, then, are perhaps more inclusive bundles than universals—but both will be endlessly complex and lack ultimate, irreducible cores. For my part, this is an utterly incredible view—something I cannot believe. Any theory having this consequence can hardly be regarded as satisfactory.

It is perhaps worth adding, as a final note, that if a bundle theorist tries to avoid this outcome by claiming that universals can be regarded as nonbundles in spite of having definite natures (or characters) that distinguish them from one another, he is open to the reply that, by parity of reasoning, particulars can also be regarded as nonbundles even though they have definite natures that distinguish them from one another. Thus, a bundle theory of particulars seems to stand or fall with a bundle theory of universals—which is to say, a bundle theory of everything.

The Failure of a Theory

If the bundle theory ultimately breaks down, the only serious alternative for a defender of the theory of immanent universals is the pincushion conception, which renders particulars fundamentally mysterious.[11] Since the nature of universals is not clearly spelled out by the theory, and the relation (or whatever) between particulars and universals is also left seriously unclear, the theory as a whole must be counted as excessively obscure—hardly the sort of theory that helps us to understand much of anything. This is a devastating objection, because the theory's chief claim to acceptability can be traced to its presumed ability to explain why different objects can be truly described by a single predicate.

As I explained in the first section of this chapter, the theory of immanent universals is based on a One Over Many argument. Stripped to essentials, the most plausible version of the argument amounts to this:

1. Different particulars are sometimes truly described by common predicates.
2. If different things are truly described by a common predicate, they must possess some absolutely determinate feature or features by virtue of which the predicate is correctly applied to them.
3. Therefore, absolutely determinate features exist or belong to the world.

Formulated this way, the argument owes its force to its second premise. But why should we, or anyone, accept this premise as true? It is silly to say that the premise is self-evident, for it is far too controversial to have that status. Those who defend the One Over Many argument generally say, when pressed, that there must be some reason (some explanation) why different objects can be truly described by the same predicate, and that the required explanation is given by that premise.

If we allow that an explanation is actually needed in this case, we should certainly ask, "Why should anyone suppose that premise 2 gives the right explanation?" The answer that is generally given to this kind of question takes the form of a question: "How else can the phenomenon be explained?" "What other explanation is possible?" The presumption is that, if no better explanation is available, we are entitled to accept premise 2 and the theory of universals that it tacitly involves.

Viewed this way, the One Over Many argument is ultimately based on what is known as an inference to the best explanation. As I shall argue in chapter 7, this kind of inference is not objectionable if (among other things) the relevant explanation is really a good one. But an explanation that, when carefully examined, has all the defects I have found in the theory of immanent universals is an extremely poor one. Such a theory cannot possibly be rendered acceptable by an inference to the best explanation. It is far too obscure, and it raises far more problems than it solves.

If the theory of immanent universals cannot successfully account for (or explain) true predication, what alternative line of explanation is available? By virtue of what, if determinate universals are not genuine components of things, is a predicate such as "scarlet" applicable to so many different things? The best thing to say here is this: The predicate "scarlet" is applicable to many different things because those things are scarlet. This is the best thing to say not just because alternative accounts break down or create unnecessary problems; it is the best thing to say because a compelling positive case can be made in its favor.

The positive case I have in mind can be developed from the notion of a world. Abstractly speaking, a world consists of certain objects that are held together, or unified, in some basic way. As I remarked in the last chapter, the objects of our world collectively constitute a spatio-temporal-causal system. Although derivative objects such as corporations and string quartets can be said to belong to a world, their existence is to be understood in relation to the fundamental objects that comprise what Kant called the world's "substance."

The fundamental objects of a world (whatever they are) can be described by fundamental predicates. Such predicates are used to characterize those objects—to say what they are like and how they are related to one another. When a fundamental predicate truly describes a fundamental object, it cannot ascribe some further object or component to it, for the object would not then be fundamental. Thus, at the fundamental level, description is not ascription. Fundamental predicates describe (or characterize) fundamental objects, and they do so without introducing objects of some further kind.

If we accept this view of fundamental predication, we must reject premise 2 of the One Over Many argument. At the fundamental level, at least, a predicate does not apply to an object because the object "possesses" some abstract component, or determinate universal. If "scarlet" is a fundamental predicate, it truly describes an object because *that object* is scarlet—not because it "possesses" or "contains" some further object of a special kind. This is the reason, basically, why I said that the best thing to say, when asked why "scarlet" is applicable to a number of different things, is "It is applicable to those things because they are scarlet."

A simple answer of this kind is not appropriate when we are asked why derivative predicates are applicable to an object. We might say, for example, that "red" is applicable to an object because it is scarlet—or vermilion, or barn red. And we might say that "brother" is applicable to a person because he is male and a sibling of some other person. Thus, in a great many cases a predicate "F" is applicable to a thing by virtue of something more elementary than the fact that the thing is F. But this is not always so: it is not so at the fundamental level. Perhaps the ultimate error of the theory of immanent universals is that it fails to appreciate this important fact. In not doing so, it ends up telling us that particular things are bare substrata or bundles of bundles of bundles. . . .

Attributes, Facts, and Truth

The theory I have just criticized is not the only theory that postulates entities called "universals." There is another theory according to which universals are components of facts rather than particular things. This theory is based on the so-called correspondence theory of truth.[12] Roughly speaking, the correspondence theory holds that simple statements and beliefs are true just when they correspond to a fact. Take the statement that snow is white, for example. This is a true statement, and it is true because it corresponds to a fact involving snow—the fact, namely, that snow is white. But what is a fact? It is certainly not the same as some particular thing or stuff, such as snow. If snow were green, the statement that snow is white would be false even though snow—green snow—exists. The fact that snow is white involves snow, but it also involves something else—and this can only be whiteness. Facts, Russell once said, are "combinations of entities"; and the fact that snow is white would seem to involve snow, whiteness, and (perhaps) the "relation" of exemplification.[13]

There is no doubt that the correspondence theory of truth has a strong initial plausibility, and the conception of universals associated with it is, at least at first sight, fairly appealing. When we make a statement like "John loves Mary," we are saying something about the world. If our statement is true, it is rendered such (it would seem) by something in the world. But while John and Mary are in the world, they are not themselves sufficient to render the statement "John loves Mary" true, for both may exist although no one is loved at all. What renders the statement true is therefore a fact involving Tom and Mary, and this fact would seem to be a complex involving at least three things: John, Mary, and the relation *loves*. This complex must also have a special structure or order, since our statement would not be true if Mary merely loved John. As a general matter, we seem forced to admit that if the statement "John loves Mary" is true, it must correspond to a fact in which John bears the relation of *loves* to Mary. If the world contains no such fact, then that statement is false.

An appealing feature of this view is that, since universals are said to be components of facts rather than of things, we do not have the problems about particulars that naturally arise for the theory of immanent universals. Thus, we are not faced with the Chinese Boxes absurdity, and there is no temptation to suppose that particulars might be either unknowable substrata or bundles of universals. On the other hand, universals themselves remain fairly mysterious entities, and the facts they are said to enter into have a dubious position in the world. It is easy to say that facts are combinations of entities, but they are certainly not made up of other things in the way in which a machine is made up of nuts, bolts, gears, and levers.

Philosophers who believe that statements are true by virtue of corresponding facts often end up saying, as Ludwig Wittgenstein did, that "The world is the totality of facts, not of things."[14] This sort of assertion ought to make us think twice about facts as objects in the world. Reflection on language may tempt us to suppose that such objects are real, but purely linguistic inquiries are a poor means of discovering what the world is really like. Observation and experimental inference are the obvious means of accomplishing this aim, and they lead to the view that the world is the totality of things, not facts. As I put it in chapter 2, the world is a space-time-causal system; and an example of something belonging to the world is a human being, John or Mary, not a fact including them. If our reflections on language lead to a view of the world seriously at odds with this one, we should suspect that they involve some kind of error.

This presumption is confirmed by a critical look at the term "fact." One who says that the facts will determine whether a certain claim is true is not using the word "fact" in some unusual way. Yet if we examine the normal meaning of the word, we find that it does not refer to a complex structure in the world. The fact that Tom loves Mary is not something that includes Tom and Mary; it is something that is *about* them. The fact that snow is white is, similarly, a fact about snow; it is not a complex that includes it. Normally understood, facts are the same as truths—and truths are propositions, not things in the world that make assertions true.

When we attempt to resolve some question by an appeal to the facts, our appeal generally consists in ascertaining key truths about the matter. Thus, we commonly determine the truth of some assertions by reference to the truth of others; this is the purpose, generally speaking, of inference. Of course, not everything can be known by inference: sooner or later we have to confront the nonlinguistic world itself. We do this when we make observations. What we observe are not facts, however. We observe things in the world—people, books, chickens—and we make up our minds about "the facts" concerning them. These facts are just relatively elementary truths.

Perhaps the basic motivation of the correspondence theory of truth is to specify, in a general way, the conditions under which elementary assertions are true. The aim is not to show how we may know that such an assertion is true; it is to explain what the truth of the assertion consists in. It is important to realize that we can do this without referring to a supposed extralinguistic "fact" to which a true assertion (or statement) corresponds. When, for example, we are dealing with the statement "John loves Mary," we can simply say that this statement is true, or is a truth, just when John loves Mary. Saying this may not be very informative, but it is certainly correct. John and Mary, we may assume, are in the world, and if John does love Mary, the statement that he loves her is true—and vice versa.

If one is convinced that true statements must represent or picture objects as they are, one can hold this view without acknowledging that true statements picture facts involving objects. Developing a suggestion from Wittgenstein's *Tractatus*, Wilfrid Sellars has argued that true statements do picture objects "as they are" just as maps picture neighborhoods as they are—with no "facts" included.[15] A map can picture a neighborhood by a configuration of named dots, each dot representing a house; and people who can read the map can find their way around the neighborhood—succeed in locating a certain house, for example—without any appeal to supposed facts or even universals. Similarly, a statement such as "John is next to Mary" can be viewed as a fragment or a more abstract (or discursive) map, which pictures John next to Mary. Instead of standing for a universal thing, *next to*, the words "next to' in the sentence "John is next to Mary" bring the names "John" and "Mary" together in such a way that the resulting sentence pictures John and Mary side by side.

Sellars claims that a metaphysically perspicuous language—one that discloses the pictorial function of sentences in the least misleading way possible—would dispense with predicates in favor of different ways of writing names and linking them together. In such a language one could say that John is next to Mary simply by writing the name "John" next to the name "Mary"—as in "John Mary." Similarly, one could say that John is tall by writing his name in tall letters. Such a language would be extremely cumbersome and inconvenient to use, but it would serve nicely to illustrate Sellars's thesis that statements can picture the world just as maps can picture neighborhoods. No reference to facts or universals would be possible in the language, for they are not objects in the world as John and Mary are.

Conceptualism

For the sake of relative completeness in my treatment of universals, I should at least mention a theory developed originally in the Middle Ages and occasionally defended even today. The theory is known as conceptualism. According to this theory, universals are concepts and, as such, are not present either in things or in nonlinguistic facts. Peter Abailard (1079-1142) may have been the first to hold this theory, though he said, confusingly, that universals are general words.

Abailard's view was approximately this.[16] General words such as "white" express general and abstract "notions" that our minds form when we perceive common likenesses between individual things. As I argued early in this chapter, things can be similar in certain respects without (even according to the theory of immanent universals) having common features. Thus, a creamy-white and a bluish-white thing may be similar in color and the predicate "white" may apply to both even though both have different determinate colors. As a conceptualist, Abailard denied that even determinate universals exist in things; a thing may be creamy white, according to his view, without having the universal *creamy whiteness* in it. Still, we recognize a similarity between creamy-white and bluish-white things, and we form a conception of their similarity, which is, Abailard said, "covered" or "expressed" by the predicate "white." Since different individual things are truly described by common predicates expressing a single conception, we can say that things truly described by a common predicate fall under a common conception—and this conception, being common (or applicable) to many, may be called a universal.

Abailard's view of a concept, or conception, was essentially Aristotelian: evidently he thought our minds form concepts by a process of abstraction. The details of this process, at least as Abailard conceived of it, are obscure, but the upshot was that we can form an abstract idea of what is common to similar things. This view does not stand up to criticism if it is granted that, strictly speaking, similar things do not have any "thing" in common.[17] If there is no single component in both creamy-white and bluish-white things, there is no common thing to form an abstract idea of. Thus, Abailard's view, carefully thought out, is in danger of collapsing into nominalism, the view that universals can be nothing but general terms. Of course, if one thinks of a concept as a mental word or predicate, as William of Ockham did, then one's conceptualism amounts to a form of nominalism anyway. But one would then have to deny that concepts are abstract ideas of common features.

It seems to me that the most satisfactory view of universals, which is probably best not called a view of universals at all, is that of nominalism. The only genuine things "common to many" are true descriptions, and these are linguistic entities. For a wide variety of reasons, cultural and otherwise, we classify certain things together or describe them by common terms, and our practice of doing this is in no way explained or rendered intelligible by postulating universal components in things. I have by now exposed the problems in the idea that common descriptions must be grounded in common features, but it may be useful to consider an example illustrating the general point that we often think of certain things as similar in some respect only because we have been taught to describe them by a common predicate.

Imagine that you are observing a large canvas painted chartreuse. Chartreuse is a shade of green, we are told; but a chartreuse canvas is no more similar to a Kelly green canvas (at least to a child) than it is to one painted bright yellow. Yet every educated person thinks of chartreuse objects as green. Nothing but custom is behind this. The same is true, though in a more complicated way, of our inclination to describe all sorts of objects by common predicates—and nothing is gained, philosophically, by postulating abstract common components or universals. If a creamy-white object and a bluish-white object can both be white without a common whiteness, two objects can be bluish white without a common bluish whiteness. Nothing is gained by a common abstract object except a good deal of philosophical perplexity.

Concluding Remarks

The arguments against universals that I have developed in this chapter do not imply that it is a mistake to say such things as "There are colors" or "There are shapes." Theories of universals postulate colors and shapes as irreducible objects of a special kind, and it is this postulation that I have been concerned to attack. Since our world contains colored and shaped objects—crimson blocks, for example—we may find it convenient to speak of colors and shapes and to say that there are such things. This way of talking is not objectionable if it is understood that colors and shapes exist only in some derivative sense. In everyday life we speak fairly loosely, and we may not have a very clear idea of how talk about colors and shapes relates to talk about fundamental objects, which may be red or white, round or square. Perhaps our talk about colors and shapes is inherently vague and indeterminate—or perhaps not. In any case, if my argument in this chapter is sound, colors and shapes are at best derivative "objects," and when we say that *there are* such things, we are not using "there are" in the primary sense discussed in the last chapter.

Chapter 4
LINGUISTIC ARGUMENTS FOR ABSTRACTA

IN THE LAST CHAPTER I discussed and ultimately rejected the principal theories of universals that philosophers have historically defended. My aim in this chapter is to consider the arguments frequently offered in support of the fundamental reality of other nonparticulars such as propositions, possibilities, and states of affairs. Since these arguments are based largely on facts about language, and since similar arguments are occasionally used to support a belief in universals, I shall begin with another section on universals and then move on to the major topics of the chapter.

Abstract Singular Terms

As a means of supporting their belief in universals of some kind or other, philosophers have recently focused attention on the common use of certain nouns and noun phrases that might be called "abstract singular terms." Consider the following assertions:

1. Honesty is a virtue.
2. The color of Mary's hair is the same as the color of my pencil.
3. Napoleon had all the qualities of a great general.

In recent years the debate about universals has been focused largely on such assertions.[1] The assertions are acknowledged to be true, and the controversy has turned on the question whether they can be paraphrased in terms referring to patently nonabstract entities. Since expressions like "honesty" and "the color of Mary's hair" seem to refer to something abstract, the assumption has been that, if we cannot find paraphrases in nonabstract terms for the true sentences in which these expressions occur, we shall have to acknowledge the existence of universals—even though we may have no idea whether universals are in things, out of things (like Plato's Forms), or whether they are mental objects or concepts.

In spite of its currency, this last assertion should strike us as exceedingly dubious. If we have no determinate idea of what universals are supposed to be, our failure to find appropriate paraphrases for statements such as 1, 2, and 3 should require us to admit that we are not really sure what those statements mean. Radical uncertainty about the meaning of familiar statements is by no means unusual in philosophy. When St. Augustine considered the question of what time is, he began by confessing: "If no one asks [it] of me, I know [the answer]; if I wish to explain it to him who asks, I know [it] not."[2] When we consider the assertion that honesty is a virtue, we may suppose that we know full well what it means. Yet when we try to offer a paraphrase of it, we may discover that, like Augustine, we know it not. If we are tempted to declare that it *must* assert something about an abstract thing, honesty, we shall have to admit, if we have no idea what such an object is supposed to be, that our declaration is tantamount to a confession of ignorance about the assertion's meaning.

There is no denying, it seems to me, that the meaning of assertions 1, 2, and 3 is fairly unclear. On the other hand, if we consider them one by one and do not try to unearth some simple strategy for interpreting them all, we can clarify their meaning without committing ourselves to mysterious abstract objects. I shall attempt to do this in what follows.

Consider assertion 1, "Honesty is a virtue." To deal with this example we might begin by considering a simpler example that a Platonist (or believer in universals) will offer anyway. The simpler example will contain the verb "exemplifies." Since honesty and virtue clearly pertain to human behavior, the Platonist will no doubt want to maintain that "Honesty is a virtue" is equivalent to "Anyone who exemplifies honesty exemplifies a virtue." In the absence of a theoretical account of what exemplification is supposed to be, we might say that to exemplify honesty is only to be honest. But what about exemplifying a virtue? The answer, I believe, is "being in a way virtuous." A liar who is courageous is not wholly virtuous; yet if (as the Greeks held) courage is a virtue, such a liar is partly virtuous, or virtuous in a way. Thus, the Platonist's assertion "Anyone who exemplifies honesty exemplifies a virtue" seems to be just a long-winded equivalent of "Anyone who is honest is, in a way, virtuous." We might therefore take our original assertion, 1, as having the sense of this last assertion.

If the notion of being "in a way" virtuous seems excessively ad hoc in this connection, the following observations may be helpful. To be perfectly virtuous is to be disposed to act only virtuously, that is, never to act nonvirtuously; to be in a way virtuous is to be at least partly virtuous, that is, to be disposed to act virtuously but not (necessarily) to act only virtuously. As far as honesty and virtue are concerned, the key idea is that honest people act honestly, and honest actions are virtuous actions. If we allow that one who is not wholly virtuous can, by acting virtuously and also (on occcasion) acting nonvirtuously, be both virtuous and nonvirtuous, we can avoid the "in a way" locution and say, more simply, that one who is honest is virtuous. This unqualified locution is quite all right so long as it is understood that "being virtuous" does not imply "being wholly virtuous."[3]

My interpretation of assertion 1 can be supported by a look at similar sentences. Consider "Tardiness is reprehensible," for example. Like assertion 1, this sentence has an abstract singular term as subject, but its predicate leaves little doubt that its subject does not refer to an abstract object. The sorts of things that are truly reprehensible are people and actions—not platonic objects, which cannot be criticized or reprehended. Thus, in spite of its abstract subject-term, "Tardiness is reprehensible" is really a sentence about tardy people or tardy actions: it means that tardy people are, in a way, reprehensible or, alternatively, that tardy actions are reprehensible actions. Parity of reasoning requires a similar interpretation of assertion 1.

To find a satisfactory paraphrase for assertion 2, "The color of Mary's hair is the same as the color of my pencil," we must appreciate certain points about quantification. As I explained in chapter 2, the existential quantifier can be interpreted in at least two different ways. According to the substitution interpretation, a statement such as "$(\exists x)(x$ is fat)" is true just when the propositional function "x is fat" has a true substitution instance, this being a true statement that differs from the propositional function only in having a name in place of the variable "x." According to the so-called range interpretation, an $\exists$-quantified statement is true with respect to a domain or universe of discourse, D, just when the relevant propositional function is satisfied by some object in D. If we take the actual universe—the system of existing things—as our universe of discourse, then the statement "$(\exists x)(x$ is fat)" will be true, interpreted in this second way, just in case something in the actual universe—Tom, say—is truly described by the predicate "fat."

When I discussed the substitutional interpretation, I observed that if the names that can replace variables in propositional functions are restricted to "logically proper" names, substitutionally quantified $\exists$-statements have the force of existence statements. It is, however, possible to generalize the substitution interpretation in a way that avoids this implication, and the result is very important for metaphysics.[4]

Consider the sentence "Tom is fat." By reference to this sentence we can identify two formulas that are reasonably called propositional functions. One is "x is fat" and the other is "Tom is F." If we allow predicate variables such as the "F" in "Tom is F" to be bound by $\exists$-quantifiers, we can interpret formulas such as "$(\exists F)(\text{Tom is } F)$" by a generalized substitution approach: we can say that they are true just when they have a true substitution instance. If "Tom is fat" is true, then "$(\exists F)(\text{Tom is } F)$" is also true, for "Tom is fat" is a substitution instance of "Tom is F." On the assumption that predicates are not names, we can no longer regard substitutionally interpreted $\exists$-statements as existence statements because the context "$(\exists F)(\ . \ . \ . \ F \ . \ . \ . \ )$" will not imply that an F exists; it will merely imply that some statement with an appropriate predicate is true.

Since $\exists$-quantifiers interpreted according to the range interpretation are always existence statements, at least if the associated universe of discourse is taken to be the actual universe, it is important to distinguish quantifiers that are interpreted in the two ways I have described. Following the practice of W. V. O. Quine, I shall do this by putting a subscript "s" on every quantifier that is to be interpreted substitutionally. Thus, "$(\exists_s x)(x$ is fat)" is to be interpreted according to the substitutional interpretation while "(Ǝx)(x is fat)" is to be understood according to the range interpretation. These two kinds of quantifiers can be combined as in formulas such as "(Ǝx)(Ǝ₅F)(x is F)."

Before turning to the example concerning the color of Mary's hair, I want to note two illustrative examples of substitutional quantification. First, suppose it is said that Tom and Sarah had the same thing for dinner. If we tried to express this claim by saying "(Ǝx)(Tom had x for dinner and Sarah had x for dinner)," we should be committed to the absurdity that there was one thing, perhaps a slice of veal, that both Tom and Mary ate. But if we said "(Ǝ₅ x)(Tom had x for dinner and Sarah had x for dinner)," we should be implying only that some substitution instance of the relevant propositional function is true. Such an instance might be "Tom had veal parmigiana for dinner and Sarah had veal parmigiana for dinner." Suppose, second, that both Mary and Sam thought about Santa on Christmas Eve. It is natural to conclude from this supposition that Mary and Sam thought about the same thing on Christmas Eve. Since Santa does not exist, we could not say that (Ǝx)(Mary thought about x on Christmas Eve and Sam thought about x on Christmas Eve). But we could use substitutional quantification and say that (Ǝ₅x)(Mary thought about x on Christmas Eve and Sam thought about x on Christmas Eve). This last formula is true because the propositional function it contains has a true substitution instance.

I now turn to the specimen assertion "The color of Mary's hair is the same as the color of my pencil." As a first step in working out a plausible paraphrase of this assertion, we might note that "The color of Mary's hair is yellow" is simply a variant of "Mary's hair is colored yellow." On this basis of this observation it seems reasonable to suppose that when we say "The color of Mary's hair is the same as the color of my pencil" we only mean, in effect, that some substitution instance of the following propositional function is true:

Mary's hair is colored F and my pencil is colored F.

What we in effect mean here can be expressed by the substitutionally quantified assertion:

(Ǝ₅F)(Mary's hair is colored F and my pencil is colored F).

The idea behind this paraphrase is similar to the idea behind the interpretation I gave to "Tom and Sarah had the same thing for dinner" and "Mary and Sam thought about the same thing on Christmas Eve." In all three cases the interpretation avoids the implication that some peculiar object is tacitly being referred to.

I now turn to the final specimen assertion, 3: "Napoleon had all the qualities of a great general." This assertion explicitly refers to attributes, which are supposed to be a species of universal. Although we constantly speak of attributes in everyday life and in science, we do not therefore have to regard them as fundamentally real or existent. Instead, we may say that they are fictions of some kind—convenient fictions that, like the average plumber, help to simplify our discourse. Even if we do not think that anything abstract actually exists, we may wish to speak abstractly about what does exist. However this may be, it seems wise, in view of the patent weakness of existing theories of universals, to seek some interpretation of assertion 3 that renders it unproblematic, not containing an explicit reference to abstract objects.

Although assertion 3 is a useful example to think about in a discussion of ontology, it is probably not true. Napoleon may have had many of the attributes of a great general, but his campaign of 1812 makes it very doubtful that he had them all. This drawback to assertion 3 may be ignored, however: we can at least assume that it is true. The question is, "How can we interpret it?" The answer is straightforward if we use substitutional quantification.

Suppose that "wise" is a predicate that truly applies to every great general. Without referring to any word or predicate, we can then say, "If every great general is wise, Napoleon is wise." To deal with (as it were) all the relevant attributes without actually referring to attributes, we can say that the following propositional function is true for all substitution instances:

If every great general is F, Napoleon is F.

Yet if all instances of this function are true, the following assertion is also true, though it refers neither to attributes nor to predicates:

$(\forall_s F)$(If every great general is F, then Napoleon is F).

We may regard this last assertion—in which the symbol "$\forall_s$" is a substitutional version of a universal quantifier—as a technical paraphrase of the problematic assertion 3. Since we know from the last chapter that predicates do not refer to attributes, the technical paraphrase, though it contains a special predicate variable, does not in any way imply that attributes exist or have some irreducible kind of being

Criteria of Ontological Commitment

My treatment of the specimen assertions in the last section illustrates a general strategy for interpreting many statements in which abstract singular terms occur. The strategy is to paraphrase the statements by technical counterparts that employ substitutional quantification. As I observed in the last chapter, this kind of quantification is not widely employed; the alternative, range interpretation is, in fact, the only interpretation that most philosophers seem to consider.[5] W. V. O. Quine, though allowing that substitutional quantification is an acceptable logical device,[6] has been particularly influential in employing the range interpretation; and philosophers who have followed his lead have found it exceedingly difficult to deal with such assertions as "Napoleon had all the qualities of a great general" or "May and Bill had the same thing for dinner."

In his highly influential paper "On What There Is," Quine proposed a widely discussed criterion of "ontological commitment," arguing that our use of an expression "E" can commit us to the existence of some entity just in case we are prepared to allow that a statement in which "E" properly occurs, " . . . E . . . ," warrants the conclusion, "$(\exists x)(. . . x . . .)$."[7] Since

Quine cannot, as he says, "countenance" attributes or universals, he will not accept as true any assertion, such as "$(\exists F)$(Tom is F)," in which a predicate variable is bound by an existential quantifier. If we ourselves do not accept the theory of universals, we must agree with Quine on this point *if* we interpret the existential quantifier as he does. As far as that interpretation is concerned, the statement "$(\exists F)$(Tom is F)" could be true only if there is some entity in the actual universe—for example, tall or tallness—that satisfies the propositional function "Tom is (or has) F." But if we do not think that there is such a thing as tall or tallness, we cannot allow that "Tom is F" is satisfied by it. Agreeing with Quine on this matter is unquestionably consistent with using substitutional quantifiers to bind predicate variables, for "$(\exists_s F)$(Tom is F)" is true just when some substitutional instance of the propositional function "Tom is F" is true; and "Tom is tall" is such an instance.

If we are prepared to use both kinds of quantification, as I am, we might wonder whether we must nevertheless agree with Quine regarding ontological commitment. I think not. It is no doubt true that we must acknowledge a "commitment" to a certain entity when and only when we can accept *some* existential statement concerning that entity, but the existential statement we thus accept does not have to be an existentially quantified formula. It can be a statement containing the predicate "exists."

In the last chapter I argued that Russell's objections (which are the standard ones) to the predicate "exists" are not satisfactory, and I proceeded to offer a definition of that predicate. The possibility of using "exists" in making existence claims does not prove that Quine's criterion is defective, but it does permit an alternative to that criterion. The alternative is that, in using an expression E, we are committed to the existence of some object just when our use of the expression warrants the conclusion that such an object exists. This alternative differs from Quine's criterion in not assuming something that his criterion presupposes—namely, that (as he put it) "the only way we can involve ourselves in ontological commitments" is "by our use of bound variables."[8] This background assumption is false: we can involve ourself in such commitments by explicitly saying that a certain thing exists.

It is, of course, true that we can use an $\exists$-quantified formula to make an existence claim. But to do this our $\exists$-quantifier has to be understood, or interpreted, in an appropriate way. If it is understood substitutionally, the relevant substitution class must contain "logically proper" names—names that we have actually attached to objects in the world. If it is understood according to the range interpretation, its associated domain must be restricted to things belonging to the actual world—that is, to things that actually exist. Quine tacitly adopts this latter alternative, but he has little to say about the means by which his intended domain is to be specified. I have argued that the actual world cannot be adequately specified in purely general terms but must involve some reference to actual objects of experience from which the rest of the world "radiates out."[9] If I am right about this, our use of bound variables involves us in "ontological commitments" only because those variables are understood as associated with things we believe to exist. From my point of view, therefore, Quine's criterion is less fundamental than the alternative I have suggested: it presupposes some means of identifying a world of existing objects.

Even if Quine's criterion of ontological commitment is less penetrating than many philosophers suppose, it calls attention to an extremely important fact—namely, that the presence of a singular expression E in a statement of whose truth we are fairly confident does not warrant our concluding that E refers to something real or existent. I discussed three unwarranted conclusions of this kind in the last section when I examined specimen assertions containing singular expressions such as "honesty" and "the color of Mary's hair." Since the use of other singular expressions have led philosophers to conclude that abstract propositions, possibilities, and even states of affairs are fundamentally real, I want to say something about them, too. As before, I shall restrict my discussion to certain representative examples.

Propositions and Adverbial Clauses

Although Russell (as we know from chapter 2) constantly spoke of propositions and propositional functions, he evidently regarded them, at least in his wiser moments, as verbal symbols—not abstract objects "expressed" by such symbols.[10] In his view the proposition that snow is white is, at least for speakers of English, the sentence "Snow is white"; and the propositional function that x is white is, for such speakers, the sentential function "x is white." This view is rejected by philosophers who believe in abstract objects of thought. They insist that sentences and sentential functions "express" propositions and propositional functions, and that the objects thus expressed are denoted or referred to by propositional clauses such as "that snow is white" and "that x is white."

Contemporary arguments for the existence of abstract propositions are commonly based on sentences containing propositional clauses. It is impossible, in a book like this, to consider every verbal construction that may be taken to support a belief in irreducible propositions, but two distinguishable kinds of verbal constructions are particularly relevant to such a belief, and we can easily consider them here.

The first kind of construction contains a propositional clause that functions as a predicate modifier. An example of such a construction is this:

Tom said that Mary is wise.

Here the clause "that Mary is wise" modifies the verb "said." Constructions of this kind lead some philosophers to believe in abstract propositions because arguments such as the following seem to be valid:

A1: Tom said that Mary is wise.
Harry said that Mary is wise.
Therefore, there is something that Tom and Harry both said.
A2: Tom said that Mary is wise.
Sarah believes everything that Tom said.
Therefore, Sarah believes that Mary is wise.

It is tempting to suppose that the validity of these arguments can be demonstrated by reference to the following schematic forms:

SA1: Tom said *p*.
Harry said *p*.
Therefore, (∃*x*)(Tom said *x* and Harry said *x*).
SA2: Tom said *p*.
(*x*)(If Tom said *x* then Mary believes *x*)
Therefore, Mary believes *p*.

But even if these schematic forms are valid, it does not follow that clauses such as "that Mary is wise" *must* stand for an abstract object. The reason for this is that the quantifiers in the schematic forms can be understood substitutionally. In fact, the substitutional interpretation of these quantifiers seems far preferable to the range interpretation.

Consider the second premise of the schematic form SA2, namely, "(*x*)(if Tom said *x* then Mary believes *x*)." If the variable here is understood as having some object for its value, we should have to allow that one can both say and believe such an object. But this seems bizarre. If Tom says that snow is white, he probably knows as well as believes that snow is white. Yet as we actually use the words "know" and "believe," about the only thing one can both know and believe are other people: we can know them in the sense of being acquainted with them, and we can believe them when they tell us something. But when we believe and know that snow is white, we don't seem to believe and know some inanimate "thing." The idea that we believe and know abstract objects is not a consequence of interpreting "Mary believes whatever Tom says" according to the substitution interpretation, for this interpretation requires only that every substitution instance of the following propositional function is true: "If Tom says *P* then Mary believes *P*." When substituends for "*P*" are restricted to quotations and propositional clauses, this interpretation seems both unproblematic and enlightening.

Since the arguments A1 and A2 can be interpreted substitutionally, the fact that they are valid cannot itself *show* that the propositional clauses they contain must stand for something, let alone something abstract. If the latter idea can be supported or demonstrated at all, it must no doubt be done by reference to the meaning of individual statements like "Tom said that Mary is wise." We shall have to attend to this now.

To clarify the meaning of a sentence such as "Tom said that Mary is wise," it is helpful to begin with the verb "to say." In general, to say something is to utter certain words and to mean something by them. Usually, people who say something mean what is normally meant by the words they use, or what a normal speaker who uttered them would mean. For this reason, we can generally relate what people say by giving their words. We do this direct discourse, as when we say:

John said, "Mary is wise."

When, for any number of reasons, we do not wish to give a speaker's exact words, we can use the device of indirect quotation and give words that, we suppose, are related to the speaker's words in special ways.[11] For example, if John spoke in French using the words "Marie est sage," we might convey his assertion by using a translation of his words in our *that*-clause, saying "John said that Mary is wise." In this case our *that*-clause contains an "indirect quotation" of John's words.

Sometimes the relation of a speaker's words to the words we use in our *that*-clause is even more indirect. Suppose a friend, Tom, actually said, "I will go to the theater with you tomorrow." If, the next day, we wish to relate what he said, we might say "Tom said that he would go to the theater with me today." Here the words we use in our *that*-clause might be called a "differently indexed counterpart" to Tom's words, for they refer to people and times in a way appropriate to a different speaker. In both these cases where we describe what someone says in indirect discourse, our description contains words that are related to the speaker's words in some special but tacitly well-understood way. In neither case do we refer to an abstract proposition; we are giving the speaker's words in an indirect way.

A minor philosophical puzzle is easily resolved by this interpretation of indirect discourse. The puzzle concerns the "referential opacity," as it has been called, of terms in *that*-clauses following a verb like "said." If I use the name "Mary" in saying "John said that Mary is wise," am I not referring to her and attributing to her the property of being said to be wise by John? An affirmative answer might at first glance seem tempting, but it is quickly refuted by the observation that one who says "John said that Zeus is insane" may certainly not intend to attribute some property to Zeus. To dispel some of the puzzlement that might arise from terms in indirect discourse, it may be helpful to say that the words following "said that" are never asserted by the speaker; they are merely *on display*.[12] If I say "John said that Mary is wise," *I* am not saying anything about Mary; I am merely conveying what John said, and for all I know Mary might not even exist. I use the words "that Mary is wise" only as an indirect means of giving his words; and I do it, in part, by *displaying* words that are related to his words in a certain way. Thus, even though I use the words "Mary is wise" in making an assertion, I should not be understood as referring to her at all.

Propositions and Logical Subjects

I turn now to the other principal context involving propositional clauses. In this second kind of context such clauses function as logical subjects rather than parts of a predicate. Examples of such contents are "That snow is white is true" and "That snow is white entails that something is white." Since propositional clauses appear as subjects in these sentences, it is tempting to suppose that they are used to refer to something and that their referent is something more abstract than a particular utterance or token. On the other hand, since an expression such as "the average plumber" can also occur as the subject of a true statement, we should be wary of supposing that these propositional clauses *must* be taken to refer to something real.

In spite of the different logical roles of propositional clauses as subjects and as predicate modifiers, there is a close logical connection between them. This can be seen by reference to the following argument, which is unquestionably valid:

> A3: That snow is white is true.
>
> Mary said that snow is white.
>
> Therefore, Mary said something that is true.

If we employ substitutional quantification and interpret the conclusion here as "$(\exists p)$(Mary said p and p is true)," the argument is easily proved valid. But although this interpretation of the argument gives us the results we want, it does nothing to illuminate the meaning of the first premise. We know that there is a close connection between the two kinds of propositional clauses, but we do not know exactly what the connection is.

To discover a satisfactory interpretation of propositional clauses as logical subjects, we might proceed in the indirect manner I adopted in interpreting verbal propositional clauses. We might, that is, begin by considering direct quotation. Here is an example:

> "Snow is white" is true.

The subject of this assertion refers to a meaningful sentence or assertion. Since no particular speaker is referred to, the sentence or assertion seems to be (in the terminology of chapter 1) a type rather than a token. Nevertheless, if the type is true, every token must be true, and vice versa. Instead of acknowledging the fundamental existence of both types and tokens, we can adopt Russell's strategy of eliminating unwanted entities (in this case, types) by contextual definition. As far as the sentence above is concerned, we could say that it asserts no more than the following: All "Snow is white" tokens or instances are true.

A similar interpretation can be given for contexts in which one assertion is said to imply one another. If P and Q are schematic letters representing propositional types, we can say that

> P implies Q =df every P-token implies every Q-token,

where our definiens means:

> $(x)(z)$(if x is an P-token and z is a Q-token, x implies z).

To avoid a possible difficulty about what to say if no tokens of P and Q exist, we can adopt either of two strategies. First, we can say that there is a sense in which such tokens are bound to exist, for a token can be a scattered object whose constituent letters may be found in different books in different libraries.[13] In fact, we can say that every sentence-token of English can be discovered among the letters of this very paragraph. Second, we can say that the "if . . . then . . . " of our definiens has a subjunctive force. The idea is that if something *were* a token of the appropriate type, then such and such *would* be true. Problems have been raised about the logic of subjunctive conditionals, but we should not be deterred from using them in the limited way suggested here.[14]

Having considered the significance of quotations or assertion-types as ostensible subjects of statements, I must now come to terms with propositional clauses as such subjects. An analysis parallel to the one just given has been urged, in effect, by Wilfrid Sellars.[15] According to him, the assertion that

[the proposition] that snow is white is true

can be paraphrased, or contextually defined, as meaning

All statements, beliefs, thoughts, etc., that snow is white are true.

The statements, thoughts, and beliefs in question here are not types but tokens: they are the statements, thoughts, and beliefs of actual people. We can make this idea more explicit by reformulating the suggested paraphrase as follows:

(x)(if x thinks, believes, or says that snow is white, then x's thought, belief, or statement that snow is white is true).

As before, the "if . . . then . . . " involved here is probably best understood as having a subjunctive force. The idea is that, if anyone *were* to say, think, or believe that snow is white, then his or her statement, thought, or belief . . . *would* (in fact or of necessity) be true.

This interpretation of propositional clauses as logical subjects discloses their intimate connection with propositional clauses used as predicate modifiers. In particular, it gives us the understanding we wanted of the argument A3 that I cited at the beginning of this section. If the assertion "That snow is white is true" means that all statements, beliefs, and thoughts that snow is white are true, then we know why, if Mary said or "made the statement" that snow is white, we may conclude that she said something that is true.

Statements and Beliefs

If the analysis I have been suggesting is to be satisfactory, a further question must be answered: "How is a belief that snow is white related to a statement that snow is white?" Saying that snow is white is producing verbal tokens with a certain meaning or, possibly, intention, but believing and even thinking that snow is white seem to be different things altogether.

This last question is very important, metaphysically, because abstract propositions have traditionally been taken to be the "objects" of beliefs, thoughts, and assertions. The assumption has been that beliefs, thoughts, and even hopes that *p* are all beliefs, thoughts, and hopes that *p* because they have a common object, the proposition that *p*. This assumption is related to the idea that a Frenchman's assertion and an Englishman's assertion can both be assertions that snow is white only because they "express" the same proposition. If these two assumptions are correct, or true, then the reduction of propositional types to tokens that I have suggested must be mistaken.

In attacking these assumptions it is easiest to begin with the second one. Suppose Jacques says, "La neige est blanche." If we relate what he says by uttering "Jacques said that snow is white," we are, as I put it earlier, *indirectly quoting* his words. We do this by using words in our *that*-clause that are, in this case, a good translation of Jacques' words. But to be a good translation of his words, our words and his words do not have to be related to some common abstract object. On the contrary, two assertions can be said to be good translations of each other just when (a) they are true under precisely the same conditions and (b) the implications of each are parallel to the implications of the other. This last condition is somewhat vague, as stated here, but it is based on the idea, which I shall defend at length in chapter 7, that an assertion's meaning is exhausted by its implications and truth-conditions.[16] Thus, if Jacques' assertion is a good translation of mine, every implication of his assertion such as "Quelque chose est blanche" must correspond to an implication of my assertion that is true under precisely the same conditions.

In recent years W. V. O. Quine has argued that assertions in different languages can be said to be good translations of one another only by reference to a "scheme of translation" that, roughly speaking, identifies words of both languages and correlates them together.[17] He has also argued that, in principle at least, two languages can be correlated in different ways, so that different schemes of translation are always possible. As a result of this, he holds that, absolutely speaking, translation is always "indeterminate." However this may be, there is no doubt that, in deciding whether an assertion in one language can be satisfactorily translated by a certain assertion in another language, we have to consider what we take to be the implications of both assertions, their truth-conditions and so forth, and then decide whether one can reasonably be considered the counterpart of the other. When we do this, we make no reference to an alleged abstract object that both assertions somehow "express." In fact, a reference to such an object would be otiose in this connection, for to determine whether one assertion—a Frenchman's, say—did "express" a certain abstract object, we would no doubt have to consider its implications and truth-conditions. When we have done this for both assertions, we would have all the information we need to decide whether they are good translations of one another quite apart from any consideration of a mysterious object that they both express.

Even if we can thus account for the fact that different assertions sometimes in different languages can be described by a common propositional clause without assuming the existence of an abstract proposition, we still have a problem about thoughts and beliefs that, say, snow is white. What justifies us in describing thoughts and beliefs, which are not uses of words, by the propositional clauses that we use in describing assertions? A detailed answer to this question is possible, but it cannot be given without a fairly detailed excursus into the philosophy of mind.[18] The following remarks will have to suffice for our purposes here.

Although it is no doubt mistaken to conceive of thoughts as literally inner speech, there is no question that we conceive of a thought—for example, the thought that it will rain, which may have occurred to Jones at a particular moment—as something analogous to a remark or utterance. The analogy concerns the semantic features of the thought. The thought that it will rain is a thought about rain; it has the same truth conditions as the assertion that it will rain; and it has corresponding implications because, if the thought that it will rain is true, it is true that something will happen, which means that every actual assertion that something will happen is true. Thus, although thoughts differ significantly from assertions in empirical respects, they have the same semantical features (they refer to things, are true or false, have implications), and this is enough to justify us in describing them by the propositional clauses that we apply to corresponding assertions.

A belief is a more complicated state of mind than a simple thought, though one who believes that snow is white is apt to entertain the thought that snow is white from time to time. However this may be, we unquestionably describe our beliefs in relation to the words that we should utter if we put them (or "expressed" them) in words. Speakers of English who believe that snow is white are inclined to say "Snow is white," and if are called upon to say what they believe about snow, they might naturally say "I believe that snow is white." By contrast, speakers of French who believe that snow is white are inclined to say "La neige est blanche," and if called upon to say what they believe about snow, they might say "Je crois que la neige est blanche." The assertions expressing the relevant beliefs of the French are thus what I called "semantic counterparts" to the assertions expressing the corresponding beliefs of the English, and the words the former would use to describe their beliefs are good translations of the words the English would use to describe corresponding beliefs. In view of this we can justifiably think of a person's belief that snow is white as a state of mind that can be put into words by the assertion "Snow is white" or some semantic counterpart thereof. Although this conception does not fully characterize a belief, it gives at least a general idea of what we can reasonably mean when we speak of a belief *that* snow is white.

A final point. In the last few pages I have been writing as if I think that beliefs and thoughts—or, more generally, states and occurrences—are irreducible entities. Reasons have been given in support of this view, but until we have come to terms with them (a topic for chapter 6) we might wish to avoid a commitment to such entities. We can do this, at least for the time being, by offering contextual definitions for statements ostensibly referring to beliefs and thoughts. The strategy for constructing the appropriate definitions can be illustrated by the following example:

John's belief that *p* is true $= df$ John believes truly that *p*.

Here a statement ostensibly referring to a belief is transformed into a statement about a person. It is true that the latter statement, by virtue of its predicate, describes a person as believing such and such, but it does not *refer* to any state or occurrence. If we say "John believes truly that snow is white," we are not *referring* to any object or thing other than John.

For what it is worth, I might add that "truly" does not indicate the manner in which something is done—as some philosophers seem to suppose. In a statement of the form "*S* believes truly that *p*" the word is, as traditional grammarians say,[19] "an adverb of affirmation," and its presence in the statement indicates that we may infer "*p*." As a consequence of this grammatical point, we might regard "John believes truly that snow is white" as an abbreviated version of "John believes that snow is white, and snow is white." If we accept this interpretation, we can reformulate the defining clause (the definiens) I gave for "That snow is white is true." We can now say that this assertion has the sense of

(x)(if x thinks, believes, or says that snow is white, then x thinks, believes, or says that snow is white, and snow is white).

Possibilities and Fictional Objects

If we are to survey the principal kinds of abstract entities that have been said to exist, we must say something about possibilities. As it happens, there are several important senses in which something may be said to be possible. There are the senses of logical possibility, physical possibility, practical possibility, and various senses of relative possibility. There are also possibilities *de dicto* and *de re*.[20] In spite of this variety of senses, two principal kinds of entities have been said to be possible: individual things and states of affairs. The notion of a possible world, which has been very widely discussed in recent years, is generally analyzed in relation to the notion of a state of affairs.[21]

People are often led to speak of possible things when they reflect on stories, plays, and myths. In Dostoevski's novel *The Idiot* there is, we might naturally say, a character named "Prince Mishkin," who exemplifies Dostoevski's Christian ideal of a perfectly good man. Since we naturally say that *there is* such a character in Dostoevski's novel, we might suppose that this character has some kind of being. On the other hand, since we know full well that Dostoevski's Prince Mishkin never actually existed and never will actually exist, we seem to be affirming the being of a merely possible person, an unactualized possibility.

When we read a first-class novel, we often become so interested in the story that we almost forget it is fiction and find ourselves speculating about the motives the characters may have had for doing this or that. In sober moments we recognize that our speculations are absurd: anything not said or implied in the novel is not part of the story; and if a certain character is not portrayed as having a particular motive, there is no such motive to think about. The essence or nature of a fictional character is exhausted by its description: it has no being apart from the description (or the story) to speculate about. A fictional character is just that—a fiction—and our remarks about such a character should be susceptible of a paraphrase comparable to the paraphrase that is appropriate to remarks seemingly about the average plumber.

When I described Russell's theory of descriptions, I presented one strategy for avoiding a commitment to the being of nonexisting objects, such as the present king of France. But Russell's strategy is not applicable, at least as he described it, to alleged fictional beings. According to Russell, a statement about the present king of France is equivalent to an existential statement about the real world: the claim that the king is bald amounts to the claim that there is exactly one person who is the king of France and who is bald. Yet if we say that Dostoevski's Prince Mishkin almost married Nastasia Filippovna, we don't mean to say that there is exactly one person who is Prince Mishkin and who almost married Nastasia Filippovna. We don't mean this because we know full well that there is not and never was such a prince.

To work our way toward a satisfactory interpretation of talk about fictional beings, we might begin with the observation that when we say, as we unquestionably do, that *there is* such and such a character in a certain novel, we can only mean that such a character is described or referred to in the novel. A novel, being a book, actually contains words and descriptions, not characters and scenes. In view of this obvious truth we might say that an assertion such as "Prince Mishkin, in Dostoevski's *The Idiot*, was not really an idiot" has the import of something like "The things Dostoevski says in *The Idiot* about Prince Mishkin imply that the prince is not really an idiot." To provide a further clarification of our remark we might add that when we say that Dostoevski said something, in his novel, *about* Prince Mishkin, we mean that he used words in that novel that, if understood as truly spoken of the real world, would be taken to refer to an actual prince fitting Dostoevski's Mishkin descriptions. A Mishkin description, we might add, is one of the form "Prince Mishkin is (was) *F*" or "*X* is *F*," where "*X*" is an anaphoric device (a pronoun, a description) that refers forward or backward (in the novel) to a use of the term "Prince Mishkin." This last claim is not perfectly precise and exact, but it does give a general idea of what we mean. The key point is that we can make sense of references to and descriptions of a certain fictional "thing" wholly in terms of certain referring and descriptive *words*.

One might object to what I have just said on the ground that a fictional thing is pretty obviously an imaginary thing, and an imaginary thing is *something* that we can imagine. The word "something" should not be taken too seriously, however. It doesn't follow that just because we can imagine something, there is in the existential sense something that we imagine. If we imagine that Santa is fat, we may assert that $(\exists x)$(we imagine that x is fat), for this is true if the propositional function "We imagine that x is fat" has at least one true substitution instance. But the truth of the instance "We imagine that Santa is fat" does not imply that something *exists* and is imagined by us. On the contrary, to imagine that Santa is fat is only to have an imaginative idea of Santa as fat.

An imaginative idea of Santa is, moreover, nothing but an imaginative Santa-idea—this being an idea that, if it did actually apply to something that exists, would apply to something that had the distinctive features our idea involves, such as a white beard, a red nose, a pot belly, and a red suit. An imaginative idea of a person is thus comparable to a description of a person: the two are not literally "directed to" some object that may or may not exist; rather, they are such that, if they did apply to something real, they would apply to something satisfying the relevant imagined conditions.

Other Possibilities

Another sort of alleged possibility that we should at least touch upon is that of a possible world. The concept of such a world has been widely discussed in recent years because of an important development in a branch of mathematics called "modal logic."[22] Although modal logic has been expanded to cover a good deal of ground, it was originally concerned with the logic of necessity and possibility. This logic is based on a traditional distinction between necessary and contingent truth. A contingent truth is said to depend on the way the world happens to be. Since, intuitively speaking, the world could have been other than the way it actually is, a truth that is contingent might (could possibly) have been false. An example of such a truth is "Many American basketball players are nearly seven feet tall." A necessary truth, on the other hand, is one that could not be otherwise: it is true in all possible worlds. The notion of a possible world is thus used to specify the conditions under which statements involving alethic modalities (necessity and possibility) are true.

Although the notion of a possible world is very useful in interpreting modal logic, it does not have to be regarded as applying to something real or existent. Nevertheless, many philosophers believe in possible worlds, regarding them as highly complex "states of affairs." In contrast to a possible world, a simple state of affairs is the supposed referent of a noun clause such as "John's kissing Mary." It seems to me that such "entities" are clear cases of logical fictions.

Philosophers who regard states of affairs as irreducible entities generally have very little to say about them. Apart from the assertion that they are the referents of various noun clauses, the most common claims about them are that they "obtain" or "do not obtain"; that they stand in entailment relations to other states of affairs; and that they may be funny, sad, or the like. Claims of the first two kinds should raise a strong presumption that states of affairs can be nothing but fictions. To say that John's kissing Mary "obtains" is only to say, in a long-winded way, that John is kissing Mary; and to say that this alleged state of affairs "did obtain" or "will obtain" is only to say that John did kiss Mary or that he will kiss her. As for the supposed entailments between states of affairs, the claim that S's doing A entails G's doing B seems to be only a clumsy way of saying that the statement or proposition that S does A entails the proposition that G does B. The predicate "entails" applies in the first instance to statements or propositions because we define it in relation to truth: roughly, the statement P entails the statement Q just when Q must be true if P is true.

The claim that a state of affairs may be funny, sad, or unfortunate is more difficult to interpret than the claims just considered. There is no doubt that we commonly employ verbal nouns and say such things as "Mary's mimicking the professor was funny" or "Tom's hitting Bill was unfortunate." But there is no evident reason to suppose that these verbal nouns must stand for irreducible objects that are funny, sad, or unfortunate. If we say "Mary's mimicking the professor was funny," we probably mean that she mimicked him in a funny way or that her action, a concrete temporal occurrence, was funny. And if we say that Tom's hitting Bill was unfortunate, we probably mean either that Tom's act was unfortunate or, more simply, that Tom should not have hit Bill. In neither case should we mean that some abstract object has some property or is describable in a certain way.

However sound this last point may be, the notion of a possible world required for interpreting formulas of modal logic is essentially formal: it is simply the idea of a system of determinate objects standing in various relations to one another. It is easy enough to imagine a system of this kind, and we can imagine a more determinate system if we imagine the actual world varied in certain ways—with different kinds of animals, with men we know to be bald having dark, curly hair, and so on. As I have emphasized, however, we can imagine something without thereby having to acknowledge that there is (existentially speaking) something that we imagine. To imagine something is to have an imaginative idea of (substitutionally) something; and to have an imaginative idea of, say, Mishkin is to have an idea of such a kind that, if it actually applied to anything x, x would be a person having the Mishkin features Dostoevski described in *The Idiot*.

Apart from the considerations prompted by reflection on modal logic and fictional descriptions, examples of familiar verbal constructions lead people to speak of possibilities. Such constructions are apt to contain words such as "something" and "that"—words which seem to require a referent. If I describe what I think might happen if my friend's car is not lubricated, he might say "That's a real possibility" or "Something like that is, I must admit, possible." We know by now, however, that many apparent substantive or referring expressions are not genuinely referential. If it is a real possibility that my friend's engine will be damaged, we may infer that $(\exists_s C)$(it is a real possibility that C), and this seems to express adequately enough the import of "Something is a real possibility." The word "that," though it often serves to pick out some object of attention, is also used anaphorically to direct attention to some other expression. When my friend says "That is a real possibility," he is claiming that what I suggested is a real possibility; and what I suggested is *that his engine will be damaged*. But we have seen that *that*-clauses of this last kind do not stand for anything. The one used here indirectly quotes my suggestion by displaying words that are semantic counterparts to the ones I used. All things considered, the import of my friend's "That is a real possibility" could be made explicit by "It is a real possibility that my engine will be damaged."

If, as I believe, talk about possibilities is ultimately reducible to assertions of the form "It is (logically, conceptually, physically, practically) possible that *p*," then the task of clarifying such talk reduces to the task of clarifying the sentential prefix, "It is possible that. . . . ' Since this prefix is used in a variety of senses, it is worth mentioning, in a general way, how these various senses might be clarified. It seems to me that the following definitions are approximately correct:[23]

1. It is logically possible that *p* =*df* the proposition that *p* is formally consistent, that is, does not logically imply a contradiction.
2. It is conceptually possible that *p* =*df* the proposition that *p* is not false by definition.
3. It is physically possible that *p* =*df* the proposition that *p* is consistent with the laws of nature.
4. It is practially possible that *p* =*df* human beings are capable of bringing it about that *p*.

These four definitions do not exhaust the possible meanings of "It is possible that *p*," but they are representative of these meanings.[24] Although the defining clause in each case contains the expression "the proposition that *p*," we have seen that such expressions can be eliminated in favor of expressions referring to thoughts, statements, and beliefs—and that these last expressions can be eliminated in favor of expressions referring to human beings. Thus, the various claims we commonly make about possibilities do not, if they are true, require us to postulate a new category of existent or subsistent things. As far as assertions about possibility are concerned, the fundamental realities still seem to be particulars.

Concluding Remarks on Abstracta

Lengthy as my discussion in this chapter has been, it has in no way exhausted the subject, for it has not dealt with every consideration that those who believe in abstracta as irreducible furniture of the world might seize upon. It has, however, brought out one crucial fact that should be kept firmly in mind when such considerations are advanced: No determinate conception of an abstract entity has ever been adequately developed. Thus, even if the analyses I have suggested for various linguistic forms are ultimately faulty in some degree, we can reasonably deny that there is some presumption in favor of admitting abstract entities as irreducible realities that nominalists must defeat. There could be a presumption in favor of accepting a certain general theory, but the presumption could exist (as it were) only if the theory is relatively clear and determinate. But no such theory is actually in hand for abstract entities. We have the words "abstract entity," but almost no theory to back them up.

These last considerations are very important, because it is sometimes said that, to explain various linguistic phenomena, we must postulate abstracta as theoretical entities in just the way that physical scientists postulate such things as photons to explain natural phenomena. As I shall argue in chapter 8, there is no tenable objection to postulating theoretical (or unobservable) entities to explain observable phenomena. Yet when such postulation is reasonable, a fairly determinate theory or at least conception of the relevant entities must be in hand—and this is precisely what is lacking when philosophers postulate abstracta.

For the sake of clarity here, I might mention the kinetic theory of gases. To explain why observable gases conform to the Charles and Boyle laws, physicists postulated unobservable atoms whose energy is correlated with observable temperature—roughly, with measurable warmth and coldness. These atoms were conceived of as tiny elastic objects whose behavior conforms to Newton's laws of motion. As their energy increases in proportion to increases in observable temperature, they interact more vigorously, exerting greater force on the walls of the relevant container and thereby increasing observable pressure. Other observable effects are similarly explained by atomic interactions. The key fact for our purposes is that the theory characterizes the postulated entities in such a way that we can understand how their collective behavior brings about the effects that we can observe. Thus, it is only because the postulated entities are conceived of in a determinate way that the theory postulating them is capable of explaining anything at all.[25]

Nothing comparable to this is found in "theories" of abstract entities. Such entities are fundamentally mysterious, and no account is given of what they are like, how they interact with other things, and so forth. For the most part, they are merely said to be "exemplified" by things (universals), to be "expressed" by things (propositions, concepts), to "obtain" or not (states of affairs), to have members and so on (classes or sets). Obviously, such descriptions are far too skimpy and formal to render such alleged entities explanatory; and if no fuller, more determinate account of them can be given, we should have no doubt whatever that they are, at best, logical fictions—in the same general category as Prince Mishkin and the average plumber.

A final remark. In my second chapter I described Russell's reductionist approach to mathematics in sympathetic terms. Since I do not accept properties (or attributes) as irreducible realities, I cannot, obviously, accept the details of his approach. Although I did not mention the fact, his approach also involves technical difficulties not apparent at the time he wrote.[26] Nevertheless, there is no good reason to suppose that numbers and sets are irreducibly real or existent. In fact, it is far from clear what one could mean in speaking of the fundamental existence of a number or set; such things are certainly not located in our space-time-causal system. Leibniz seems to have held that an abstract entity could be said to exist (in a derivative sense) if an appropriate description or conception were consistent. Similar views have been expressed recently.[27] I have no doubt that mathematical objects are best understood as fictions of some kind or other, but I am frankly uncertain about the preferred strategy for analyzing statements "about" them.

Chapter 5
CHANGING THINGS

ACCORDING TO THE ARGUMENT of the last two chapters, only particulars are fundamentally real or existent. The main question to be discussed in this and the following chapter is "What are particulars?" As we know by now, this question has been answered in different ways by different philosophers. A good share of the disagreement springs from problems about the notion of a changing thing, and these problems will be my chief topic in the present chapter. Since selves or persons are particularly interesting examples of changing things, problems about personal identity—or the identity, through time and change, of selves or persons—will eventually dominate the discussion.

Continuants and Change

As we ordinarily conceive of the world, the particulars it contains are, in the first instance, continuants—things that, like trees and people, persist in time and undergo change. On the face of it, such particulars are either simple or complex. A complex particular is one that is made up of more elementary particulars. If complex particulars are viewed as aggregates, then complex particulars are really derivative objects: they exist only in the sense that the simple particulars making them up exist and are related in appropriate ways. As we shall see in chapter 8, plausible reasons can be given for thinking that some complex particulars are not mere aggregates; such particulars have been called "organic unities" or "emergents."

In addition to continuants, particulars seem to include happenings or events, processes, and such things as shadows, ocean waves, and sensations—the latter including pains, itches, and feelings of dizziness. Philosophers in the Aristotelian tradition generally claim that only continuants have fundamental reality or existence; as they see it, happenings, processes, and the like are only adjectival to, or "modes" of, continuants. According to these philosophers, when we say that a movement occurs, we can only mean (if we have our philosophical wits about us) that some thing, some continuant, moves; and when we say that a process occurs, we can only mean that some continuant or continuants did this or that, acting alone or in sequence. As for waves and the like, these are only perturbations in a body of water, and a body of water is a continuant. Since shadows may persist in time, they too are continuants, though they depend for their existence on the thing casting them. Sensations, finally, are sensory states, not individual existents. I shall have more to say about these matters in the pages to follow.

Aristotle called continuants "primary substances" and said that their most distinctive characteristic is that, while remaining one and the same, they are capable of possessing contrary qualities.[1] By saying that they are capable of possessing such qualities, he meant that they are capable of undergoing a change from having some quality Q to having a quality incompatible with Q. The idea that an individual thing can actually undergo such a change while remaining the very same thing has caused a good deal of perplexity in the history of metaphysics, and a discussion of some of the main problems involved is a good way to approach the subject of particulars. I shall, in any case, adopt this approach here.

One of the oldest, simplest, and yet most persistent problems about change can be expressed as a question: "How can a thing possibly remain one and the same if it has changed?" The suggested answer is that it cannot: If a thing has changed, it is by definition different from before. Given this, we shall have to say that if a continuant is supposed to be something that can remain one and the same while undergoing change, no continuant ever did or could exist. The very idea of such a thing is contradictory.

To undermine this last claim we need only attend more carefully to the definition of a continuant. According to the definition, a continuant is a thing that persists through at least some interval of time and that is capable of undergoing change while remaining the same *thing* as before. But "remaining the same thing" does not imply "staying exactly the same and not changing"; it implies only that the same particular continues to exist. When Aristotle said that the mark of a primary substance is that it is capable of admitting contrary qualities, he did not mean to suggest that a substance could admit contrary qualities at the same time; as I pointed out, his idea was that a substance could change, this being a matter of losing a quality and gaining another quality incompatible with the one it lost. Thus, when a maple tree exists for a year in a mature state, it will have light green leaves in the spring, dark green leaves in the summer, brown or reddish leaves in the fall, and no leaves in the winter. These changes are entirely compatible with its remaining the very same tree throughout the year.

As this rejoinder might suggest, some changes are more significant for a thing's continued self-identity than others. According to Aristotle, the changes compatible with a thing's continued existence are "accidental" changes; a change in a thing's substance or "essence" brings the thing to an end. A woman could change in size or shape, as after diet or surgery, while remaining the same woman; but she would not remain the same thing if, like Daphne, she changed into a laurel bush. If she changed enough to become a bush, "she" would not longer be a woman, a female human being, and thus would not be the same *thing* as before.

Aristotle thought that the substances or primary things in nature belong to natural kinds and that the essence of a natural thing is determined by the smallest natural kind to which it belongs. I speak of the smallest natural kind because kinds can be conceived of more or less abstractly. Every natural thing, Aristotle says, is either a plant or an animal; and if it is an animal, it is either rational or nonrational. The smallest natural kind (the "infima species") to which a human being belongs is that of humanity, or rational animality; thus, rational animality constitutes the essence of a human being. Since two human beings have the same essence on this view, they are generically the same; they differ as particulars because their common essential nature, or "Form," is embedded in different portions of flesh.

For anyone who believes in Aristotelian Forms, the notion of a "real" essence, or essence of a thing, may seem natural and unproblematic, but philosophers in the modern period have generally found such essences to be highly dubious entities. Bertrand Russell is a case in point. After remarking that the notion of an essence is "hopelessly muddle-headed," Russell added:

> The "essence" of a thing appears to have meant "those of its properties which it cannot change without losing its identity." . . . In fact, the question of "essence" is one as to the use of words. . . . The "essence" of Socrates thus consists of those properties in the absence of which we should not use the name "Socrates." The question is purely linguistic: a *word* can have an essence, but a *thing* cannot.[2]

Although Russell's view here is fundamentally correct, it is badly stated. The view he is trying to express can be summarized by the slogan "Essences are purely nominal," but one who accepts the slogan need not deny that things can have essences—particularly if essences are not Aristotelian Forms. Socrates' essence may consist of those properties that we happen to associate with the name "Socrates"; yet if Socrates exists, he (and not his name) will possess those properties. This claim can be allowed even by one who, like me, does not accept properties as ultimately real. Suppose that we assign the name "Socrates" to *a certain man*. If we conceive of a man as a rational animal, we shall then be assigning the name to a rational animal—and any descriptions applicable to Socrates will then be applicable to a *certain* rational animal.

Russell's reasons for thinking that the notion of essence is hopelessly muddle-headed are not included in the passage I have quoted above. To understand his reasons it is helpful to recall the example of Daphne, who escaped Apollo's amorous advances by changing into a laurel bush. If we reflect on the series of changes that took place during her so-called transformation, it might occur to us that it is really objectionable to say that one thing, a woman, gradually changed into another thing, a bush. What actually exists in such a case is, we might insist, a complex series of events—with no persisting things involved. This is Russell's view: the notion of a persisting thing is, he says, "merely a convenient [means] of collecting events into bundles." Apart from the events or occurrences that we can observe in Daphne's transformation, the persisting "things" are "mere imaginary hooks, from which the occurrences are supposed to hang." But the occurrences, he insists, "have in fact no need of a hook, any more than the earth needs an elephant to rest on."[3]

Two sorts of considerations lie behind Russell's remarks here. The first is that there appears to be something highly arbitrary in supposing that, in cases where we ordinarily say that one thing is transformed into something else, we first have one thing and then, a little later, have something entirely new. The other is that, if "we think of a substance . . . as a thing possessing various properties," the thing as opposed to the properties is a very mysterious entity. As Russell put it, "when we take away the properties, and try to imagine the substance by itself, we find that there is nothing left." Thus, if we abandon the notion of a persisting thing, we can achieve a far more realistic view of what actually exists in the world. We shall not then suppose that things pop in and out of existence at certain points in a continuous process of change, and we shall not have to wonder about the nature of certain mysterious hooks that are supposed to hold occurrences together.

The considerations involved here are quite distinct: the first is tempting, and possibly sound; the second is erroneous, the result of accepting properties as basic realities. Russell seemed to think that the second consideration exposed the confusion specifically involved in the notion of a substance or continuant, but if that consideration were tenable, it would expose confusion in *any* notion of an irreducible particular, even in the notion of an irreducible event or process. Russell wrote that the occurrences we observe are not imaginary hooks on which properties are hung; yet if those occurrences have properties, we can follow Russell himself and ask what would be left if we took away the properties and tried to imagine the occurrences by themselves. As we saw in the last chapter, Russell was led by his belief in irreducible properties (or universals) to accept a bundle theory of particulars generally; and according to that erroneous theory, irreducible events or occurrences are just as illusory as irreducible substances.

Russell's first consideration is, as I said, tempting and possibly even sound. In the next chapter I shall offer a detailed criticism of Russell's view that a changing thing should be understood as a series of momentary events; here I shall simply say that, if there is something highly arbitrary in conceiving of Daphne's transformation as one "thing" turning into another "thing," the arbitrariness is in no way minimized by Russell's approach. Russell contended that Daphne should be viewed as a series of Daphne-events; but any decision as to when this series ends and the bush-series begins will be no more and no less arbitrary than the conventional decision as to when she ceases to exist and the bush begins to exist. In both cases we are faced with something odd—certain intermediate events that do not clearly belong in either bundle, and a particular "thing" that is neither a familiar sort of a woman nor a familiar sort of bush.

If I am right in what I have been arguing, Russell's reasons for thinking that the notion of a thing's essence is "hopelessly muddle-headed" were not satisfactory. In spite of this Russell was, as I said, fundamentally correct when he said that Socrates' essence consists in certain "properties" that we associate with the name "Socrates." If, as he also said, a thing's essence consists of the properties "it cannot change without losing its identity," then the manner in which we conceive of what we are referring to when we use a name is no doubt crucial for settling questions about that thing's identity. I want to pursue this idea a bit further by considering another example.

As a contrast to the example of Daphne and the laurel bush, it is interesting to consider the metamorphosis of a caterpillar. If, like a child, we conceive of caterpillars and butterflies as different sorts of things, we should have to say that the butterfly that emerges from the cocoon is a different thing from the caterpillar than spun the cocoon. But as matters stand, we do not actually conceive of butterflies and caterpillars this way. To put it somewhat roughly, we conceive of a caterpillar as a certain kind of insect in an early stage of its development, and we conceive of a butterfly as an insect in a later stage of its development. Given this, we can truly say that the butterfly emerging from the cocoon is the same insect as the caterpillar that created the cocoon. So long as the referents of "this butterfly" and "that caterpillar" are taken to be a certain insect, there is no tenable objection to identifying the two animals: the thing (the insect) that is now a butterfly is one and the same as the thing (the insect) that was a caterpillar.

The claim I am making here should not be misunderstood. Some contemporary philosophers have argued that identity is always "relative," meaning by this that a thing a cannot be said simply to be the same as (or identical to) a thing b, but only the same K as b, where "K" picks out some kind or sort of thing.[4] I am not saying this. The caterpillar I spoke of may be identified with the butterfly in the nonrelative sense expressed by the symbol " $=$ ": that caterpillar $=$ this butterfly. The truth of this statement will depend, however, on the manner in which the referents of the expressions "this butterfly" and "that caterpillar" are to be understood. If they are understood as referring to a certain insect—one capable of undergoing metamorphosis—the identity statement may be true; if they are understood in some different way, the statement may well be false. To evaluate an identity statement we thus have to know what things are being identified or referred to. The notion of a kind or sort is crucial for the evaluation because, as Aristotle rightly observed, we conceive of things as instances of natural or artificial kinds. Daphne and the laurel bush are different things because, as we distinguish the individuals of our world, they are instances of incompatible kinds.

The approach I am taking to essences and identity statements is compatible with an idea that has become popular in recent years—namely, that F is an essential feature of a thing a just when a has F in every possible world in which it "exists."[5] Although a possible world is, at best, a logical fiction, we can certainly describe possible situations and imagine that, in so doing, we are describing possible worlds to which those situations (as it were) belong. The question whether, in describing such situations, we are dealing with a thing a can be settled only by reference to the sort of thing we regard the term "a" (or some counterpart term) as picking out. If "a" is supposed to pick out Socrates, a certain man, then Socrates must possess the features that we associate with human beings—animality, say. If that man does not belong to the situations, or possible worlds, that we are describing, then *a* (or Socrates) does not belong to that world.

There is, of course, more to being a *certain* person than being a mere human being, but being a human being (or, more generally, being an instance of the relevant kind of thing) is particularly important for deciding whether we are dealing with Socrates rather than something else. The question whether, in referring to a thing *a* and a thing *b* that belong to the same sort or kind, we are referring to the same individual thing raises special problems that I shall discuss in the sections to follow.

The Problem of the Ship of Theseus

One of the classic problems about the identity of particular things can be brought out as follows. Imagine that a certain ship, the Theseus, has seen long, hard service. Over the years it has required numerous repairs, and old boards have been replaced by new ones. The old boards have not been destroyed, however; they have been stored away in a shed at the shipyard. In spite of the many repairs, the crew have never doubted that they are sailing the very same ship, even though they have suspected that most of its original boards have been replaced by new ones. Like the body of a human being whose cells are constantly being cast off and replaced by others, the Theseus has evidently remained the same ship over the years even though its original parts have been replaced.

Why does it seems reasonable to say that, in spite of the changes, the Theseus still exists? Apparently, because of this: No particular change or replacement of parts was sufficiently dramatic to suggest that the original Theseus was destroyed; each change seems purely accidental. The Theseus was christened at a certain place on a certain day. From that time and place a continuous series of positions in space and time was occupied by a ship that everyone called the Theseus. No change in the ship seem dramatic when it occurred, and there was no change in deed or ownership. Thus, the resulting ship could be nothing but the Theseus.

Suppose, now, that a young man at the shipyard, needing a ship and finding that the cost of a new one is beyond his means, decides to build a ship from cast-off lumber in the shed. As it happens, he uses all and only the cast-off boards of the Theseus, and he puts them together in exactly the way they were originally assembled. The ship is leaky and creaky, to be sure, but it is seaworthy and it serves the young man's purposes, which we may assume to be limited. Yet, since his ship, which he calls "the Phoenix," has exactly the same parts as the Theseus had when it was new and has those parts assembled together in exactly the way the parts of the Theseus were originally assembled, it would seem that the Phoenix can be nothing but the Theseus resurrected. But this conflicts with the claim, made earlier, that the ship with the new parts is the Theseus. Which ship is the *real* Ship of Theseus?

The problem is particularly acute here, because the considerations favoring each alternative are decisive for many familiar cases. Here is an analogy to the last case. When my maternal grandfather bought his first car, a Model T Ford, he said he wouldn't drive any machine if he didn't know what made it tick. So when his car was delivered, he and his eldest son took it apart, scattering parts all over the yard. Surprisingly, they managed to reassemble the parts correctly, and the car performed as it was supposed to. There is no doubt, I think, that the car he had put together was the car he bought. He took that car apart and put *it* back together again; the same parts were assembled in the way they were originally assembled. This case seems analogous to that of the Phoenix, for the Phoenix consists of the original parts of the Theseus assembled in the original way. This favors the hypothesis that the Phoenix is the same ship as the Theseus.

But analogies from familiar cases also support the alternative hypothesis. I have heard it said that all the cells of a human body are replaced within a period of seven years. Suppose this is true; it is certainly possible. I have no doubt that I have the same body that I had seven years ago even though, like the ship now called "the Theseus," the parts (cells) of my body may be new. To avoid complications concerning the alleged soul or spirit of a human body, we might also consider a parrot—an old, fierce one named "Henry." Even if it is true that every cell in Henry's body has replaced some original cell, there is no doubt that Henry is the same parrot that I bought eight years ago. There is also no doubt, at least in my mind, that Henry is nothing but a highly complex system of cells. The fact that Henry has undergone so many bodily changes—so many replacements of "parts"—does not show that he is not the same parrot as before. The analogy with the Theseus here is obvious: If the individual boards of the Theseus are replaced by new ones in the right way, the unity and therefore the identity of the Theseus would seem to be preserved.

If the conflicting considerations about the Theseus lead us to wonder which of the two ships is the real Theseus, we shall naturally seek some principle, at least if we are philosophers, that will settle the matter for us. One standard principle concerning identity is known as Leibniz's Law, and some philosophers might suppose that this principle will help us with our problem. In my view the principle is actually useless for our purposes here, but it is instructive to consider it anyway.

To appreciate the meaning of the principle, we should first note that when we ask whether something *a* is or is not the same as (or identical with) something *b*, we generally have in mind two names or descriptions, say "the Phoenix" and "the Theseus," and we could equally ask whether the thing named or described by the one is the thing named or described by the other. This is why, even if the Phoenix *is* the Theseus, the "cognitive value" (as Gottlob Frege put it) of the assertion "The Phoenix = the Theseus" differs from that of "The Theseus = the Theseus."[6] Now, Leibniz's Law formulates a general condition that holds when and only when an assertion of the form "a = b" is true. The law may be expressed as follows:

$a = b$ just when whatever is true of *a* is true of *b* and vice versa.[7]

It might be thought that this law could help us with the problem of the ship of Theseus.

As I have remarked, Leibniz's Law, though in my judgment unquestionably valid, cannot help with the sort of problem we are concerned with, and here is why. Suppose that every wooden board of the Theseus was replaced with an aluminum board. If we ask whether the ship now made of aluminum is identical with (the same as) the ship once made of wood and called "the Theseus," Leibniz's Law will require us to consider whether everything true of the aluminum ship is true of the ship once made of wood and called "the Theseus," and vice versa. Now, one thing true of the ship now made of aluminum is that it is *now* made of aluminum. Is the ship *once* made of wood and once called "the Theseus" *now* made of aluminum? If we can answer this question, we can solve our problem, but we have no way of answering it if we don't know what we are trying to find out, namely, whether the ship made of aluminum is or is not the same as, or identical with, the ship once made of wood. Leibniz's Law cannot, consequently, help us with our current problem. To apply the law successfully, we should have to know what we are trying to find out.

If Leibniz's Law cannot help us with our problem, how can we possibly resolve it? The answer, I think, is the one Thomas Hobbes gave: we are free to decide the matter either way.[8] Our decision will be, of course, a philosophical one, and it need not agree with, say, the legal practices of our community, which are arbitrary in their own way. My reason for saying the latter is this. Although we may be able to make very drastic repairs or replacements of parts in our automobile and yet have what is, in our community, the car to which we possess the title, certain parts—perhaps the part on which the registration number is stamped—cannot be changed without obtaining what is, legally speaking, a different car. Since the parts critical for the possession of a given car may not be open to view and may not be familiar to us, what is to our sentiments a fairly trivial change in the car we drive every day might possibly render it a different car in the eyes of the law. Also, since the parts critical for the continued identity of a car may vary significantly in different towns, states, or countries, it seems fair to say that the legal principles or criteria that may be used, in our community, to decide whether, after making certain changes, we still have legally the same car as before are, at least philosophically speaking, arbitrary.

But my claim, like that of Hobbes, is not just that the legal principles governing the identity through change of a piece of property are arbitrary; it is that there are no nonarbitrary principles by which we can settle the philosophical problem of the Ship of Theseus. The fundamental reason for this claim is that, in the case of the Ship of Theseus, all the relevant facts are open to view, and none of these facts dictates a particular solution to the philosophical problem.

The situation is this. A ship made of wood and called "the Theseus" is constantly repaired over a long period of time, and its wooden boards are gradually replaced by aluminum ones. The old wooden boards are retained and eventually reassembled. If we want to call the reassembled ship "the Theseus" and say that it is *the* ship that properly bears the name, that was built in a certain shipyard and sailed for a certain period, then we shall have to deny that the aluminum ship is the Theseus. But this raises problems. At what time did the aluminum ship begin its existence? At the time "it" became wholly aluminum? If we say yes to this, we shall have to make a decision about the ship that is exactly like the aluminum ship except for one wooden board. Did this ship cease to exist when the final aluminum board was added? The idea seems absurd: you don't get a different ship by adding a single board. But if the ship with the single wooden board *was* the same ship as the one now made entirely of aluminum, when did that ship stop being the Theseus? When the first aluminum board was added? Again, the idea is absurd: you might as well say that you have a new man every time you cut his fingernails.

Quite clearly we are faced with a special case in which our usual principles for establishing a thing's identity conflict, and the only way to resolve the problem is to *make a decision*. There is no fact of the matter by which one could possibly determine that one of the ships now in the harbor, the wooden Phoenix and the aluminum one still called "the Theseus," is "really" the Theseus. Our attitudes to the two ships may differ—we may feel a sentimental attachment to one, for example—but such attitudes do not show us that any one decision is more reasonable than the other. Philosophically speaking, we are free to choose.

Before moving on to problems about the identity over time of persons, I want to consider a traditional objection to what I have said about the problem of the Ship of Theseus. The objection was expressed in the eighteenth century by Joseph Butler.[9] According to Butler, the word "same" is apt to be used in two different senses in speaking about continuants. One sense of the word is, he said, "loose and popular." If a man claims that the same tree has stood fifty years in the same place, he means only that the tree is "the same to all the purposes of property and the uses of common life, and not that the tree has been all the time the same in the strict philosophical sense of the word." The reason he does not mean that it is the same in the strict philosophical sense is that "he does not know whether any one particle of the present tree be the same with any one particle of the tree which stood in the same place fifty years ago." For Butler, it is a "contradiction in terms to say that two things are the same when no part of their substance and no one of their properties is the same."

Butler's objection to the idea that, in the strict sense, the same tree could stand in the same place for fifty years is not just that the particles composing the tree fifty years ago are *all* different from the particles composing the tree now. Evidently, he would have claimed that, in the strict and philosophical sense, tree A would not be the same as tree B if many, or perhaps even one, of their parts were different. However this may be, the grounds for his objection are absurd. Without doubt, there would be a contradiction in saying that $A = B$ if even a part of tree A is different from a part that B has, but this does not imply that there is a contradiction in the idea that tree A had a part that tree B does not now have. If you cut off a dog's tail, it will have had a part, a tail, that it does not now have, but there is surely no "contradiction" in the claim that the dog that once had a tail is the same dog as one that doesn't now have a tail. To assume that there is a contradiction here is tacitly to assume that the very idea of a changing thing is, in the strict sense, an impossibility—and as we have seen, there is no good reason to think this.

Problems of Personal Identity

The idea that it is actually up to us to decide, rather than to discover, whether after certain radical changes we still have the same thing may seen credible for inanimate objects such as cars, ships, and trees, but it is not easily believed when it is applied to the special case of human beings, or persons. I shall devote the rest of this chapter to a consideration of this special case.

The claim I made earlier—that in deciding whether, after various changes, we still have the same thing or not, we have to know how the thing is being classified—has a particularly important application to the case of personal identity. As John Locke observed in the seventeenth century, a person is not necessarily a human being. In his view, which I think is at least roughly correct, a person is "a thinking intelligent being, that has reason and reflection, and can consider itself as itself, the same thinking thing, in different times and places."[10] So conceived, a monkey or bird could conceivably be a person. Locke described the case of an old parrot of whom it was reported that it "spoke, and asked, and answered common questions like a reasonable creature; so those of [its owner's] train there generally concluded it to be witchery or possession."[11] Although Locke had his doubts about the story, it is certainly conceivable that a rational parrot should exist, even if hatched only on another planet. If we encountered such a parrot, we might well regard it as a person but not, obviously, a human being.

As a sidelight, it is interesting to note that Locke seemed to have felt some doubt about whether every man (or human being) must be a person. As he observed:

> Whatever is talked about other definitions, ingenious observation puts it past doubt that the idea in our minds of which the sound "man" in our mouths is a sign is nothing else but of an animal of such a certain form. Since I think I may be confident that whosoever should see a creature of his own shape or make, though it had no more reason all its life than that of a cat or [ordinary] parrot, would still call him a man.[12]

I take it that a man with the "reason" of a cat would not be a person in Locke's sense of the word. He would be some kind of human brute.

The very great importance, for Locke, of the distinction between human beings (or "men") and persons is that the idea of disembodied personal survival was very much alive in the seventeenth century. Since Descartes' idea that the human soul is a thing that thinks (and thus a person in Locke's sense) was widely accepted in Locke's time, the possibility that a man's soul could be separated from his body made it important to distinguish the survival of the person from the survival of the man, conceived of as "an animal of a certain form." When the man dies, his body soon rots and eventually ceases to exist, but the man's soul—the person that did inhabit his body—may continue to exist. Thus, the continued existence of a person must be distinguished from the continued existence of a human body.

I shall take up the idea of alleged human souls or spirits at a later stage of my discussion. To open the subject of personal identity I want to consider some simpler and less controversial cases. It is quite clear, to begin with, that many radical physical changes are compatible with the continued existence of a human being. People can lose their hair, their arms and legs, their sight, and even (I shall argue) their memory of past events and still be the same person as before. It goes without saying, of course, that they are different from before, but they remain the same person, or human being, that they were. Not all parts of a person's body, taken individually, are equally accidental for his continued existence, however. The brain, at least if it remains in good working order, is an obvious exception.

Consider the following case. An airplane crashes in the mountains. The pilot is very badly burned and smashed, but he is still alive. After a few days in the hospital generalized infection sets in and the pilot, a very unusual man with specialized knowledge, is near death. Most of his head, except for his lower jaw, is relatively undamaged, however; and to preserve his special knowledge and expertise, the government undertakes to finance an experimental operation in which the diseased part of his body, which amounts to everything but the top of his head, is replaced by a "bionic" replica. What we have, in other words, is a more radical version of the kind of replacement featured in the television series "The Six Million Dollar Man." The bionic replacement is a success; the resulting individual becomes conscious, expresses great satisfaction at "his recovery," and claims to be the pilot who crashed. By virtue of its rational consciousness, the individual here is quite clearly a person in Locke's sense. But is it true that this person is, as he claims, the pilot who crashed?

It is not entirely clear that a *man* (= human being) has survived; the person who survives might well be described as "part man, part machine—mostly machine." However this may be, there is no doubt that the "survivor" is a person; and if I had been the pilot, and the thing with my brain (to speak as neutrally as possible) became conscious, it might well think: "Well, I'm alive; I survived, though I now have an artificial body and I might not, strictly speaking, qualify as a real man." It seems to me that if the consciousness of the resulting person is of the right kind or character, we should find it entirely natural to say that the pilot, as a rational being, did survive the crash. He still lives.

An important question arises at this point: "What must the consciousness of the survivior be like if he is to count as the same person as the pilot who crashed?" John Locke offered an answer to this question; he said, in effect, that the survivor must be conscious of what (or perhaps most of what) the pilot *was* conscious of before the accident.[13] Locke's idea, which he did not express in the clearest possible terms, seems to have been that the survivor must *remember* what (or most of what) the pilot was conscious of before the crash. I put "most of what'' in parentheses, because Locke would no doubt have allowed that, to be the same person as the victim, the survivor need not remember everything the pilot was conscious of prior to the crash. I don't remember everything I was conscious of even yesterday, but there is no doubt (to anyone who knows me) that I am the person I was yesterday.

Locke's claim about personal identity is very strong and thus subject to attack on a number of counts. In the first place, he is claiming that the survivor is the same person as the victim *if and only if* the survivor remembers most (let us say) of what the victim was conscious of before the crash. To claim this is to imply that if a person *a* does not remember, at a time *t*, most of what a certain person *b* was conscious of at a time prior to *t*, then *a* and *b* are not the same person. This is dubious because it seems entirely possible for a person to have lost his memory, as Locke puts it, of certain parts of his life "beyond a possibility of retrieving them, so that [he] shall never be conscious of them again." But Locke denies that this is really possible. He says the following in support of his view:

> We must here take notice what the word *I* is applied to; which, in this case, is the *man* only. And the same man being presumed to be the same person, *I* is easily supposed to stand only for the same person. But if it be possible for the same man to have different incommunicable consciousness at different times, it is past doubt the same man would at different times make different persons; which, we see, is the sense of mankind in the solemnest of their declaration of opinions, human laws not punishing the mad man for the sober man's actions, nor the sober man for what the mad man did—thereby making them two persons.[14]

Locke's remarks here are not entirely convincing, but they point to a problem that is difficult to resolve.

Consider the story *The Three Faces of Eve*, which purports to relate a true case history.[15] According to the story, a young woman developed at least three distinct personalities. Each personality was so different from the others that, when it was "in charge" of the woman, it spoke of the other personalities as different women and gave them different names. One woman was prim, proper, and dowdy; another was racy and promiscuous; the third was sensitive, thoughtful, and well balanced. Curiously, the personalities became aware of one another—knew a good deal of what the others thought and did—but did not like one another and sometimes had quarrels. People who were acquainted with Eve Black, Eve Green, or Eve White did not think of them as the same person, and when, say, Eve Black "came out" from, say, Eve White, a new person seemed to appear.

In spite of the differences between the three Eves it seems reasonable, in view of the psychoanalytic treatment that "they" received, to view them as three related personalities of the same woman, not three distinct persons. It is not necessary to view them this way, and it may be, as we shall see a little later, that the very concept of a unitary consciousness is more problematic than we naturally suppose. But the reasons for thinking that the three Eves are just personalities of one Eve, one woman or rational being, is not that each Eve has memories of the other Eves. In fact, the extent to which each Eve did remember what the other Eves thought and did is not entirely clear, and appeared to vary over time. It seems to me that even if each Eve has no consciousness (as Locke would say) of what the other Eves thought and did, it would still be natural to think of them as different personalities, or mental "faces," of the same actual person.

As my last remark suggests, I think it is really unsatisfactory to hold, with Locke, that remembering most of what a person was conscious of at a particular time is necessary for being that person. My view here can be supported by two further examples. Suppose, first, that I now remember most of what I was conscious of yesterday and that yesterday I remembered most of what I was conscious of the day before. If we assume, with Locke, that remembering most of what X was conscious of at a certain time is sufficient as well as necessary for being the same person as X, then Locke's view is easily undermined by another fact about myself—namely, that my memory is so bad that, on any day, I can remember only what I experienced the day before. If I remember most of what I was conscious of yesterday, I am, by Locke's test, the same person as "I" was yesterday; and if, yesterday, I remembered most of what I was conscious of the day before, then the person I was yesterday is the same as the person I was the day before. But if the person I am today is the same as the person I was yesterday, and if the person I was yesterday is the same as the person I was the day before, then the person I am today is the same as the person I was the day before. This follows from the law that if $a = b$ and $b = c$, then $a = c$. But if I cannot, today, remember most of what I was conscious of the day before yesterday, then, if remembering most of what a person was conscious of at a particular time is *necessary* for being that person, I could not be that person —even though this is required in the present case by a fundamental principle concerning identity.

My second example is this. Suppose that, as the result of a car accident, I (the man, as Locke would say) lose all recollection of my early manhood. In spite of this, my qualities of character, my habits and enthusiasms—in fact, my personality—remains exactly the same, and no one who knew the person Bruce Aune during his early manhood would doubt that I am he. I still love the same kind of music, I like to read the same kind of books, I have the same sense of humor—in a word, I am entirely the same except for the fact that I am a little older and have no recollection of a certain period in my life. It seems to me that no philosophically unbiased person who had an intimate knowledge of the man Bruce Aune at these two times, now and during his early manhood, would seriously doubt that he is, then and now, the very same person.

It is clearly not a necessary truth that, if a and b have, as we should say, the same personality, they are the same person. It is possible, after all, that identical twins could be indistinguishable in personality as well as looks and yet be two distinct persons. Nevertheless, if the bodies of a and b are the same, the sameness of their personalities would leave no reasonable doubt that they are the same person, the same rational being. The crucial objection to Locke's view of personal identity is that he exaggerates the importance of memory for such identity. It may be, as we shall see in a moment, that "sameness of memories" provides rationally compelling evidence for personal identity, but it is not necessary for personal identity, and this is what we have been concerned with in the last few paragraphs.

The other part of Locke's view, that sameness of memories may provide sufficient evidence for personal identity, is also subject to attack. The standard objection, generally attributed to Joseph Butler, is that an appeal to a subject's memories cannot possibly settle a philosophical puzzle about personal identity.[16] The basis for the objection is this. Anyone who actually remembers having seen or heard something must, by virtue of the meaning of "remembers," have seen or heard that thing. You can't remember something that didn't occur. Now, suppose that Jones actually remembers being alone in his garden last Wednesday. Since Jones actually remembers this, *he* must have been in his garden on that day. If the person who recovered from the plane crash actually remembers the same thing, then he must be Jones. But if there is any question about whether the man who recovered from the plane crash is Jones, the question will arise whether the man's claim to remember being alone in that garden at that time reports an actual or true case of remembering. For this reason, an appeal to a person's actual memories cannot, in general, settle a philosophical question about personal identity. Philosophical doubts about the identity of person *a* and person *b* will inevitably become attached to the question whether *a* or *b* actually remember what they think they remember.

To defend the relevant part of Locke's view it is only necessary to modify it a little. If we interpret him as holding that sameness of ostensible or apparent memories is sufficient for personal identity, then the objection can be avoided. Thus, if the person surviving the crash *seems* to remember doing or thinking what a certain man—Jones, say— was conscious of doing or thinking before the crash, and if the survivor's ostensible memories are sufficiently comprehensive, then, we may say, he *is* Jones: "they" are the very same person.

This modified version of part of Locke's view is also open to objection, however. The objection is that the sameness of ostensible memories, or the agreement of a person's ostensible memories with most of what someone was conscious of thinking and doing at some previous time, cannot provide a "sufficient criterion" of personal identity because it is conceivable that two different persons might have the very same ostensible memories. To make this possibility vivid, suppose that a super scientist, Dr. X, discovers a method of inducing ostensible memories in people by stimulating their brains in some exotic way. Suppose, also, that Dr. X has invented a means of ascertaining what people are conscious of at particular times. If we assume that Dr. X is concerned to refute the modified version of Locke's thesis, we can imagine that she should ascertain what Jones was conscious of thinking and doing during a certain period and then produce corresponding ostensible memories in another person, Smith. Smith will then seem to remember most of what Jones was conscious of thinking and doing at that time, but Smith will not be the same person as Jones.

There is no doubt that this example succeeds in showing that Locke's thesis, or a modification of it, does not provide a sufficient "criterion" for personal identity, at least if the satisfaction of a "sufficient criterion" is supposed to yield absolutely certain results in every case. But there is no good reason to suppose that the revised version of Locke's thesis is intended to provide such a criterion, and no obviously compelling reason to suppose that such a criterion is even possible. If the revised thesis is capable of providing very strong evidence of personal identity in most or even many actual cases, it would seem to be acceptable even if it does not give the right results in some hypothetical cases. This should not be surprising, because if the identity over time of persons is like the identity over time of continuants such as the Ship of Theseus, then we should expect that some hypothetical cases of personal identity may not be decidable by any means at all, let alone by some "criterion." Personal identity may, it is true, differ significantly from the identity of other continuants, but this cannot simply be assumed in criticizing Locke's thesis.

Memory, Personality, and Self-Identity

Why should we suppose that the revised version of Locke's thesis is capable of providing strong evidence for personal identity in any cases at all? The answer, I believe, is that when we reasonably rely on the thesis, we are tacitly employing what is known as "an inference to the best explanation."[17] The key consideration is this: An ostensible memory is a natural occurrence that, like a smile or shrug, has some explanation; and in most cases, at least, the best explanation for an ostensible memory is that it is a genuine memory—the result, that is, of some past occurrence that the agent has actually experienced.

Suppose that someone who calls himself Smith seems to remember a good deal of what Jones's diary tells us he was thinking and doing when he spent a winter in Madrid. Unless we have positive evidence to the contrary, the most natural explanation of Smith's ostensible memories is that Smith really is Jones and actually remembers what Jones was conscious of thinking and doing that winter. "How," we might ask, "could Smith possibly seem to recall so much of what Jones was actually conscious of if Smith is not Jones himself?" Even wives and husbands, who are as intimate as two persons can be expected to be, have only a highly incomplete knowledge of what the other is conscious of thinking and doing during the period of a week; and if Smith's ostensible memories are both correct and extensive, it is reasonable, contrary evidence aside, to suppose that they are actual memories.

Contrary evidence can, as I say, undermine this kind of explanation. If we know that the remembered event did not occur, then we know that the subject did not remember it. An example of this would be a case in which the subject was given a posthypnotic suggestion that he would later seem to remember having done something we know he didn't do; here we should naturally take the posthypnotic suggestion as the cause of the ostensible memory. Again, if the ostensibly remembered event is one whose occurrence is extremely unlikely—such as the experience of seeing a spaceship unloading little green men—we should want to deny that the ostensible memory is an actual memory, and we might naturally speculate about a psychologically more exotic cause. Yet if contrary evidence of this kind does not exist, the rational presumption is that the ostensible memory springs from a prior experience and is an actual memory, a mental record of something that really occurred.

With these points in mind, I now want to return to the fancied example, described in the last section, of the person, "part man, part machine," who survived the plane crash. When we discussed the example, we were confident that the survivor, though physically very different from the victim, was the same person as the latter, and our confidence as based on the fact that the consciousness of the survivor was of the "right kind or character." Our subsequent discussion was largely motivated by the wish to understand what the "right kind or character" of the survivor's consciousness might be. Our discussion of Locke's thesis puts us in a position to say at least two things about the character of this consciousness.

The first thing we can say is that *if* the survivor ostensibly recalls most of what the victim was conscious of thinking and doing at the time of the crash, then, in the absence of fancied Dr. X's, we are justified in regarding him as the same person as the victim. The term "most" here is admittedly vague, and we might reasonably be prepared to regard the survivor as the same person as the victim if he ostensibly remembers just a good share of what the victim was conscious of. But we are concerned merely with a materially sufficient condition for the survivor's being the same person as the victim, and ostensibly recalling "most" of what the latter was conscious of before the accident provides such a condition. The basis for considering this a "materially" sufficient condition—a condition that provides a reasonable ground for personal identity—can be traced, as before, to inductive (or explanatory) considerations. We are assuming that most of the head (including the brain) of the victim literally survives the crash, and we have good scientific reasons for thinking that memory and, indeed, self-consciousness is dependent on a reasonably healthy, well-functioning brain. Thus, although the survivor might not be considered a whole man or human being, it is clearly a rational being, and it seems reasonable to add that it possesses the rationality and the memories of the victim.

The second thing we can say is that, to be the same person as the victim, the survivor need not perhaps have to remember even most of what the victim was conscious of before the crash. I say "perhaps" because this case is more controversial than that in which I suffer a significant memory gap. Yet it seems to me that if the victim's brain is connected to the artificial body in such a way that the body expresses the person's wishes, habits, and so forth as it ideally should, then the case is comparable to that of me after the car accident. To see this, suppose that after what is, in effect, a body replacement the victim returns home and, except for the memory lapse, behaves pretty much the same as before. He does not recognize his family and friends, to be sure, but he enjoys the same things, tells the same kinds of jokes and stories, is equally religious, enjoys the same writers and composers (whom he does not remember having read or heard), has the same urges to jog or swim, and so on. Having the same personality as the victim and having the same brain, it seems that he is reasonably regarded as the same person—memory lapse or not.

If I am right in what I have been saying, there are, then, at least two materially sufficient conditions for the identity of the victim and the partially reconstructed survivor of the plane crash. *If* the survivor recalls most of what the victim was conscious of before the crash, then he is reasonably regarded as the same person as the victim; and he is equally so regarded *if*, possibly lacking the appropriate memories, he has the same personality as the victim. Although I have claimed, *contra* Locke, that having appropriate memories is not necessary for personal identity, I have not claimed that sameness of personality is equally unnecessary. I prefer to leave this possiblity open at present. Sameness of personality is often associated with sameness of soul or human spirit, which some philosophers have claimed to be both necessary and sufficient for personal identity. I shall discuss this claim and the grounds on which it is based in the next section.

The case of the survivor just considered adds some plausibility to Locke's claim that a person is not necessarily a man or human being. I say "some plausibility" here, because someone might argue that the person who is "part man, part machine" is, after all, a man, though a partly artificial one. To offer further light on the relation between being a person and being a human being I want to say something about two further cases.

The first case is simply a development of the one concerning the survivor of the plane crash. Suppose that, after the crash, the only viable part of the pilot's body is his brain. Suppose, also, that bionic bodies are merely pipe dreams, but that some physiologist has devised a means of keeping a brain alive and conscious in a container that looks something like a large fishbowl. By numerous tiny tubes, he is able to supply the cells of the brain with the necessary oxygen and nutrients, and, by means of countless tiny tubes connected to a computerlike machine, he is able to communicate with the brain. Suppose, further, that the brain is able to convey the information, by means of the machine, that it is the pilot, that it realizes its predicament, that, though considerably gloomy, it wants the scientist to reassure its wife that "he" is still alive, and so on. It seems to me that, given these suppositions, most people would allow that the pilot, as a person, has survived the accident.

The possibilities for the pilot's manifesting his personality are, of course, extremely limited by his predicament, but he can still tell jokes, discuss philosophy, and the like. Fundamentally, he is a person for the same reason that the "part man, part machine" survivor is a person: He possesses the consciousness, as Locke would say, of the victim. In spite of this identity of consciousness, the survivor is not a man in Locke's sense, for he does not possess the "outward form" of a human animal. He is, however, a man in the biological sense, for his cells contain the genes of a man and they could, at least in principle, be developed into normal human beings by the process known as "cloning."

Consider, now, a contrasting example. After the crash the pilot's brain is transplanted into the body of a man whose brain has been destroyed by a large tumor. The operation is successful, and some person recovers. The person has the ostensible memories and the personality of the pilot, but he has the body—the strength and agility—of the man whose brain was destroyed. The questions to ask are: "What man survived?" "What person?"

The last question seems the simplest: the person who survived would seem to be the pilot, for the survivor has his consciousness—his memories and intellectual abilities. The first question is more difficult because there are grounds for answering it either way. If the person who survived were to procreate by normal sexual means, his offspring would have half the genes of the athlete. If he procreated by cloning, using a brain cell for the process, his offspring would be genetically identical to the late pilot. Biologically, therefore, the survivor could be viewed as either the pilot or the athlete—or as a hybrid of the two. From a philosophical point of view, it would seem preferable to say that the man who, as a pilot, experienced the terrible crash and underwent very radical surgery simply got a new body, a transplant. The man who was an athlete and had the brain tumor died; and when a human being dies, he or she ceases to exist. The fact that the man who survived was given the body of an athlete should not be taken to imply that he is not the same *man* as before. I say "should not be taken to imply" because there is no need to describe the case in a different way.

In two of the cases thus far described a person who was a man is changed into a person, the same person, who is at least partly not a man. In one case the man-person (or human being) becomes, at least on the face of it, part man and part machine; in the other case the man-person becomes a living brain in a fishbowl, one connected to a machine. In both cases the surviving person is at least partly alive, and his consciousness is entirely owing to his living part, his brain. I now want to consider a case suggesting that a living person might become a nonliving person.

As a preliminary to the main case I wish to discuss, consider the example of Harris, who, as the result of brain disease, is rapidly losing his ability to remember. No known therapy exists for his disease, but a neurologist interested in electronics develops a "memory packet," as she calls it, that can store information and that can be connected to a man's brain, thus permitting him to recall what he has experienced in a way that is truly extraordinary. The neurologist suggests that Harris might wish to have such a packet installed, so that he can avoid the baleful consequences of his fading memory. Harris agrees, and is delighted with the result. He finds, for example, that he never has to take notes when he reads and never has to memorize anything. Everything he has experienced since the operation is at his fingertips.

In spite of his operation Harris is still a human being, though he has an artificial memory device that permits him to remember. But suppose that the brain disease that destroyed Harris's natural memory eventually extends to other areas, or mechanisms, of his brain, and that Harris loses other cognitive abilities. Suppose, further, that other artificial brain parts become available—parts that, though mechanical, perform the functions of living brain tissue. After a series of operations in which artificial parts are implanted, one by one, in place of diseased tissue—and after which, in each case, Harris regains consciousness and expresses delight with the outcome—Harris's brain becomes entirely mechanical. He is still a living thing—his heart pumps, his kidneys secrete, and so on—but his behavior is guided by a mechanical brain. In spite of this he tells us, through his living lips, that his consciousness has not appreciably changed as the result of his new brain parts; and we who knew him well before his many operations can testify that his personality has not, to our knowledge, changed at all. Is he the same person as before? If, as I am inclined to do, we answer yes to this question, we can move on to an even more exotic one. Supposing that Harris's body becomes smashed by a tractor and his artificial brain is removed and connected to a machine that keeps it working, so that the cognitive activities it performs continue as before, can we reasonably regard the mechanical brain as *the* person who had the history I have described? If we answer this question with a yes, we shall have to say that a person who was a human being eventually became a nonliving machine.

Descartes on the Self

I have not tried to urge that the answers to these last questions must be yes, because anyone tempted to offer an affirmative response must first come to terms with traditional arguments to the contrary. According to the view supported by these traditional arguments, a person is not really a living animal of flesh and blood, but a mind or spirit—one that, as Descartes put it, is not only "in a body as a pilot in a ship," but so "intermingled" with the body as to form what *seems* to be a unitary whole.[18] So conceived, a person can possibly survive the destruction of his body, and his spiritual life might possibly be everlasting.

The conception of a person as a soul or spirit was introduced into Western philosophy by the ancient Pythagoreans in the sixth century B.C.; it was espoused by Plato nearly two hundred years later; and as the result of Plato's enormous influence on subsequent philosophers, it has played a central role in Western philosophy. The most important arguments for the identity of persons and souls were given by René Descartes in the seventeenth century. I shall not attempt to give a detailed exposition of Descartes' arguments, for they involve technical ideas peculiar to his philosophy. But their basic import is easy enough to describe.[19]

Descartes' first and most important argument is based on the idea that he can clearly and distinctly conceive of himself as existing without a body. He arrived at this idea by a method of systematic doubt. Seeking to discover an absolutely certain foundation for scientific knowledge, he adopted the principle that anything he could reasonably doubt is not certainly true, and vice versa. Since he could not reasonably doubt his own existence as a thinker (if he doubts, he must exist as a doubter), he concluded that the proposition "I am, I exist" is, as he put it, "necessarily true" each time that he "pronounces it or mentally conceives of it." But although he could not reasonably doubt that he exists as a thinking thing, he could reasonably doubt that he has a body, for his natural belief that he has a body is based on sensory experience (sight, feeling, and so forth) and he has no absolute assurance that his sensory experiences are not mere figments of his imagination, like the experiences he has in dreams. Since he can reasonably doubt that he has a body but cannot reasonably doubt that he exists as a "thing that thinks," he concluded that his conception of himself as a thinking thing is "entirely distinct" from his conception of his body.

Having proved to his satisfaction the existence of a God who, being "absolutely perfect," would never deceive him about what he clearly and distinctly conceives, Descartes proceeded to reason as follows:

> Because all things which I clearly and distinctly conceive can be created by God as I apprehend them, it suffices that I am able to apprehend one thing apart from another clearly and distinctly in order to be certain that the one is different from the other.[20]

Since Descartes' conception of himself as a thinking thing is, as he believes, entirely distinct from his conception of his body, he can clearly and distinctly conceive of himself, *qua* thinking thing, apart from his body. Given the assumption expressed by the last clause in the quotation above, Descartes therefore concluded that, as a thinking thing, he is "entirely and absolutely distinct from [his] body and can exist without it."

Descartes' argument, as I have given it here, is fairly complicated, and a lengthy discussion would be required to evaluate it fully. For our purpose, fortunately, it is sufficient merely to point out certain points of weakness in it. One point of weakness concerns his attempted proofs (he gives more than one) for the existence of God; I have not given those proofs here, and they are not, as it happens, satisfactory.[21] Another point of weakness concerns his claim, not actually defended in his argument, that if God exists and is not a deceiver, any things that Descartes can clearly and distinctly conceive as distinct must really be different from one another. A final, and in my view more important weakness, concerns his claim that he can clearly and distinctly conceive himself (as a thinking thing) and his body as "distinct." Although Descartes' notion of "clearly and distinctly" conceiving something can be satisfactorily clarified, if at all, only by a somewhat elaborate discussion of what he says about it, we can readily see, I think, that he has failed to show that his conceptions of himself and his body are sufficiently "distinct" to establish the certainty of his conclusion.

Why does Descartes conclude that his conception of himself as a thinking thing is "distinct" from his conception of his body? The reason he gives, in the argument above, is that his certainty about his existence does not involve certainty about anything other than his nature as a thinker. As he says:

I am, I exist, that is certain. But how often? Just when I think; for
it might possibly be the case that if I ceased entirely to think, I should
likewise cease altogether to exist. I do not now admit anything which
is not necessarily true: to speak accurately I am not more than a thing
which thinks, that is to say a mind or soul, or an understanding, or
a reason.[22]

Here Descartes claims that, because the only thing he is certain about himself
is that he is a thinking thing, he is nothing more than a thing that thinks, that
is, a thing whose nature is exhausted by mental attributes. But this inference is
surely invalid. I may be wholly certain that someone is hitting me on the back
of the head and yet be completely uncertain about who is thus hitting me; yet
it does not follow that the person hitting me is "not more than" a person who
is hitting me—not, say, a mathematician or a wrestler. If Descartes is *merely*
certain that he is a thing that thinks, he cannot *also* be certain that the thinking
thing he is has no nonmental features—in particular, that it does not have the
physical features of a body. To relate this point to the matter of distinctness, we
might say that although Descartes' conception of his self does not include the
notion of anything physical, his conception of his self has not been shown to
exclude the notion of anything physical. Consequently, for all that Descartes
actually knows at this point in his argument, he might be a physical thing that
thinks, that is, a thinking animal.

The argument I have been discussing occurs in the second part of
Descartes' famous *Meditations on First Philosophy*. In the sixth part, "Meditation VI," Descartes supports his conclusion by further premises, but he holds
to the fallacious inference that I have just mentioned:

Just because I know certainly that I exist, and that meanwhile I do
not remark that any other thing necessarily pertains to my nature or
essence, excepting that I am a thinking thing, I rightly conclude that
my essence consists solely in the fact that I am a thinking thing (or
a substance whose whole essence or nature is to think).[23]

But, again, just because Descartes does not "remark" that nothing besides
thinking necessarily pertains to his "essence or nature," it does not follow that
nothing besides thinking actually does pertain to his nature. For all he knows,
his nature might include animality.

I said that Descartes supports his conclusion about the nature of his self
by further premises in "Meditation VI"; these premises concern the subject of
divisibility, and they have been very influential in the history of philosophy. The
premises can be extracted from the following passage:

There is a great difference between mind and body, inasmuch as
body is by nature always divisible, and the mind entirely indivisible . . . . [When] I consider the mind, that is to say, myself inasmuch as I am only a thinking thing, I cannot distinguish in myself

any parts, but apprehend myself to be entirely one and entire . . . ; yet if a foot, or an arm, . . . is separated from my body, I am aware that nothing has been taken away from my mind.[24]

The relevant premises here might be expressed by saying:

1. Any body is by nature divisible into parts.
2. A thinking thing does not have parts and is not diminished by the separation of any part of the body with which it is associated.

If these premises are true, then Descartes' conclusion is sound, for an indivisible thinking thing, or self, could not be the same as a divisible body. The question is: "Are both premises true?"

If the word "body" in premise 1 refers to macroscopic bodies, we may accept the premise as true. But premise 2 is certainly doubtful. If we do not simply assume what Descartes is trying to prove—that a self or thinking thing is not a body—then it is far from obvious that a thinking thing does not have parts. As we have seen, Aristotle conceived of earthly thinking things, or persons, as rational animals, and rational animals certainly have parts. If this view is mistaken, why? A possible answer is this: A thinking thing is, by definition, a kind of unity that a physical body is not; it makes sense to speak of half of a physical thing, but no sense to speak of half of a thinker. This answer is unsatisfactory. I think of my friend, a certain human animal (as I conceive of her), as a thinker, but it certainly makes sense, at least, to speak of half of her—her left half, say. She would remain a thinker if I removed some of her parts—her nose or a finger—but if I removed enought of her brain, I am sure that no thinker and no living body would remain.

The argument from divisibility, as we might call it, seems plausible only if, like Descartes, we think of a person's consciousness as a thing or continuant. One's consciousness or reason or understanding does not seem to have parts, and thus seems indivisible in a way that one's body is not. But if one's consciousness or reason is adjectival to one's self—if, that is, one may be conscious or rational without possessing some "thing" that is one's consciousness or reason—then the argument from divisibility loses all force. Consciousness and reason are then features or attributes of a person; and the fact that they cannot be divided into parts is no more significant, metaphysically, than the fact that running or being fat cannot be divided into parts. In the passage where Descartes introduces the argument from divisibility, he speaks of a thinking thing as a "mind," thereby conceiving of a person as an immaterial being. But persons, as we normally conceive of them, "have" minds; they are intelligent animals, not immaterial minds or consciousnesses. It is true that we sometimes speak of a person as *a* mind, as when a teacher says that she has several good minds in her class. But this kind of speech seems metaphorical; the teacher means that she has several students in her class—several creatures of flesh and blood—who *have* good minds, that is, who are intelligent, curious, intellectually creative, and so on.

In view of these considerations I think we must conclude that Descartes' argument for the thesis that thinking things, or persons, are really minds or souls must be counted a failure. Our conception of a person as a thinking "thing" is different from the conception of a rational animal, but both conceptions may apply to the very same things—namely, human beings. The caveat "may apply" is important here, because it is possible that things other than human beings may qualify as persons. When I discussed the possibility of human brains being preserved, live and functioning, in containers resembling fishbowls, or of human brains being replaced by mechanical substitutes, I emphasized that things other than normal human beings might reasonably be considered persons. This possibility is not entertained only by philosophers. When distinguished astronomers express an interest in transmitting messages to distant solar systems, the possible listeners (or audiences) they have in mind are unquestionably supposed to be rational beings and therefore, in Locke's sense at least, persons, but even the least imaginative of these astronomers do not insist that the listeners will be human beings: for all they know, such beings may be similar, physically, to birds, reptiles, or possibly even spiders.

Although these considerations adequately demonstrate that the conception of a person is broader than that of a human being, they also call attention to an important limitation in a contemporary argument purporting to show that Descartes' view of persons as minds or souls must be erroneous. The argument is that, since we conceive of persons as beings who *have* minds (who are intelligent and so forth), it is an out-and-out blunder to suppose that persons might literally *be* minds. The argument is weak because it ignores the possibility that people, or even well-functioning brains in glorified fishbowls, are conscious only when rational souls or spirits "inhabit" them. The possibility is theoretically significant because, if a good scientific case could be made for the view that a person's covert mental activities consist in, or are, changes of state in his or her spirit, we might reasonably conceive of a person pretty much as Descartes did— namely, as a spirit that inhabits and thereby controls a human body. Such a view seems exceedingly implausible on scientific grounds, but our current habits of speech are patently inadequate to render it erroneous—just as they are inadequate to render it unreasonable to speak of a normally functioning brain in a life-supporting container as a person. The tendency of philosophers to try to refute or establish hypotheses concerning what Hume called "matters of fact and existence" by purely armchair methods is largely what gives metaphysics its bad name among empirical scientists.

Cerebral Commissurotomy and Survival after Death

To round out this discussion of philosophical problems pertaining to personal identity, I want to consider two final matters: the philosophical significance of certain recent discoveries concerning the results of severing the connection between the cerebral hemispheres of a human brain, and the possibility of personal survival after death. I shall discuss these matters in turn.

As every student of psychology knows, the human brain contains two cerebral hemispheres that are directly connected to one another by a large bundle of nerve fibers called the corpus callosum. Although the function of these fibers was not understood until the late 1950s, important experiments by R. W. Sperry and others have shown that the corpus callosum coordinates the activity of the two hemispheres in normal human beings. The experiments of Sperry leave no doubt that, when the corpus callosum is severed in a living person, each disconnected hemisphere, as Sperry puts it, "develops its own private chain of learning and memory experiences that are actually cut off from, and inaccessible to, recall through the opposite hemisphere."[25] As an illustration of this conscious independence, Sperry has described cases in which, when the dominant hemisphere provides an erroneous answer to a certain question, the other hemisphere, "alert and consciously cognizant of what is going on externally," discloses its awareness that the answer is incorrect by producing a "disgusted shaking of the head or irked facial expressions."[26]

In a normal right-handed person the left hemisphere is "dominant," the right "minor." According to Sperry's experiments, the dominant hemisphere has greater verbal ability than the minor hemisphere; it plays the major role in speech, writing, reading, and calculation. The minor hemisphere, by contrast, plays a dominant role in the discrimination of geometrical forms, though it is capable of "substantial," yet "limited and selective," linguistic functions. In the apparently undivided consciousness of a normal person, both hemispheres make an appropriate contribution; but when the hemispheres are disconnected by cerebral commissurotomy, not only the brain but "the mind" (says Sperry) seems to be divided. As he says: "Two separate realms of subjective awareness are [then] apparent: one in each disconnected hemisphere, and each in itself seems to be remarkably whole, unified, and capable of supporting behavior comparable in many respects to that of the combined intact system."[27]

The experiments of Sperry and his colleagues are fascinating and deserving of more extensive discussion than we can undertake here. For our purposes, the interest of the experiments concerns their implications for the problems of personal identity that we have been discussing. One such implication is relevant to Descartes' claim that our consciousness is an indivisible whole. The implication is that, in spite of appearances, our consciousness may have only a synthetic unity, consisting in the "integration" of distinct mental activities associated with different parts of our brain. Another implication is that this synthetic unity may be broken up, by a cerebral commissurotomy operation, into two conscious unities. This last possibility might seem to create a special problem about personal identity, but I think that such a problem is really an illusion; at any rate, the perplexities it might generate seem resolvable in a fairly straightforward way.

Consider the following case. Jones, a philosopher and scientific genius of the first order, is horribly maimed in an automobile crash. His body is irreparably damaged but his brain is unscathed. As it happens, Jones has a brain of very unusual size, and although brain-transplant technology is perfected, no available head is capable of housing Jones's enormous brain. To preserve his valuable mind, the only possibility is to divide his brain and transplant each part in a different body. The operation is performed and is successful; two intelligent beings survive, each of whom has some of Jones's extraordinary mental abilities. The questions that obviously arise here are "Does Jones himself survive?" and "If Jones does survive, which person is he?"

If Jones was right-handed, the survivor receiving his left hemisphere will no doubt claim that he is Jones, and he will possess many if not most of Jones's distinctive verbal abilities. The other survivor will not be very accomplished verbally, but he will have some of Jones's verbal abilities and will possess most of Jones's distinctive powers of visual and perhaps musical expression. Since one person cannot be two people, we have to make a choice: either Jones does not survive, or he survives as just one of the people with a single hemisphere. What are we to say?

No particular answer is correct here; a choice has to be made. If I were Jones and were told, before the operation, that only one half of my brain were to be transplanted, I would choose to have the dominant hemisphere preserved. But this does not prove that the survivor with the dominant hemisphere must be considered Jones. The facts are clear: different parts of Jones survive in the two patients. If Jones also happened to be a very great painter, the survivor with the right hemisphere might well possess Jones's artistic abilities; and admirers of Jones's artistic productions, who think of Jones as an artist and are not even aware of his other remarkable abilities, might regard this survivor as Jones. But neither view is correct. Jones, as a rational being, has been divided; and though each survivor is a rational being, there is no need to regard either as Jones. The most natural thing to say, I should think, is that "parts" of Jones survive in two different people. The fact, if it is a fact, that this is the most natural thing to say does not imply, however, that it is the correct thing to say. The notion of correctness does not imply here.

It may be interesting to consider a more exotic possibility at this point. Suppose that, as the result of exposure to some novel form of radiation, my friend Mary undergoes binary fission, as if she were an amoeba. Both survivors have the same ostensible memories and both are genetically identical. Could both be versions of Mary? Well, the survivors are different people—one here, one there—so both cannot *be* any individual person. Since neither survivor has a better claim than the other to be the actual Mary, the most reasonable thing to say, I should think, is that Mary split apart and two similar people resulted, both distinct from her, who ceased to exist. Similarity of ostensible memories, character traits, intellectual abilities, and physical appearance provide only a limited basis for affirming personal identity. There is no compelling reason for thinking that the original person survived at all.

I now want to say something about personal survival after death. This ancient subject has been understood in different ways by different philosophers and theologians, but I shall discuss it briefly under just two headings, which raise standard philosophical perplexities. The headings are "survival as physical resurrection" and "survival of the human soul or spirit."

From my point of view, the least problematic view of physical resurrection is that the cells or microparticles that were dispersed when the body decayed become reassembled in the original way. It seems to me that if the resurrected body is alive, functioning, and possesses the same mental traits, abilities, and ostensible memories, then there would be little reason to doubt that the person who died has come back to life. The survival here would be similar to that of a watch that has been taken apart for cleaning and then put back together again. If the same parts are put back together in the same way, there is no doubt (at least in the absence of Ship of Theseus complexities) that we have the same watch as before. The same should be true of a person, *if* we think of a person as a living human body. For the time being, we can ignore the possibility that a living human being possesses a nonphysical spirit or soul whose existence is not dependent upon, or inextricably associated with, a properly functioning human body.

The possibility of physical resurrection seems far more dubious when the resulting body does not consist of the original parts properly reassembled. In such a case we seem presented with what is, at best, a duplicate of the original person—and a duplicate will be a different thing from the original even if it has the same ostensible memories and so forth as the original. This claim can be supported by a thought-experiment. Suppose that God created a replica of a living person—Ronald Reagan, say. Clearly, the replica will be different from the actual president, however similar to the president he may be. If we suppose the real Reagan were to die, the replica would remain a different person, and he would have been a different person even if the original had died before he was created. The possiblity of this kind of case suggests that the hypothesis of radical resurrection (as it may be called) either does not make clear sense or involves an error, the error of mistaking a replica for a person who died and turned to dust.

The argument here, which is based on a materialist's conception of what a person is, may not seem fully convincing. Haven't we all seen vampire movies in which the body of Count Dracula is reconstituted when the stake is pulled from the ribs in which it was lodged? And doesn't it seem perfectly natural to say that the revived evil person *is* the Count himself? The answer, I think, is that unless special assumptions about a surviving spirit are made, what is natural to say in this case is not thereby correct. We must still deal with the question whether we have a mere replica or the real thing. If, as we have supposed, a living (or "undead") person is simply an appropriately functioning body, there is no reason to conclude that the reconstituted vampire is anything but a replica of the original—a new, equally evil creature of darkness.

These difficulties with radical resurrection can be avoided, I will allow, if we suppose that living human beings possess some nonphysical component, a spirit or soul, in which reason, memory, and personality are somehow lodged. As I mentioned earlier, we commonly think of a human being as an animal that *has* memory, personality, and so forth; but as Socrates observed in the *Republic*, this way of thinking is compatible with the view that human beings are rational because they possess a rational soul, something that is rational (has personality and the like) in a more fundamental sense.[28] Although compatible with our normal way of thinking, this view is extremely dubious, however. The considerations are fundamentally empirical or scientific rather than philosophical. As I remarked when I criticized Descartes' arguments, there is no tenable philosophical argument supporting the existence of a soul or spirit, and Sperry's split-brain experiments are illustrative of the scientific considerations that render the view doubtful.

Quite apart from the fact that terms such as "soul" and "spirit" are conspicuously absent from the language of experimental psychology, we really have no determinate conception of what a soul or spirit is supposed to be and thus no evidence in favor of such a thing. In the absence of a satisfactory conception of the soul, we can't pretend to know what the hypothesis of spiritual survival actually amounts to. We might *believe*, if we are religious, that consciousness and personality are somehow based on a nonphysical thing that will continue to exist after we die. But this belief is, at best, a matter of faith, and it is too indeterminate to yield a coherent account of what disembodied survival might be. Our belief here is very much like John Locke's belief in a material substratum, which he confessed to be a belief in "a thing I know not what."

Chapter 6
WORLDS, OBJECTS, AND STRUCTURE

THE PARTICULARS I have discussed thus far are continuants, things that persist through time and typically undergo change. In this chapter I shall be concerned with particulars of other kinds or categories—specifically, with events, processes, times, and places. My discussion of these things will lead me into a discussion of such topics as causation, alternative ontologies, and metaphysical realism.

The point in discussing these other kinds of particulars is that they have a doubtful ontological status. To be sure, some philosophers contend that there is no problem about these things: they are fundamentally real and must be acknowledged in addition to continuants. This view is not shared by all philosophers, however. According to the ontological tradition represented by such figures as Aristotle, Leibniz, and Kant, the fundamental objects of our world are "substances" or continuants: events and processes are derivative realities and exist only in a manner of speaking. Philosophers such as Russell hold the opposite opinion. As they see it, events are fundamental and continuants are reducible to them. This controversy about particulars is neither trivial nor uninteresting; it leads to some of the most important questions of metaphysics.

Continuants and Events

On the face of it, a process is a complex entity consisting of happenings or events: Socrates' running, for example, is a process that consists of numerous movements that Socrates makes during an extended interval of time. Philosophers who believe that the world ultimately consists of continuants generally contend that statements about processes are reducible to statements about events and that statements about events are reducible, in turn, to statements about changing things. Thus, the statement that a motion occurred would be understood by such philosophers as just another way of saying that some thing (perhaps a person) moved; and the statement that a buzzing sound occurred would be understood by them as an abbreviated way of saying that something, perhaps a bee, buzzed. Philosophers holding this latter view would argue that to speak of events in addition to things is to speak just as redundantly as a person does who says that he is wearing a right glove, a left glove, and a pair of gloves. This kind of redundancy is no doubt harmless in common life, but in philosophy it generates needless problems about the relation between entities of different categories and about how such entities make up a single world.

This last point deserves a little elaboration. As I remarked in chapters 2 and 3, a world, abstractly considered, is a totality of objects interrelated in some fundamental way. Kant, in his famous *Critique of Pure Reason*, argued that our world—that is, the world of our experience—is a spatio-temporal-causal system whose fundamental objects are substances. This view of the world has been implicitly shared, I noted, by a long line of philosophers beginning with Aristotle. Those who accept it say that a substance (or continuant) exists just when it belongs to the world—just when it is an element of the ultimate totality. But they give another account of the existence of things that, though in some sense belonging to the world, are not substances. This other account is "reductive" in the way I explained in chapter 2. According to it, aggregates exist, or belong to the world, only in the sense that their elements belong to it and are suitably related to one another; corporations exist, or belong to the world, only when people in the world adopt appropriate conventions and carry them out in certain ways. A related claim holds for the occurrence (or the presence in the world) of events and processes: they can be said to occur when certain things are true, ultimately, of the fundamental objects that define the world's totality.

Although attractive and metaphysically penetrating, this abstract view of the world raises various problems. One problem emerges in connection with time. Consider the assertion "Socrates is walking." This assertion is tensed; it has the import of "Socrates walks now." Yet the moment to which "now" refers does not, apparently, include any part of the past or future: what did happen is over and done with; what will happen has not yet taken place. If this is right, it is hard to see how the assertion about Socrates (or any comparable assertion) can possibly be true. To walk, a person must move; yet to move is to proceed from one place to another, no matter how close together the two places may be. But to go from one place to another, a person must first be in one place and then, eventually, be in another place. Yet when a thing is in one place, it is not yet in another place; and when it is in another place, it is no longer in the first place. If a now includes neither the past nor the future (relative to it), a movement cannot therefore occur. This means that a statement like "Socrates is walking" cannot possibly be true, for such a statement implies that the relevant now contains both an end and a beginning of movement, these being successive (nonsimultaneous) occurrences.

If we accept the idea that the present moment is instantaneous, containing nothing of the past and the future and, therefore, no before and after, we can defend the common view that "Socrates is walking" may be true only by insisting that the "now" it tacitly contains does not actually refer to such a moment. It refers, we shall have to say, to a temporal interval that contains such a moment. If we add, as we should, that an interval of time actually consists of a continuous series of durationless moments or instants, we shall then have to admit that, when one says that Socrates is in continuous movement during an interval *i*, one can only mean that, at each of the infinitely many instants of which *i* consists, Socrates' body is in a slightly different position from what it is (was or will be) in adjacent instants. Although the ancient Greek philosopher Zeno argued that no series of instants in which no motion occurs could possibly add up to an interval that contains a motion, we shall have to insist that the idea of a moving thing actually does apply to a series of durationless instants each of which contains "things" that are closely related to what its neighbors contain. Thus, the statement about Socrates walking during a certain interval i will be true if, and only if, the series of instants or durationless moments m has a content that can be pictured schematically as follows:

In this picture or diagram Socrates himself exists (is present) in each of the moments belonging to i; at each such moment, and there are countlessly many of them, Socrates' body is in a position that is slightly different from the position it occupies at other moments. Although this picture seems reasonable, many philosophers have argued that it cannot be correct. Socrates, as a person, is a continuant—something that, as Aristotle said, endures in time and undergoes change. Yet a continuant cannot be wholly present in an instant, for it has a past and, usually, a future. What can be wholly present in an instant can only be a "temporal slice" of a continuant, an entity that might be described in this case as "Socrates-at-time-t." A slice of this kind is not, obviously, a person; it is momentary reality that constitutes part of the history of a person.

If, like Russell and Carnap,[1] we use the term "event" to refer to the temporal realities of which momentary slices are instances, we must then say (if the argument is sound) that a changing thing is not an irreducible reality but an enormously complicated system of events. Saying this amounts to acknowledging, in Russell's terms, that continuants are derivative realities—specifically, logical constructions out of events. The general conclusion to draw from this is that the Aristotelian conception of the world as a totality of continuants or substances ultimately breaks down. The world is really a totality of momentary events.

Although theoretical physics might provide good reasons for decomposing a moving photon into a series of events in space-time, the argument above does not provide compelling reasons for decomposing a moving Socrates into a series of Socrates-events or Socrates-stages. Even if moments are timeless, containing within them no before and after, and even if Socrates is a thing with a past and a future, we do not have to conclude that Socrates does not himself exist at such a moment. To say that a thing has a past is only to say that, from some temporal standpoint, certain things were true of it; and to say, from such a standpoint, that a thing has a future is only to say that certain things will be true of it. To say, as we naturally do, that Socrates exists at a certain moment or instant is only to say, therefore, that Socrates, of whom such and such is now true (true at this instant), has had other things true of him and will (no doubt) have certain further things true of him. Consequently, if Socrates exists at adjoining instants—these being times when, from the perspective of one instant, he had or will have certain features—he can be said to exist at the present instant, even though that instant is durationless. To show that a continuant cannot occupy a durationless present, one must show that adjoining moments cannot contain it. But nothing like this was actually shown in the argument above.

In the last chapter I discussed some of the classic problems associated with the idea of identity over time. One of these problems—a confused one, I argued —naturally arises when we speak of the same thing existing at different instants. If one looks at the schematic picture above, which represents Socrates at different instants, one sees that he is different at those instants. Since no thing can possibly be different from itself, it is tempting to suppose that what I describe as Socrates at different instants cannot possibly be the same thing: Socrates at instant *mj* cannot be the same as Socrates at instant *mk*. But this is sheer confusion. The diagram does not picture such "things" as Socrates-at-instant-*mj* and Socrates-at-instant-*mk*. It pictures only Socrates; it pictures *him* at different instants. Since he is a changing thing, he is different at one instant from what he is (was or will be) at other instants: at one instant his left leg is on the ground; at a later instant it is in the air. But *he* remains the same thing, the same person, throughout the interval *i*. He is never, strictly speaking, different from himself; his left leg, for instance, is never simultaneously on and off the ground. When I say that he is *never* different from himself, I mean that there is no time, no instant, when he is different from himself. This is wholly compatible with saying that what is true of him at one instant may not be true of him at other instants. There is no contradiction in the idea of a changing thing.

Events and Time

Although the phenomenon of change does not require us to reject continuants in favor of events, it is often said that we must acknowledge irreducible events if we are to give a satisfactory analysis of time, or of temporal intervals and instants. I think this view is mistaken, at least if we are concerned with time as it is understood in everyday life, but it is very instructive to consider the principal reasons behind it.

In Chapter 2 I argued that "exists" is a tensed predicate, having the sense of "exists now," and the preceding discussion makes it clear that "now" does not refer to a timeless instant. (If it did refer to such an instant, the statement "You are now reading" would have to be false—and you know it isn't.) Assuming that "now" does refer to something, we shall want to say that it refers to a temporal interval of short but somewhat indefinite duration, the shortness depending on the context in which "now" is used. The notion of a timeless instant is abstract; we never experience such instants, at least as discrete units, but we naturally think of temporal intervals as consisting of them—just as we naturally think of lines as consisting of dimensionless points. This way of viewing temporal intervals seems to imply that instants are irreducible realities, as Newton thought they were; but Russell argued that if we accept events as irreducible entities, we can regard instants as logical fictions. Since it seems advisable to avoid a commitment to unobservable entities that, because they do not interact with other things, have a very dubious position in the sort of causal system we take our world to be, the possibility of viewing them as logical fictions would seem to add reasonable support to Russell's conception of an event.

Russell's analysis of time (or temporal discourse) is based on the idea of temporal precedence.[2] If *e1* and *e2* are events neither of which wholly precedes the other, we can say that *e1* and *e2* overlap temporally or are, at least in part, simultaneous. The events we observe are not, Russell said, instantaneous; they have some duration. Since Russell wanted to reject Newton's theory of absolute time, he had to interpret "duration" relationally. He did this by saying that an event has duration just when other events occur while it occurs. In more exact terms his definition was this:

> *e* has duration $=df$ there are nonoverlapping events *x* and *y* both of which overlap *e*.

Generally speaking, Russell proposed to construct appropriate instants from temporally related events. Specifically, he wanted to show, by constructing appropriate definitions, what it means to say (a) that ordinary events exist (or occur) *at* various instants and (b) that instants, understood as logical constructions, make up an appropriate series—the kind of series required by classical physics. He eventually extended his theory to accommodate the temporal (or "timelike") relations postulated by Einstein's theory of relativity, but this extension of his theory raises special problems that I shall not consider here.

Russell's basic idea was that an instant can be understood as a set of overlapping events. To understand his basic idea, suppose that *e1* and *e2* are events that overlap as in diagram D1:

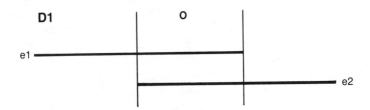

Consider the area of coincidence between *e1* and *e2*, which I have represented as *O*. If other nonoverlapping events *e3* and *e4* overlap the events *e1* and *e2* in the area *O*, then, according to Russell's definition, the parts of *e1* and *e2* in *O* have duration. Thus can be seen in the diagram D2:

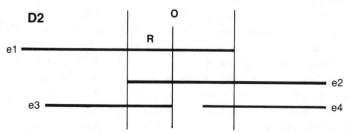

Now consider the area of overlap between *e1*, *e2*, and *e3*, which I have represented by *R*. If no other events—that is, no events outside the group {*e1*, *e2*, *e3*}—overlap the area of coincidence *R*, then the segments of *e1*, *e2*, and *e3* in this region will have no duration; they will be instantaneous. Russell defined an instant as a set of events that overlap as *e1*, *e2*, and *e3* do here. More exactly, his definition was:

> *i* is an instant =*df i* is a set of events such that (a) every member of *i* temporally overlaps every other member and (b) nothing outside *i* temporally overlaps everything in it.

On the basis of this last definition Russell proceeded to say that an event occurs at an instant just when the event is a member of that instant, that is, a member of the relevant series of events. He also said that an instant *I* wholly precedes an instant *J* just when some member of *I* (some event occurring at that instant) wholly precedes some member of *J* (some event occurring at *J*). He claimed that, given certain assumptions, the series of instants ordered by the relation *wholly precedes* yields a mathematically satisfactory series. If Russell was right, therefore, we can make good sense of our talk about instants and durations of time without assuming that instants and durations are ultimately real: talk about such things can be understood as talk about sets of overlapping events.

A little earlier I said that, according to Russell, the series of instants as he defines it is mathematically satisfactory—that is, satisfactory for the purposes of classical mathematical physics—*if* certain assumptions are made. Russell fully realized that some of these assumptions are not obvious truths.[3] One such assumption—one that must be made if the series of instants is to have the mathematical property of compactness—is that it is impossible for an event not to overlap at least one of the events that precedes or succeeds it. Abstractly speaking, this is a dubious assumption, for there is no compelling reason, either a priori or empirical, to suppose that it is actually true. If this assumption is not made, however, Russell's series of events cannot be assumed to be compact, even though its compactness is assumed for the events postulated by classical physics.

This possible drawback to Russell's construction is not of crucial importance for metaphysics, however. From a metaphysical point of view, theoretical physics could be seen as involving certain simplifying assumptions that, though not exactly true, can in practice be accepted with advantage. Thus, even if Russell's series of instants does not, on the basis of patently acceptable assumptions, actually have such properties as compactness, so that between any two instants there is another, the requirements of mathematical physics might well be met if we suppose that it has such properties.

While I am on the subject of mathematical physics, I should repeat something I mentioned earlier—namely, that Russell did not advance his construction of instants as adequate for the purposes of the special theory of relativity. For these purposes he offered a revised construction.[4] In what follows I shall not be concerned with the "timelike" intervals postulated by relativity physics, for my aim is to deal with basic metaphysical problems about time. I shall argue that our ordinary, nontechnical thought about time and places can be understood without assuming irreducible times, places, *or* events. Such things might have to be assumed if theoretical physics is to be acccepted at face value, but the question of how particular physical theories (such as the theory of relativity) are to be interpreted or understood is a highly technical one that I cannot pursue here. It is often said—in fact, it is said by Russell—that irreducible events must be assumed if the theory of relativity is accepted, but this kind of claim can be supported only by a painstaking logical analysis of that theory. I shall have more to say about this matter toward the end of the chapter.

Time without Events

Although Russell's construction of a temporal order allows us to contend that instants, or times, are not irreducible realities, it is based on the idea, fatal to the substance ontologist, that events are such realities. I now want to offer a construction of time that is not based on such an idea.

The key to my construction is the substitution of temporal connectives for Russell's primitive temporal predicate "wholly precedes."[5] Instead of saying, with Russell, that irreducible events wholly precede one another or overlap temporally, we can say that things (substances) do this or that before, while, or after they or other things do something or other. Given this way of speaking, we can proceed to define the predicates "has duration" and "is instantaneous" without assuming irreducible events. In fact, we can proceed to develop a theory of time without events.

Since we want to say, in a manner of speaking, that events are instantaneous, we shall have to make sense of the idea that a thing does something exactly once. To avoid the implication that something done is an irreducible reality, we can employ substitution quantification and say that "*S* does something" has the sense of "$(\exists_s A)(S$ does $A)$," *where the quantified variable takes action predicates such as "move," "run," or "laugh" as substituends.*[6] With this point in mind, we can then say that "*S* does something exactly once" has the sense of "$(\exists_s A)(S$ does A & ~ (S does A after S does A) & ~ (S does A while S does A))." The reason for the middle clause in this last formula is obvious; the last clause is needed to rule out the possibility that, intuitively speaking, S does A more than once at the same time. If I snap my fingers with my left hand while I snap my fingers with my right hand, I shall be snapping my fingers while I am snapping my fingers. But if I snap my fingers just once with my left hand, I shall not be snapping my fingers *while* I am snapping them.

We can now construct the required definitions of "has duration" and "is instantaneous with." Intuitively, "*S*'s doing *A* has duration" is a shorthand way of saying "*S* does *A* noninstantaneously." This idea can be captured by the definition:

D1: *S*'s *A*-ing has duration =*df S* does *A* exactly once & (∃x)(∃y)(*S* does *A* while *x* does something *B* & *y* does something *C*, & *x* does *B* before *y* does *C*).

We can now add:

D2: *S*'s *A*-ing is instantaneous =df *S* does *A* exactly once &~ (*S*'s *A*-ing has duration).

D1 shows us that when we say that an event has duration, we can be understood as meaning that something a bit complicated is true of nonevents or substances. Speaking of events in this way can thus be viewed as a mere manner of speaking: the relevant events need not then be understood as irreducible realities. Since the statement ostensibly about an event in D2 (namely, "*S*'s *A*-ing has duration") can be replaced by the equivalent provided by D1, D2 shows us that we can speak of an event as being instantaneous without assuming that such events are irreducibly real. When we say such a thing, we can be understood as saying something a little more complicated about persisting things.

If we assume that the definition D2 is actually satisfied by some thing doing "something," we can proceed to say, with Russell, that an event *e* occurs at an instant, though we shall not mean what he means in saying this. Our meaning can be given by the definition:

D3: *e* occurs at an instant =*df* (∃x)(∃ₛA)(*x*'s *A*-ing is instantaneous & *x* does *A* while *e* occurs).

We shall, of course, interpret a statement to the effect that an event occurs as meaning that some thing *a* does something *D*, that is, that (∃a)(∃ₛD)(*a* does *D*).

To make sense of claims to the effect that things happen at specific times and dates, we must introduce the notion of a standard clock. Such a clock is simply a thing (a continuant) that behaves in a way we regard as regular; it could be a pendulum, a tuning fork, a device with a moving hand, or, as is now standard in physics, a cesium-133 atom, which vibrates at a "standard rate." Although the choice of a standard clock is ultimately arbitrary, we may regard one choice as preferable to another (particularly if we have scientific interests) if the first choice permits us to simplify our assumptions about such things as moving bodies. If, for convenience, we think of our standard clock as a mechanical device with a circular dial and three hands, we can easily explain the meaning of such statements as "John ran for one hour."

To construct the appropriate definition schema for statements of this last kind, it is helpful to begin with the notion of temporal congruence. This notion can be clarified without assuming irreducible events as follows:

>   D4: *S*'s doing *A* is temporally congruent with *R*'s doing *B* =*df S* does *A* exactly once & *R* does *B* exactly once & *S* begins doing *A* when *R* begins doing *B* & *S* finishes doing *A* when *R* finishes doing *B* & *S* does *A* without interruption & *R* does *B* without interruption.

Given this definition, we can clarify the meaning of such claims as "John's running lasted for one hour" by two further definitions:

>   D5: *S*'s doing *A* lasted for one hour =*df S* did *A* for one hour.
>
>   D6: *S* did *A* for one hour =*df S* did *A* & *S*'s doing *A* was temporally congruent to one temporal revolution of the hour hand around the dial of the standard clock.

The definiens in D6 contains event expressions, but they are eliminable by virtue of the definition D4. Since the dial of a standard clock can be divided into progressively smaller segments, we can introduce generalized definitions corresponding to D5 and D6 that will allow us to say, in a manner of speaking, that events last for longer or shorter periods of time.

Earlier, I explained how we could make sense of assertions to the effect that events occur "at" instants. Since we do not always or even usually date events by reference to instants, a more general notion of a thing's occurring at a time is worth specifying. This can be done, in principle, by reference to a standard clock. For example, we can say that "John did *A* at four o'clock" means "John did *A* when the hour hand of a standard clock points to four and the other hand points to twelve." To be more specific about dates as ordinarily understood, we have to appeal to the familiar periodicities that are conventionally represented by calendars. These periodicities concern the behavior (or "movements") of the earth, the moon, and the sun, which rises and sets. Roughly, Tom does *A* in January if and only if Tom does *A* when the moon is beginning a new series of twelve "lunations"; and Tom does *A* in a certain year if and only if Tom does *A* when the earth is making a certain journey around the sun— either a standard journey, such as the one that occurred when Christ was (or is supposed to have been) born, or one that preceded or succeeded such a journey by *x* number of trips.

To make clear sense of this last suggestion in a way that does not presuppose the reality of irreducible movements or journeys, we can use the temporal connective ". . . and then . . . ," which is just a variant of " . . . after . . . ." The strategy for defining instances of the schema "*S* did *A x* times in succession" is illustrated by the following definitions:

>   D7: *S* did *A* twice in succession =*df S* did *A* and then *S* did *A*.
>
>   D8: *S* did *A* three times in succession =*df S* did *A* and then *S* did *A* and then *S* did *A*.

Together with the examples just given, the following definitions will allow us to explain how nominal occurrences can have dates with reference to the birth of Christ:

D9: *S* did *A* just after *R* did *B* =*df S* did *A* when *R* finished doing *B*.
D10: *R* did *B* just before *S* did *A* =*df S* did *A* just after *R* did *B*.

On the basis of D9 we can say the following:

S did *A* in *x* + 1 A.D. =df *S* did *A* while the earth was moving around the sun just after it had, without stopping, moved around the sun *x* times just after Christ was born.

Finally, if we indicate the meaning of a certain use of "now" by reference to something that we are (present tense) doing, we can employ both D9 and D10 to say this:

Christ was born 1984 years ago =*df* Just before now, the earth had made, without stopping, 1984 trips around the sun just after Christ was born.

Since the right-hand side of this last definition can be interpreted, by virtue of definitions I have given earlier, in a way that does not imply the irreducible reality of trips or movements, we can assert that "Christ was born 1984 years ago" does not assert such things either.

As these last few examples show, the reduction of statements about times, dates, and motions to statements containing temporal connectives yields locutions of surprising complexity.[7] Yet from a metaphysical point of view, the complexity of the resulting locutions is enlightening rather than problematic. After all, if talk about times, dates, and motions can be understood as a kind of shorthand for a metaphysically more penetrating form of speech, we should *expect* the latter to be complicated, cumbersome, and difficulty to use. Why have a shorthand if it does not make things easier for us?

Space and Causation

Although I am fully confident that the strategy I have outlined for interpreting everyday talk about time, instants, dates, and so forth is philosophically illuminating, some contemporary philosophers will no doubt object to it on account of my use of temporal connectives. I shall discuss the most plausible grounds for this kind of objection in the next chapter. In this section I want to say something about space, spatial locations, and causation. My treatment of time has important implications for the proper treatment of these subjects, and I want to develop these implications before I consider any general objections to my analysis of instants, dates, and the like.

Philosophers who have metaphysical objections to Newton's view of absolute time have metaphysical objections to his view of absolute space—to his view, that is, that time and space are irreducible realities. Although time and space seem to have a similar metaphysical status, they are also very different as ordinarily understood: the entities said to occur in time are, on the face of it, very different from the entities said to exist in space. The sort of things that occur are events or processes; the sort of things that exist in space are "substances" or continuants. A philosopher who admits the irreducible reality of both events and continuants faces a problem of how such categorially different entities fit together in a single world. The usual strategy for resolving the problem is to argue that just one of the two is irreducible. As we know, Russell claimed that events are fundamental and that continuants are reducible to events; thus far I have adopted the opposite strategy, taking continuants to be irreducible and suggesting, if not arguing, that events are reducible to continuants. If the task of interpreting scientific theories (particularly the theory of relativity) is not in question, my strategy has an obvious advantage over Russell's, for the task of reducing discourse about space and time to discourse about continuants is easier and more natural than his task of reducing such discourse to talk about events. On the face of it, events can be said to occur *where* objects (continuants) are, just as acts are performed where the actors are—and not, figuratively speaking, the other way around.

The claim that one strategy is "easier and more natural than another" is not, of course, decisive, and one might insist on asking the questions "Which strategy is really preferable?" "Which is wrong and which is right?" Unfortunately, these questions are extraordinarily difficult to answer, and they can be approached from different points of view. Thus far I have assumed the perspective of traditional ontology. Having expressed my sympathy with the classical view that the world is a system of "things" or continuants, I have been concerned to criticize metaphysical arguments purporting to show that, owing to certain facts about time, this traditional view of the world breaks down and *must* be rejected. In the present section I intend to show that a world of continuants can also accommodate crucial facts about space and causation. This way of defending the traditional view cannot prove that it is correct to say that the world ultimately consists of continuants, or that this view is really preferable to others. The most it proves is that the view is internally coherent, not objectionable on a priori grounds.

As I mentioned in passing, Russell thought that the traditional view is, in fact, scientifically out-of-date, incompatible with the requirements of the theory of relativity, which assumes, he said, an ontology of events. P. F. Strawson, on the other hand, has subsequently argued that the "basic particulars" in relation to which objects of a common, intersubjective world can be identified must be continuants.[8] More recently, Nelson Goodman has argued that no sort of object is intrinsically fundamental to the world: we can conceive of the world in different ways, and different "versions" (or pictures) of the world may involve different sorts of basic objects.[9] If Goodman is right about this, Aristotle's picture of a world of things and Russell's picture of a world of events might be legitimate alternatives—neither one being more correct, absolutely speaking, than the other. I shall comment on these possibilities at a later stage of my discussion; my task in the present section is to show how space and causation fit into a world of continuants.

If our world consists ultimately of continuants, the events "occurring" in it are derivative objects that exist only in a manner of speaking. To say "The car crash occurred on 14th Street" is then tantamount to saying something like "A car, or certain cars, crashed on 14th Street." Ostensibly, 14th Street is a place, a region in space, but instead of thinking of space as a thing, perhaps an infinite container, we can regard it as, on first approximation, a system of relations between things. More exactly, we can say that genuine things (that is, continuants) are *spatially related* to one another, and that spatial relations generate a three-dimensional order in the sense that things are not only side by side but above, below, behind, and in front of one another. In the first instance, a place such as 14th Street is where something is; in the second instance, a place is where something would be, relative to other things, if it moved this or that way for this or that number of inches, feet, yards, miles, and so on. Since the continuants (the fundamental objects) of our world are invariably here or there, they are, in a sense, in space; and since they also do A or B after (while, before) they or other things do C or D, they are equally "in time." This view fits together nicely with the Kantian conclusion I reached in chapter 2—namely, that the things existing in the fundamental sense collectively constitute a spatio-temporal-causal system. I shall have something to say about causation very shortly.

It is possible to conceive of locations in a more fine-grained way than my remarks above might suggest. If we wish to speak of spatial points, we can conceive of them as idealizations of the positions occupied, or potentially occupied, by parts or subregions of continuants. We can do this in at least two ways. First, we can conceive of points as limits of a series of converging positions. The idea, more exactly, is this: A spatial point is an ideally small position x such that, if the position occupied or potentially occupied by any part or subregion of a continuant is progressively and uniformly reduced in size, a position p will eventually be reached that (a) has x at its center and (b) differs in area from x by no more than an arbitrary fraction f, where f is as small as we may wish to specify. Second, we can follow the example of A. N. Whitehead and conceive of a point, not as the limit of a series of converging positions, but as that series itself.[10] Whichever approach we take, we can reasonably contend that points are not fundamentally real: like instants, they are, we may say, logical fictions. Our basic or true realities are thus continuants: collectively, they make up or define the spatio-temporal system of objects that is the real world.

I must now say something about causation. Ever since David Hume focused critical attention on the concept of causation in the eighteenth century, philosophers have generally assumed that causation is a relation between events. If this conception is acceptable, it seems to follow that anyone who denies that events are ultimately real must also deny that causation is ultimately real. This outcome should be disturbing to anyone seriously tempted by the traditional idea that the world is a spatio-temporal-causal system whose fundamental constituents are things or substances.

As a first step in dealing with this matter, we should observe that things of many different kinds (or categories) are commonly spoken of as causes. Remarks of the following sort are by no means unusual:

1. John caused an uproar when he insulted the speaker.
2. The fire was caused by an explosion.
3. The collapse was caused, not by the fact that the bolt gave way, but by the fact that it gave way so suddenly.

If we reflect on these remarks, we can see that continuants, events, and even facts are often thought of as causes. Philosophers who accept Hume's view of causation will concede that, although the statements above may all be true, they must be interpreted, for they do not all mean what they seem to say. Such philosophers will insist that, in spite of appearances, they all really affirm some causal relationship between events. I agree that all three statements might well be true, and I also agree that they all require interpretation. But I do not agree that a metaphysically satisfactory interpretation of them *must* show that they affirm a causal relationship between events.

The question whether continuants—in particular, human beings—can reasonably be regarded as irreducible causes will assume some importance in chapter 9, and I shall defer my comment on it to that chapter. At the moment I can ignore it, because the possibility that a continuant could be a cause casts no doubt on the metaphysical thesis I am exploring—namely, that fundamental existents are continuants and that they collectively make up a spatio-temporal-causal system. I have already argued that continuants can be said to exist both in space and in time; if they are, or may be, causes, they fit even more securely into the system to which (according to the thesis) they belong. The question I want to consider now is whether alleged causes other than continuants must be interpreted as events.

A useful way of approaching this matter is to attend to a suggestion that Donald Davidson made in his influential article, "Causal Relations."[11] Although Davidson was specifically concerned to defend the thesis that singular causal statements should be understood as affirming a causal relation between events, he eventually had to admit that certain statements—in particular, the statement 3 above, which is, in effect, one of his examples—require a different analysis. His suggestion was that 3 and others relevantly like it should be interpreted by the use of the predicate "causally explains." Since this kind of interpretation accords nicely with the substance ontology I am defending here, the absence of independent reasons for admitting the irreducible reality of events makes it desirable to extend the interpretation to all singular causal statements—with the exception, perhaps, of statements like 1 that ostensibly identify continuants as causes.

Davidson did not elaborate upon his suggestion for interpreting such statements as 3, and I am not sure just how he would want to develop that suggestion.[12] Yet if we attend to 3 ourselves, we can easily develop Davidson's suggestion in a way that suits our purposes here. On first approximation we might say that 3 could reasonably be interpreted as 4:

4. The fact that the bolt gave way so suddenly causally explains the fact that the collapse occurred.[13]

Since anyone who denies the irreducible reality of events would want to rephrase the final clause of 4, we have to know what collapse is tacitly being spoken of. Suppose it is the collapse of a cerain bridge. On this supposition we can interpret the final clause of 4 as ''The bridge collapsed.'' Our second approximation to the analysis of 3 would then be this:

5. The fact that the bolt gave way . . . causally explains the fact that the bridge collapsed.

If we ignore, for the moment, the apparent reference in 5 to facts, which a final analysis should eliminate, we can easily see how other causal statements can be interpreted by reference to ''causally explains.'' Take the statement 2 above, for instance. If we suppose that the relevant explosion occurs to a thing *A* and the fire is associated with a thing *B*, we can say that the statement 2 is simply a convenient way of expressing 6:

6. The fact that *A* exploded causally explains the fact that *B* caught fire.

Or take the metaphysical assertion that every event has a cause. The simplest way of expressing this assertion without referring to events is to say that there is a causal explanation for every matter of fact.

When I discussed facts in chapter 3, I argued that they can be nothing but true statements or propositions, and I eventually argued that true statements and propositions are logical fictions rather than irreducible realities. If I am right about this matter, we can say that assertions such as 5 affirm that certain true statements are related in a certain way. To understand what this relation is, we must understand, at least in general terms, what a causal explanation is. It is easiest to do this by referring freely to events, but we shall quickly see that our reference to events is merely a matter of convenience and has no metaphysical significance whatever.

According to the received view of scientific explanation, a fully explicit explanation of why an event *E* occurred under the conditions *C* would identify some law or causal principle that, taken together with a statement affirming the conditions *C* to have obtained, warrants the conclusion that *E* occurred. It is generally agreed that some further condition must be satisfied by an ideally complete explanation, but there is no general agreement on what this further condition is.[14] However this may be, there is no doubt that a fully explicit, satisfactory explanation of why a phenomenon *P* occurred shows that the statement that *P* occurred is inferable from a group or conjunction of statements that (a) express the conditions under which *P* occurred, (b) express some law or causal principle, and (c) express some condition that is not yet understood.

From a metaphysical point of view, the crucially important feature of this conception of an explanation is that when, as we ordinarily say, we explain some phenomenon, we are really explaining *why it is true* that the phenomenon occurred—and we explain this by showing that the statement (which we assume to be true) that the phenomenon did occur, can be inferred from true statements expressing laws or causal principles as well as the occurrence of certain conditions. Understood this way, the predicate "causally explains" quite clearly applies to statements rather than events or occurrences: certain true statements causally explain why a given statement is true. The reference to events or occurrences that is commonly present in our ordinary talk about explanation is thus unimportant, metaphysically. The statement that a certain event occurred can be replaced by the more perspicuous statement that some thing or continuant behaved in this or that way.

If we return, now, to the specimen statement 3, we can say that the suggested interpretation 5 is best expressed in the form of 7:

7. The true statement that the bridge collapsed is causally explained by the true statement (among others) that the bolt gave way. . . .

I have put the words "among others" in parentheses here because statements such as 3 do not provide ideally complete explanations. What they actually do is to identify some matter of fact that, together with certain causal principles that we may or may not be able to identify, yields an ideal explanation of why some special statement is true. I make this qualification without apology because it is well known that the causal explanations we offer in everyday life are generally only fragments of ideal explanations. They help us to explain why things behave as they do because they provide crucial information on the basis of which ideal explanations can be constructed.[15]

Although the topic of causal explanation is a large and intricate one, I have said enough about it to clarify the main lines of a "substance" approach to causation. By way of summary, I can say this. Statements such as 2, which ostensibly concern causally related events, may be accepted as true, but their truth depends on a metaphysically satisfactory interpretation. According to the interpretation I have developed here, they really affirm that certain matters of fact (that is, certain true statements) can be causally explained in a particular way. The standard empiricist contention that events are causally related can therefore be interpreted as the claim that true statements describing changing things are causally explainable, at least in large part, by other true statements describing changing things. The further claim commonly made by empiricists that events are explainable by natural regularities can be interpreted as the claim that true statements about changing things are causally explainable by statements expressing (among other things) causal laws or principles. As for my basic ontological claim in chapter 2 that fundamental existents are the things belonging to the space-time-causal system, I can now say that, if fundamental existents are understood as continuants, they are spatio-temporal entities that behave *according to causal laws*.

Causal Laws

Although my argument in the last section shows us that we can make sense ₌of causation without assuming irreducible events, it does not show us how to deal with the notion of a causal law. This notion has been an important source of controversy in metaphysics, and it is appropriate, therefore, say something about it here.

A causal law is a special case of a law of nature, the latter being a universal statement, or proposition, about the natural order. Two principal interpretations of such statements have been defended since the Renaissance. The most popular interpretation among empiricist philosophers is the "regularity" interpretation espoused by David Hume.[16] According to him, natural laws are generalizations from experience. When, for example, events of kinds A and B are "constantly conjoined" in our experience, A preceding B, we speak of A as the cause, B the effect. Strictly speaking, there is no real "necessary connection" between cause and effect. We do, it is true, think that certain events, being causes, *must* have certain effects, but our idea of this "must" (this necessity) merely reflects our expectation that, when the cause occurs, the effect will also occur. For Hume, a law of nature is merely a statement affirming that events of one kind are invariably (or "regularly") accompanied by events of another kind; if there is temporal succession between the events, the statement is a causal law.

The other principal interpretation of causal laws may be called the "entailment" view. According to this interpretation, natural laws affirm natural necessities. If events of kinds A and B are lawfully related in nature, they are necessarily connected: the occurrence of one necessitates or physically entails the other. This view of a causal law does not require (as the regularity interpretation is often thought to do) an ontology of events. The relevant necessary connection or entailment can be interpreted as holding between facts or propositions: If it is a natural law that if P then Q, then the fact or proposition that P can be said to necessitate, or physically entail, the fact or proposition that Q. The facts or propositions involved here need not concern events; they may concern substances or things. The fact that a certain thing is moving in a certain direction with a certain velocity physically entails (or necessitates) the fact that it will continue to move in that direction with that velocity unless it is acted on by some other object or thing.

I have expressed these rival interpretations of natural laws in a simplified form; both involve difficulties, and both have been qualified in various ways by different writers.[17] As far as my argument in the last section is concerned, either could be correct. The regularity interpretation is often thought to require an ontology of irreducible events, but this is a mistake: the claim that events of kind A are constantly conjoined with events of kind B can be reinterpreted as the claim that things of one kind act in a certain way *where* and *when* things of another kind act thus and so. As I explained, natural regularities can be understood without reference to irreducible events. It is natural and often highly convenient to speak of events in connection with natural laws, but such speech can be understood as a mere *façon de parler*.

Which of these interpretations do I favor? The answer is, the regularity interpretation, though it requires some spit and polish to be fully acceptable. The key idea is that things in nature behave, in point of fact, in regular ways—and natural laws express, or describe, these regularities. We commonly say that things in nature *must* conform to natural laws, but this "must" expresses our attitude to the relevant regularities: lawful regularities are those to which there are no exceptions. As C. S. Peirce observed, the notion of a natural "law" was developed from the notion of a prescriptive law or ordinance.[18] Originally, natural laws were understood as divine prescriptions that created things are "required" to obey. The metaphor of being required to obey still clings to the notion of natural necessity. Yet inanimate objects do not choose to obey the laws that "govern" their behavior; they simply do behave, we believe, in ways that conform, without exception, to the regularities *described* by natural "laws." Our belief on this matter is not self-evident, for undetermined or random behavior is at least conceivable. Yet we do *expect* natural things to conform to objective regularities, and this subjective attitude is expressed in our talk of what "must" happen in nature.

I should mention that the notion of an objective regularity is more problematic than one might initially suppose. As Peirce observed in the 1860s, the behavior, no matter how chaotic, of any finite class of objects will always conform to some "regularities."[19] Suppose that, for centuries, emeralds have invariably been found to be green but that blue emeralds are now occasionally discovered. Does this variation in the color of emeralds exhibit a distinctive regularity? The answer is yes: emeralds are invariably green *or* blue. Since green objects are green or blue, this last "regularity" will be exemplified by emeralds if they are invariably green. If we are prepared to speak of a natural law covering the color of emeralds, we therefore have two possibilities to consider: according to one, they are green; according to the other, they are green-or-blue. Which is the true law? I think we should say that, given the evidence we have, the first is the true or fundamental law; the second expresses a derivative and uninteresting regularity. The regularities that we are prepared to regard as lawful are not only exceptionless but belong to a system of regularities that are, in a sense difficult to define, fundamental for the explanation of natural phenomena.[20] However this may be, natural laws may still be viewed as describing mere regularities, though regularities of a special kind.

The alternative interpretation of natural laws—the one according to which they express genuine necessities or entailments—can be traced back to Aristotle's discussion of intuitive induction.[21] Although Aristotle was concerned with primary general truths rather than natural "laws," his discussion influenced the interpretation later thinkers placed on natural laws. According to Aristotle, primary general truths are necessary and, being primary, are not known by syllogistic inference from other truths. They are known intuitively, by reflection on the nature of particulars. Such reflection makes us aware of the universals involved in the relevant particulars, and in some cases, at least, we are able to "see" that certain universals are necessarily connected. Aristotle's position here is sometimes clarified by reference to the notions of color and extension. If we reflect sufficiently on our experience of colored and extended objects, we can "see" that color and extension are necessarily connected: nothing could possibly be colored without being extended. Thus, the proposition "Everything colored is extended" is a primary, necessary truth about the world.

Philosophers who conceive of natural laws as principles of natural necessity do not suppose that natural laws are invariably known by Aristotle's process of "intuitive induction," but they often claim that the necessity of a natural law is the same as the necessity of an Aristotelian primary truth.[22] Their opponents, typically empiricists, reply to this claim with two principal lines of objection. First, they say that if the idea of natural necessity is supposed to apply to something "seen by the mind," the alleged idea is excessively obscure and deserves to be rejected. To speak of mentally seeing a connection is to use a crude metaphor, for we literally see objects with our eyes and, as Hume observed, alleged necessary connections are in no way present to our senses.[23] Second, they insist that our knowledge of natural laws is based on inductive or experimental inference, and this kind of inference cannot be used to conclude that a proposition is necessary. Strictly speaking, such inference allows us to conclude that something is probable or practically certain. If our experimental evidence favoring some *general* principle is exceptionally strong, we may find ourselves *saying* that exceptions to the principle are "impossible." But in saying this we are merely expressing our confidence that exceptions *will not* be found, that it is useless to contemplate them.

Current debate about natural laws is focused on issues belonging to three distinct areas of philosophy: metaphysics, semantics, and the theory of knowledge. The key metaphysical issue was clearly identified, I believe, by C. S. Peirce: it concerns the ontological staus of natural laws.[24] As I see it, the most reasonable view of a natural law is one that Peirce called "Ockhamist." According to this view, laws are statements or propositions whose truth is determined by natural regularities of the sort I have indicated. Ontologically speaking, necessary connections are as fictional as facts or universals. The issue appropriate to the theory of knowledge concerns the means by which laws, thus understood, are known or rationally accepted. On this matter the empiricist view of, say, Hume is seriously defective. As I shall explain in chapter 8, the basic form of experimental inference is not generalization from experience but, roughly, inference to the best explanation. Fundamental regularities are postulated, not observed, and the postulation is rationally defended by the explanations and predictions that it allows us to make.[25]

The remaining issue is the semantic one, and it dominates current discussions of natural laws. Historically, the semantic issue concerned the meaning of "necessity" or the "must" in "*X* must happen if *Y* happens." Today, the issue is focused on the interpretation of conditional statements expressed in the subjunctive mood. Many uniformities are merely accidental, as it were: if American males happened to shave every morning, this would be a merely accidental uniformity, not a matter of natural law. When we think that a regularity is lawful, we express the regularity in subjunctive terms: If a certain thing *were* to occur, something else *would* then occur (always, 90 percent of the time, or whatever). The semantic problem concerning natural laws is now focused on the proper interpretation of the subjunctive statements (or their technical counterparts) used to formulate natural laws. The notions of natural necessity and physical possibility, which express our attitude toward lawful regularities, can be defined in relation to natural laws: It is physically necessary that *p* just when the proposition that *p* is entailed by natural laws, and it is physically possible that *p* just when the proposition that *p* is consistent with natural laws.

The semantic problem about subjunctive conditionals arises from the fact that such conditionals may be "counterfactual": A conditional "*P* → *Q*" may be true, that is, when its antecedent, "*P*," is false. The idea is that if "*P*" *were* true, "*Q*" would be true as well. This idea raises a semantic problem because the conditionals best understood in logic are truth-functional: "If *P* then *Q*" requires that "*Q*" be true when "*P*" is true, but if "*P*" is false, the truth-functional conditional is held to be "vacuously" true. Since conditionals expressing laws often have unfulfilled antecedents, they are not truth-functional. The key semantic problem about them is, therefore, that of explaining their peculiar logical structure.

One metaphysically attractive interpretation of the subjunctive conditionals used to express causal laws may be called the "inference-ticket" interpretation.[26] The idea is that a lawlike conditional, though having the syntactical structure of a statement, functions as a principle of inference: it tells us, in effect, that certain conclusions are properly inferable from certain sorts of premises. Since, in science, we are often interested in drawing conclusions from premises we know to be false, this interpretation accords with scientific practice. Thus, even though we know that there are no perfect gases in nature, we are often interested in reasoning about such things. In such reasoning we do not allow any conclusion to be properly inferred from a false supposition; the conclusions properly drawn on nonformal grounds from a false supposition are often based on scientific rather than on logical principles; and often these scientific principles are regarded as laws of nature.

Other semantic interpretations of lawlike statements have been offered in recent years,[27] but the metaphysical conception of laws that I have suggested here still seems defensible. Like Ockham, we can reasonably contend that natural laws are general statements applicable to the world because of natural regularities. And like Hume, we can reasonably contend that their truth does not require us to postulate special necessary connections in nature. A qualified version of the "regularity analysis"—one not requiring irreducible events—can, therefore, be appended to the remarks about causation given in the last section.

More on Things and Events

If my argument thus far is correct, there are no a priori or purely philosophical difficulties with the classical idea that our world is a system of irreducible continuants and that events belong to the world only in a derivative sense. This outcome does not prove, however, that our world actually is such a system. The question I propose to discuss now is whether the classical conception of our world is actually preferable, all things considered, to alternative conceptions such as the event ontology proposed by Russell.

I mentioned earlier that this kind of question is extremely difficult to answer because it can be approached from different points of view. One approach is to consider the implications of currently accepted scientific theories. As I noted, Russell thought that even the special theory of relativity—the one concerned with time and motion—requires an ontology of "events." If he was right about this, the classical conception of the world as a system of irreducible continuants must be rejected as scientifically inadequate. Similar claims have been made by other philosophers who appeal to such things as the electromagnetic field. As they see it, the classical conception of the world loses all plausibility when we pass beyond the views of the so-called plain man and come to terms with contemporary physics.

Although these ontological claims must be taken seriously, they presuppose debatable interpretations of scientific theories. Such interpretations are, in the first place, "realistic"; they construe physical theories as literally true descriptions of the ultimate nature of reality. Not every philosopher of science will agree with such interpretations, however. In fact, realistic interpretations of physical theories have recently come under attack by very able philosophers.[28] Yet even if realistic interpretations are, on the whole, acceptable (as I believe they are), claims such as Russell's can be supported only by a correct analysis of particular scientific theories. Since Russell held, mistakenly, that the classical conception of a persisting thing or "substance" is objectionable on logical grounds, we cannot dismiss the possibility that his claim about ontological implications of the special theory of relativity is equally mistaken.

On the face of it, this last possibility is not negligible, for the paper in which Einstein formulated his special theory was called "On the Electrodynamics of Moving Bodies,"[29] and this title suggests that Einstein's theory was concerned with *moving bodies*, not exotic events. To evaluate Russell's claim that an ontology of events is required by contemporary physical theories, one must, therefore, subject the relevant theories to a careful logical analysis—a task, I regret to say, that I am unable to carry out. Nevertheless, we must, as students of metaphysics, take seriously the idea that the classical view of the world, however coherent it may be, might be shown to be false on scientific grounds.

A contrary view may appear to be required by P. F. Strawson's arguments in his influential book, *Individuals*. As I mentioned in the last section, Strawson argued that to make sense of intersubjective discourse, we must assume that the "basic particulars" of our world are continuants—things that, because they persist in time, can be identified again and again.[30] Such objects are basic to a publicly understandable conceptual scheme because, he said, hearers must be able to identify what speakers are talking about, and this is possible only if there is a fairly stable background of enduring objects in relation to which identifications can be made. Thus, if I say that the cat is on the mat, the cat and mat to which I am referring can be identified by others only if these things, or perhaps the room in which they are now placed, can *later* be singled out by those with whom I am speaking. They must be able to say, for example, "Is this the cat you referred to?" or "Is this the house in which the cat and mat you spoke of were located?"

Although Strawson's arguments do seem to show that intersubjective discourse must in some way be tied to persisting objects of reference, they do not prove that our world must be understood as containing irreducible continuants. We may, at some preliminary stage of our linguistic development, conceive of the world as containing persisting things to which we can repeatedly refer, but this conception does not have to be regarded as immutable: it can be revised as our theories develop. True, we could not have begun by conceiving of a tree or animal as biologists now do—that is, as a complex of cells, molecules, or their exotic constituents. Yet just as observable spatial objects can be conceptually decomposed into systems of unobservable spatial objects without destroying the possibility of intersubjective reference, enduring temporal objects can, it would seem, be conceptually decomposed into systems of momentary events—again without destroying the possibility of intersubjective reference. High-level theoretical developments are compatible, after all, with the retention of conceptually primitive linguistic habits.

The possibility that the objects of everyday discourse might be understandable as, or reducible to, systems of exotic events raises an interesting question: "Might thing ontologies and event ontologies reasonably be viewed as noncompeting alternatives?" To see what I mean by a noncompeting alternative, consider the following possible world *W*:

According to a theory T1, the world *W* consists of six elementary objects (lines), standing in the relation *R* to one another: the odd and even lines are, we might say, parallel to one another. According to theory T2, on the other hand, the world *W* consists of three elementary objects (crosses) standing in the relation *R*∗: they are side by side. Although these theories describe *W* differently—identifying different basic objects and describing them as standing in different relations to one another—they are, in an intuitive sense, equivalent theories: they exhaustively describe the same reality, though in different ways.

The question is: "Could a thing theory and an event theory be equivalent and noncompeting in the way that T1 and T2 are equivalent and noncompeting?'' As I see it, the answer is yes. Suppose that a thing theory is truly descriptive of our world in the way that T1 is truly descriptive of the miniworld W. In this case an alternative event theory is, I believe, equally satisfactory from an ontological point of view. Since our world is not static—since the "things" it contains undergo change—an event theory can also be applied to it. The intuitive idea is this: where a thing theory postulates a continuant (Socrates, say), the event theory postulates a series of events (Socrates stages, if you will). If there is no metaphysical presumption that the series of Socrates stages, or Socratic events, is truer to the facts than a persisting Socrates, these two conceptions of the world are not, ontologically speaking, incompatible: they are alternative and noncompeting in the sense in which T1 and T2 are alternative descriptions of the world W.[31]

My claim, above, was that a thing theory and an event theory (or ontology) *could* be alternative and noncompeting; I did not say that such theories are bound to be alternative and noncompeting. This qualification is extremely important. According to Russell, the concept of a persisting thing should be replaced, in the interests of an "improved" ontology, by the conception of a certain R-family of events: instead of speaking of a persisting Socrates, we should speak of a series of Socrates-stages or Socrates-events. Russell's philosophical arguments for this view were, I claimed, untenable, but he did succeed in calling attention to an important fact—namely, that the counterpart, in an event theory, to a continuant is a certain "family" or sequence of events.[32] This fact is ontologically important because it shows us that a thing theory is an acceptable alternative to an event theory only when the events postulated by the latter invariably fall into appropriate R-families. If this condition does not hold—if, that is, the world contains events that cannot reasonably be viewed as belonging to the history of some persisting thing—then a thing ontology cannot provide an acceptable alternative to an ontology of events.

Since the existence of events not belonging to appropriate R-families is a purely factual matter, one to be ascertained by empirical investigation, it appears that the ultimate nature of our world cannot be discovered by purely philosophical speculation. In saying this I am not only endorsing the thesis of scientific realism but expressing my agreement with a more fundamental kind of realism that bears some similarity, at least, to what has recently been called "metaphysical realism." This last kind of realism is currently under attack by a growing number of philosophers, and I want to end this chapter with some comments about it.

Metaphysical Realism and Descriptive Metaphysics

In a number of articles and in a new book called *Reason, Truth, and History*, Hilary Putnam has argued that metaphysical realism is an erroneous doctrine.[33] According to this form of realism, the world consists of a "fixed totality of mind-independent objects." Since the totality of real objects is fixed, there is, in principle, "exactly one true and complete description of the way the world is.'' This ideally complete description is true in the sense that its ingredient words or thought-signs "correspond" to mind-independent objects and represent them as they really are. Although our aim, as scientists and philosophers, is to contribute to the discovery of this ideally complete description, our view of the world is limited by our circumstances and our sensible natures, and we cannot reasonably suppose that the ideal description will ever actually be achieved.

Since Putnam believes that equally acceptable, alternative conceptions of the world are possible, and since he also believes that our best-founded views about what exists involve a conceptual apparatus (or system of descriptions) to which there are alternatives, the thesis of metaphysical realism cannot, in his opinion, be correct. He supports his opinion by some remarks about reference and truth. As he sees it, if the objects of the world are truly independent of our opinions about them, they must collectively constitute a "ready-made" world of Kantian things-in-themselves—one that our system of concepts is intended to fit but may misdescribe. Yet this view is, he insists, utterly untenable. We can conceive of the world only by means of concepts we freely invent, and our concepts, words, or thought-signs can refer or attach to objects only if those objects are singled out by us and are *not* utterly independent of us. As a consequence of this, the truth of our opinions is not determined by a correspondence, or fit, between our concepts and ready-made things-in-themselves but by their "warranted assertibility"—their assertibility under "optimal conditions" for creatures with our "sensible natures."

As I see it, the metaphysical realism Putnam attacks is a confused doctrine that deserves to be rejected. On the other hand, few if any philosophers have (to my knowledge) actually held it, and the consequences of rejecting it are not, in any case, what Putnam takes them to be. In particular, we do not have to reject the traditional view that our world consists, at least in part, of mind-independent objects and that the truth of our opinions consists in a "correspondence" between them and the objects they concern. My view on this matter can be supported by the following considerations.

To begin with, although a "real" object is properly definable as one whose existence does not depend on our opinions about it,[34] this definition does not commit us to the idea that real objects are anything like Kantian things-in-themselves or that only one means of truly describing the world is possible. To see this, suppose that the possible world W given in the last section *is* the real world. As we saw, this world can be adequately described by two alternative theories, T1 and T2. It can also be described by a theory T3, according to which W consists of spatial regions (mostly triangular) related in a manner $R**$. Although the fundamental objects of these three theories are different, they would still exist even if the three theories had never been developed. As Leibniz observed in his *Nouveaux essais*, "whatever we truthfully describe or compare is also distinguished or made alike by nature."[35] In other words, the objects identified by the three theories really exist: the world W *is really such* that the concepts of these alternative theories truly apply to it.

The idea that the world consists of mind-independent objects—objects whose existence does not depend on our opinions about them—does not imply, therefore, that "there is exactly one true and complete description of the way the world is." It also does not imply that real objects are Kantian things-in-themselves, for such objects are, as Kant insisted, incomprehensible and indescribable. Traditional "realists" have insisted, to be sure, that truth consists in some kind of correspondence between thought (or proposition) and object, but no philosopher holding this view of truth has ever supposed that the real objects to which true statements correspond might be Kantian things-in-themselves. The paradigmatic statement to which the correspondence theory is applied is one like "The cat is on the mat," yet the reality to which this statement (if true) would apply is one containing a cat on a mat. The concept of a cat—or, better, the concept of a reptile[36]—may be a peculiarly human creation, but this does not mean that the reality to which it applies is a Kantian thing-in-itself. If the statement really is true, it has, as Leibniz would have said, its "foundation in reality."

When Putnam criticized metaphysical realism, he assumed that, if the objects we recognize are inevitably singled out from our distinctively human point of view, they cannot properly be regarded as mind-independent. But this assumption is extremely dubious. If I single out certain people as *my* ancestors, they are not thereby "dependent" on me. I single them out by reference to myself, but the subjectivity of my means of reference does not in any way detract from their objectivity or reality. In chapter 4 I claimed that "essences are purely nominal"—that objects are singled out as unities by, ultimately, conventional criteria.[37] But my claim did not, if sound, cast any doubt on the reality (in the traditional sense) of those objects. However conventional our means of identifying objects, or sorts of objects, may be, those objects are, if they exist, real: they are not mere figments of our imagination. A God's-eye view of the world may be more comprehensive and more discriminating than ours, but it is still one view among others. Even highly limited views single out elements of reality.

If the remarks I have been making are correct, the metaphysical realist's claim that (in Putnam's words) "the world consists of some fixed totality of mind-independent objects" is not necessarily objectionable. If alternative conceptions of the world are possible, different totalities of objects can be singled out and regarded as "fixed" from different points of view. In saying this I am, to a degree, agreeing with Putnam's "internalism." Although the truth of particular assertions may consist in an appropriate "correspondence" with reality, questions about the "ultimate reality" of this or that kind of object can still be regarded as, in a sense, internal questions—to be answered by reference to some well-founded conception (or theory) of the world. Such questions are internal only in a sense, however, for alternative conceptions (or theories) are not always equally well founded: some are better than others.

In the earlier sections of this chapter I supported the idea that the basic objects of the ordinary, nontechnical view of the world can be understood as continuants, but in the last section I argued that a noncompeting alternative to this view might have events as basic objects. I also admitted that continuants might not be basic in the technical view under development in the physical sciences. To clarify my total position and to relate it to what I have just been saying about metaphysical realism, I want to add some further remarks.

Although events theories are, in principle, noncompeting alternatives to thing theories, the ordinary view of the world involves, as I see it, an ontology of things. Not only do we naturally think of the world as made up of things—of people, animals, plants, and mountains—but the predicates we use are suited to the description of things: they are not, on the whole, suited to the description of events or object-stages. Take Socrates, for example. Although it is easy to describe *him* as, say, bald, snub-nosed, short, and wise, it is not easy to describe his "stages": they are not wise, short, bald, or snub-nosed. We can, it is true, find some predicates that are applicable to Socrates-events—his conversation with Phaedrus was lengthy, interesting, and thought provoking—but it remains true that, if we use ordinary language in an ordinary way, the most natural and most detailed description of the world that we can provide will be Aristotelian in basic categorical structure.

P. F. Strawson, in *Individuals*, introduced a useful distinction between "descriptive" and "revisionary" metaphysics. To resolve the metaphysical problems that have arisen since the time of Aristotle, it is important to understand the categorial structure of ordinary, nontechnical thought about the world. This kind of understanding can be achieved only by an excursus into descriptive metaphysics. But there are alternatives to ordinary thought about the world, and these can be appreciated only by speculation that amounts to revisionary metaphysics. Such alternatives are extremely important, because ordinary views about the world are subject to criticism, both scientific and philosophical. Such criticism can be evaluated—shown to be sound or worthless—only if the categorial structure of ordinary views is clearly understood.

It is obvious that some theories about the world are better than others. It is, perhaps, not obvious, though I believe it is true, that some large-scale views of the world are also better than others. Yet if the claims I have made in connection with metaphysical realism are true, we cannot say that, judged solely by the criterion of representational adequacy, some single view of the world is ideally the best one. If noncompeting alternatives are, in principle, possible, such alternatives are equally adequate so far as their truth—their correspondence to reality—is concerned. But there are other respects in which one view or theory can be judged better than another, one of which is very important for metaphysics.

When I discussed the notion of a causal law, I remarked that many natural regularities are derivative and uninteresting, and that only some regularities correspond to natural laws. A similar point is applicable to the notion of a fundamental object. Objects can be singled out in various ways and from different points of view; but the objects regarded as basic in a scientifically preferred theory, or "view," provide a preferred means of making predictions, giving explanations, and, in short, organizing our experience. To say this is not to imply, again, that the objects singled out by a preferred theory are not real: if we single them out, they are there to be singled out. The point is rather that one way of singling out objects may be preferable to others for scientific purposes. I am speaking, of course, of representationally adequate theories—of theories whose objects can actually be found in reality. Many theories of the past are, we now believe, not adequate in this sense—for example, those that postulated ghosts, devils, phlogiston, or even Cartesian egos. The representationally adequate theories I have in mind *might* differ in the postulation of things and events as basic realities. Even if both theories are equally adequate in representational fidelity (as they might not be) one theory might be preferred on other grounds.

Chapter 7

MEANING, TRUTH, AND METAPHYSICS

ALTHOUGH THE THEORY of meaning is not a standard topic in metaphysics, contentions about the nature of reality have often been supported by an appeal to facts about language. I discussed and rejected one contention of this kind in the last chapter—namely, Strawson's contention that we can make sense of another person's remarks about the world only on the assumption that the world contains continuants as basic particulars. Another, more recent contention of this kind has been advanced in favor of the idea that a proper understanding of our language requires us to admit events as basic realities. Since this last contention is at odds with what I have argued in the last chapter and is also widely accepted at the present time, I propose to discuss it here. My aim in doing so is not just to defend my ontological views against likely objections but to introduce further subjects of metaphysical importance. These further subjects are associated with the concept of truth.

Adverbs and Ontology

When, in the last chapter, I developed an analysis of time without events, I employed temporal connectives such as ''while' and ''after'' as part of my basic vocabulary. Some contemporary philosophers, taking their cue from Gottlob Frege,[1] will object to my procedure on logical grounds. As they see it, temporal connectives have a derivative status: they are verbal shorthand for conceptually more primitive expressions that refer to times or intervals of time. If these philosophers are right, my analysis of time actually puts the car before the horse. Instead of providing an acceptable basis for the philosophical construction of times, statements containing words like ''while' and ''after'' involve a tacit reference to such things. This view deserves some discussion.

The reasoning supporting the view is this. A statement such as ''Nero giggled after Rome burned'' implies the simpler statement ''Nero giggled.'' If we are to account for this implication, we must appreciate the logical complexity of statements containing the temporal connective ''after.'' Gottlob Frege exposed this complexity when he observed, in effect, that ''Nero giggled after Rome burned'' is a shorthand version of ''$(\exists t)(\exists t')$(Nero giggled at t & Rome burned at t' & t is later than t'),'' where the variables of quantification range over a domain of times or numbers correlated with times.[2] This observation shows us why "Nero giggled (at a time)" is a logical consequence of "Nero giggled after Rome burned": the former follows from the latter by standard principles of deductive inference.

I can agree that "Nero giggled" follows from "Nero giggled after Rome burned," but I deny that this implication *must* be understood as a logical one—that is, as an implication based on the logical structure of the statements in question. As Carnap emphasized, not everything reasonably regarded as an implication is a formal relation; some implications are "material," based on the meaning of nonlogical words.[3] An example of such a nonformal implication is that between "*a* is warmer than *b*" and " $\sim$ (*b* is warmer than *a*)." The latter follows from the former, but it does so for nonlogical reasons. I submit that, from a basic metaphysical point of view, the implication between the two statements about Nero is best understood as a nonlogical one. Properly understood, the implication is based on the meaning of the temporal expression "after," not on the logical structure of a formula that the vernacular statement containing "after" supposedly abbreviates.

As I explained in the last chapter, our conception of a time or a determinate temporal interval is an empirical one. It is founded, moreover, on some objective periodicity, which serves as a standard by which temporal units are defined. Generally speaking, a periodicity is a regularity in the behavior of some thing, a regularity in which something happens before or after something else. Whether we conceive of temporal units (times) as constructions or as irreducible realities, we identify them in relation to a conceptually more primitive notion of temporal succession—of before and after. This more primitive notion can be used in saying that Nero giggled *after* Rome burned, and it is part of the content of this notion that if A occurs after B, then A occurs.

To say this is not to deny that, if we have introduced the notion of a time by appropriate definitions, we can proceed to prove that if A occurs after B, then there are times t and t' such that A occurs at t, B occurs at t', and t is later than t'. A proof of this kind can, indeed, be constructed, and the proof will be formally valid. Yet the possibility constructing such a proof does not show us that the implication between the vernacular statements "A occurs after B" and "A occurs" is also formally valid, for it is not. This last implication is, at best, material, based on the meaning of the temporal expression "after"; it is not derivative and formal, based on the definition of times or temporal units.

An analogy may be helpful at this point. In ordinary life we employ all sorts of comparative expressions such as "is warmer than," "is sweeter than," and "is bluer than." Our use of these expressions does not always presuppose an underlying metric. If it is true that x is bluer than y, it must be true (as most people use the word) that x is, if not blue, at least bluish; yet the implication between "x is bluer than y" and "x is bluish" does not depend on a tacit quantification over some exotic entities—degrees of blueness, say. Similarly, the implication between "x is warmer than y" and " $\sim$ (y is warmer than x)" does not depend on a tacit quantification over degrees of warmth. It is true that, according to a sophisticated conception of warmth, the statement that x is warmer than y might have the sense, for certain speakers, of "$(\exists d)(\exists d')$(the degree of warmth of $x = d$ & the degree of warmth of $y = d'$ & $d > d'$)," and those speakers may be able to deduce from this formula their canonical counterpart to "$\sim (y$ is warmer than $x)$." Yet the possibility of this kind of deduction does not show us that the implication between the vernacular "x is warmer than y" and "$\sim (y$ is warmer than $x)$" can be understood only on the assumption that these statements involve a tacit quantification over degrees or even numbers that represent degrees.

A metaphysical argument related to the one I have just discussed has been used by Donald Davidson to show that statements describing people as doing this or that should be understood as involving a tacit quantification over events.[4] Since I have claimed that the ordinary view of the world can be understood as a thing or substance ontology in which events have only a derivative reality, Davidson's argument poses a challenge that I must meet.

Davidson began by calling attention to statements such as this:

1. Jones buttered the toast with a knife at midnight.

He rightly noted that this statement implies the simpler statement,

2. Jones buttered the toast.

The implication between 1 and 2 is, Davidson added, a logical one, which must be accounted for. According to standard logical theory, 1 has the logical form of

3. Bjtkm,

where "B" expresses the property of buttering . . . with . . . at. . . . Yet if 1 has the logical form of 3, the statement 2 would not be a logical consequence of it. Thus, Davidson concluded, 1 must have some other logical form—one not taken account of in logical theory. He contended that 1 tacitly involves a quantification over events, as in

4. $(\exists x)(Bxjt$ & Wxk & $Axm)$,

which has the sense of "There is an event x that is a buttering by Jones of the toast, that is (done) with a knife, and that occurs at midnight."

If this last formula represented the only means of interpreting the statement 1, Davidson's contention would raise a serious problem, at least, with a reductive approach to events. But other interpretations are, in fact, available— and some of them are preferable to Davidson's interpretation because they follow from a general theory of predicate modification. In spite of Davidson's confidence in the soundness of his approach, he has not actually offered a general theory: he has merely offered certain suggestions about how specimen sentences containing adverbs are to be interpreted. Obviously, a fully adequate account of adverbial modification requires a general theory that covers all instances whatever.

One general theory of this kind—one that I find attractive— has been worked out by Romane Clark.[5] According to him, prepositional phrases of the sort Davidson discussed are predicate modifiers. Logically speaking, such modifiers are operators: when applied to a predicate, they generate a predicate of greater complexity. Thus, if we start the simple predicate "butters" and conjoin it with the modifier "with," we obtain the complex predicate "butters . . . with." It is by virtue of the meaning of this complex predicate that the sentence "Jones butters *t*" is inferable from "Jones butters *t* with *k*." Although the former sentence is, as I say, inferable from the latter sentence, the inference is not formally valid, warranted by the logical form of the two sentences. It is warranted, rather, by the meaning of the complex predicate "butters . . . with." In this regard the inference is comparable to that of "*x* is blue, or bluish" from "*x* is bluer than *y*." Such an inference may be said to be valid, but its validity is not logical (in the narrow sense) or formal, since it depends on the meaning of a nonlogical expression.

Although this book is not the place to develop a theory of predicate modification such as Clark's, the idea on which his theory is built is easy enough to understand. It is also easy to see that, if predicate modifiers simply serve to make complex predicates out of simpler ones, their presence in a sentence does not require us to interpret such sentences as tacitly referring to events. If "Jones butters the toast" refers only to Jones and some toast, and describes them in a certain way, then the statement containing the more complicated predicate "butters . . . with"—namely, "Jones butters the toast with a knife"—refers only to Jones, the knife, and some toast, and describes *them* in a certain way. Unless we have some special reason to suppose that predicates refer to events—and my earlier chapters have shown that no such reason exists—the possibility of treating adverbial modifiers as predicate modifiers, as expressions that make complex predicates out of simpler ones, undermines Davidson's argument for an ontology containing events.

The temporal connectives I discussed earlier are not predicate modifiers, but they are similar to them in a respect worth noting: Just as predicate modifiers make big predicates out of littler ones, temporal connectives such as "before" and "after" make big sentences out of littler ones. Logical connectives such as "and" and "or" also make big sentences out of littler ones, but temporal connectives are not logical words and the inferences they warrant are not logically (that is, formally) valid. There is no doubt that if "Mary smiled after John left" is true, then it must be true that Mary smiled. But the implication here is no more logical (in the narrow sense) than that between "Jones buttered the toast with a knife" and "Jones buttered the toast." In both cases the validity of the inference depends on a nonlogical word or expression, and it is simply a mistake to suppose that formal logic must be stretched to account for them.

As it happens, Davidson is fully aware of the approach Clark takes to predicate modifiers and of the kind of approach I am taking to temporal connectives, but he rejects them for reasons associated with his theory of meaning. As he sees it, a theory of meaning for a natural language is best given by a truth theory for that language, one having the basic structure of Alfred Tarski's original definition of a truth predicate. The requirements of such a theory show us, Davidson believes, that theories of predication such as Clark's and the use I have made of temporal connectives must be viewed as inadmissible.

Although a general theory of linguistic meaning is not, as I observed earlier, a standard subject in metaphysics, the nature of truth is such a subject, and for this reason I shall discuss it in the section to follow. Eventually, I shall relate the theory of truth to the theory of meaning and then discuss the latter in sufficient detail to make it clear why I believe a satisfactory account of truth and meaning does not have the consequences for ontology that philosophers such as Davidson suppose. My remarks about meaning will also provide the basis for a criticism of classical empiricism that I shall offer in the next chapter.

Theories of Truth

Although we can reasonably speak of a true friend or of true love, the kind of truth of principal importance in metaphysics concerns beliefs, propositions, and statements. The aim is to explain what the truth of these premissory entities consists in. For the reasons set forth in chapter 4, I shall assume that the truth of beliefs and propositions can be understood in relation to the truth of statements—that is, declarative sentences meaningfully produced. My aim in the present section is therefore to give a general account, or "theory," of truth as it applies to statements.

Historically, three theories of truth have been at the center of philosophical concern: the correspondence theory, the coherence theory, and the pragmatic theory. These theories all try to identify what is properly asserted of a statement when one says that it is true. The first theory, at least in its most familiar traditional form, claims that a true statement is simply one that corresponds to a fact.[6] According to this theory, the statement "Snow is white" is true just when it corresponds to an appropriate fact involving snow—specifically, the fact that snow is white. According to the coherence theory, a true statement is one that coheres with certain other statements, presumably the totality of statements that an ideal knower having ideal evidence would affirm.[7] According to the pragmatic conception, finally, a true statement is one that an enlightened community of scientists would eventually assert if, roughly, they were able to carry out their scientific investigations as far as possible. As C. S. Peirce put it: "Truth's independence of individual opinions is due (so far as there is any 'truth') to its being the predestined result to which sufficient inquiry *would* ultimately lead."[8]

The coherence theory was originally proposed by so-called Absolute Idealists, followers of Hegel.[9] The theory is difficult to discuss in short compass because it is extremely obscure. Perhaps the main difficulty is to identify in a useful way the totality of statements to which a true statement must cohere, and also to characterize the vague notion of coherence. If one believes, as Hegel did, that reality is ultimately spiritual, so that there is no dualism between reality and the thoughts (beliefs, opinions) of an ideally developed mind, one might be strongly inclined to accept the coherence theory, at least in some form, as an adequate account of the nature of truth. But if one thinks that true statements often concern objects external to minds, however well developed the latter may be, the theory has little plausibility.

One might grant, to be sure, that a true statement must cohere with the totality of beliefs accepted by some ideal reasoner who has some ideal body of evidence. Yet this coherence would be merely incidental to a statement's truth; the latter would consist in some relation to reality —to the subject matter of the statement. The statement that snow is white would be true, that is, *because* of its relation to snow. The fact that this statement also coheres with certain other statements might, if we knew enough, provide us with a way of deciding whether it is true. Such a fact might even, in the end, provide us with the only *test* for a statement's truth that we can possibly have. Still, its truth would not consist in such coherence.[10]

A similar criticism can be made of the pragmatic theory, which is simply a development (as Peirce acknowledged) of the coherence theory. We might reasonably believe that the ultimate truth about the world is what scientific investigation would ideally discover; in fact, we might contend that this is the only reasonable way to conceive of ultimate truth. Nevertheless, an opinion or belief is not true because it is formed by enlightened inquiry but because it describes the world correctly. Inquiry is enlightened, we might say, only when it employs methods that are apt to yield true opinions, or opinions that are a decent approximation to true ones. In either case the opinions sought by enlightened inquiry are supposed to describe the world, to tell us what the world contains and how it is put together.

As I mentioned in the last chapter, some contemporary philosophers believe that one who thinks of true statements as describing a mind-independent reality is committed to the absurdity that such a reality would be a system of Kantian things-in-themselves. But this belief does not stand up to criticism. We may conceive of the world in human terms and describe it from a human perspective, but as Leibniz observed, if such conceptions and descriptions are applicable to the world, they will have a "basis" in reality. Thus, if an object is successfully singled out even by a clumsy, crude, and anthropocentric description, reality must contain it: it must, as it were, be there to be singled out. As we saw in connection with the miniworld *W*, alternative theories can be equally applicable to a single reality.

The remaining and intuitively most plausible conception of truth thus seems to involve some "correspondence" between statements (or beliefs) and the world. Although this conception is sound in basic principle, it is questionable on points of detail. As I mentioned in chapter 3, the relevant correspondence between statement and reality was traditionally interpreted as a correspondence between statement and fact. Yet a fact, I argued, is an extremely dubious entity if it is not simply a true proposition, and a true proposition is a patently inappropriate candidate for the object in reality that makes a statement true. If the fact that snow is white is a fact *about* snow, then snow, being what it is, accounts for the existence of the fact as well for the truth of the statement. Thus, if some version of the correspondence theory is to be satisfactory, it must clarify the sense in which a true statement corresponds to its subject matter, the latter being not a fact but some thing, or things, in the world.

The Semantic Conception of Truth

The semantic conception of truth is often said to be a correspondence theory of an acceptable kind.[11] The idea is that the statement "Snow is white" is true because and only because snow is white, not because some peculiar fact exists or perhaps subsists. I employed this idea when I criticized the traditional correspondence theory in chapter 3, but I did not thereby introduce the semantic conception of truth, which involves complexities and limitations not always appreciated by philosophers.

The semantic conception of truth was originally worked out by the mathematician Alfred Tarski and expounded in a famous article written in 1933 whose title, in translation, is "The Concept of Truth in Formalized Languages."[12] As this title suggests, Tarski was concerned with truth in connection with "formalized languages," these being systems of symbols having a mathematically exact structure. What he offered, generally speaking, was a recipe by which a so-called truth predicate (for example, "is true") can be defined for languages satisfying special conditions.

The conditions that must be satisfied for a language if a truth predicate can be satisfactorily defined by Tarski's strategy are, first, that it have an exactly specifiable structure. By this is meant such things as these: (1) it must be clear which expressions are to count as meaningful elements of the language; (2) it must be known which expressions are to be regarded as definable by reference to others; (3) criteria must be available for distinguishing well-formed sentences of the language from other strings of symbols; and (4) it must be possible to identify some sentences as simple or basic, in a sense that I will explain in what follows. Also, the language cannot be "semantically closed," as Tarski put it. A semantically closed language is one in which certain contradictions are derivable. An example of such a contradiction is the one that can be obtained by reflecting on the sentence "This sentence is false," where the term "This" refers to the sentence in which it occurs. If such a sentence is included in a language, a contradiction results, since the sentence is true if and only if it is false.

To insure that the language for which we wish to define the truth predicate is not semantically closed, Tarski requires us to draw a distinction between the language in which we are giving the definition, the "metalanguage," and the language for which we are giving the definition, the "object language."[13] If a satisfactory definition is to be possible, our metalanguage must be "essentially richer," logically, than the object language. The metalanguage must not only have a logically determinate means of referring to every sentence of the object language, but must contain a "translation" of every such sentence. This last condition is required so that the metalanguage can express every instance of the following schema:

T. *X* is true (in the object language) if and only if *p*,

where the substituends for "*X*" are structure-revealing descriptions of the object-language sentences whose translations replace "*p*." To be "materially adequate" a definition for "is true" must permit one to prove that every instance of the schema T—every *T*-sentence, as they are called—is, in fact, true. Material adequacy is a crucially important feature of a truth definition because a *T*-sentence formulates the truth conditions for an object-language statement. If a truth definition is materially adequate, it supplies truth conditions for *every sentence* of the object language.

To understand Tarski's strategy in constructing a truth definition, it is helpful to begin by considering an extremely simple language. Suppose we have an object language that contains just one simple sentence, "Snow is white," and just one logical connective, " $\sim$," which means "It is not the case that. . . . " Although this "language," which we may call L1, is extremely simple, it contains an infinity of sentences, for the connective " $\sim$ " may be used to build up sentences of progressively greater complexity. Thus, not only is "Snow is white" a sentence of L1, but so are " $\sim$ (Snow is white)," " $\sim$ ($\sim$ (Snow is white))" and " $\sim$ ($\sim$ ($\sim$ ($\sim$ (Snow is white))))." As a criterion for being a sentence of L1, we can offer the following recursive definition:

> D1: *S* is a sentence of L1 $=df$ either *S* is "Snow is white" or, for some *Q*, *Q* is a sentence of L1 and *S* is the result of prefixing the connective " $\sim$ " to *Q*.

If, as I have been doing, we refer to the basic sentence of L1 by a description that, as it were, contains that sentence within quotation marks, and if, in our metalanguage, we use the sentence "Snow is white" as a translation of the basic sentence of L1, then we can define a truth predicate for L1 as follows:

> D2: The sentence *S* is true in L1 $=df$ either (1) *S* is "Snow is white" and snow is white or (2) there is a sentence *Q* of L1 that is not true and *S* is the result of prefixing " $\sim$ " to *Q*.

This last formula defines "is true" for L1 in the following sense: It gives the conditions under which the basic sentence of L1 is true (the first clause), and it provides a rule by which the truth or falsity of any other sentence of L1 can be ascertained in relation to the conditions under which the basic sentence is true (the second clause). As a result, the definition is "materially adequate," allowing us to derive every instance of the schema *T*, that is, all *T*-sentences for the language L1.

Readers unfamiliar with recursive (or "inductive") definitions might suspect that the definition D2 is actually circular, for the predicate "is true in L1" occurs in the definiens as well as in the definiendum. Such a suspicion would be mistaken, however.[14] The definition simply shows that the truth value of any sentence of L1 is a function of the truth value of the basic sentence of L1. It gives, in a noncircular way, the conditions under which the basic sentence of

L1—that is, "Snow is white"—is true, and it then shows us how to determine the truth value of any other sentence of L1 by reference to the truth or falsity of "Snow is white."

This last point can be seen as follows. If we want to know whether the sentence "Snow is white" is true, we have to find out whether snow is white. We may do this by examining the color of snow. If we find out that snow is white, we can infer, by the first clause of the definition, that the sentence "Snow is white' is true in L1. But consider a more complicated sentence of L1, namely, " ~ (~ (~ (Snow is white)))." According to the second clause of D2, this sentence is true in L1 if and only if the simpler sentence " ~ (~ (Snow is white))" is not true in L1. We therefore consider the truth value of this simpler sentence. According to D2, this simpler sentence is true in L1 if and only if the still simpler sentence " ~ (Snow is white)" is not true in L1. We must therefore consider the truth value of this latter sentence. D2 tells us that this latter sentence is true in L1 if and only if the sentence "Snow is white" is not true in L1. But we know that this sentence is true there. We may infer, therefore, that " ~ (Snow is white)" is not true in L1, that " ~ (~ (Snow is white))" is true in L1, and, finally, that the sentence we were originally concerned with, namely " ~ (~ (~ (Snow is white)))," is *not* true in L1. In this way D2 allows us to determine the truth value of any sentence of L1 by reference, ultimately, to the truth value of the basic sentence "Snow is white."

The definition D2 gives us just part of Tarski's strategy—that of providing a *recursive definition* for a truth predicate. Tarski's actual procedure was more complicated because he was concerned with a more complicated language—specifically, a language containing the quantifiers "for all x" and "for some x." To deal with sentences containing quantifiers, Tarski introduced the notion of a domain (the values of the variables of the language) and a special relation that he called "satisfaction."[15] As I noted in chapter 2, Russell sometimes spoke of objects satisfying propositional functions, but Tarski's use of "satisfies" was special for two basic reasons. First, where Russell spoke of an individual object such as Fido satisfying a propositional function, Tarski spoke of a sequence satisfying such a function. Tarski spoke of sequences rather than objects becuse some propositional functions contain more than one variable. Consider Tom, Harry, and the propositional function "x is taller than y." We can't simply say that these two men satisfy the function, for the order of the variables requires us to consider Tom and Harry in a certain order. Since the sequence < Tom, Harry > differs in just the right way from the sequence < Harry, John >, Tarski chose sequences as satisfiers of propositional functions, saying that a sequence $< a,b >$ satisfies the function "x is taller than y" if and only if the first member, a, is taller than the second member, b. The other special feature of Tarski's usage is that he also spoke of sequences satisfying *sentences*—that is, formulas not containing "free" variables.

Tarski's procedure in defining a truth predicate for languages containing quantifiers involved two fundamental steps. The first was to construct a definition of "the sequence s satisfies the formula F of L2," where L2 is the object language in question. The second was to define the predicate "is true in L2" (with respect to the domain *D*).

As we might expect, Tarski's definition of satisfaction is recursive. To construct such a definition for L2 we first specify the conditions under which the simplest or basic formulas of L2 are satisfied by a sequence. We then lay down recursive clauses, showing how the satisfaction conditions for more complicated formulas can be calculated by reference to the satisfaction conditions that we have specified for the basic formulas. To get a general idea of what we might include in some of our recursive clauses, suppose that "*A*" and "*B*" are formulas of L2. Our clause for conjunction would be to the effect that a sequence *s* satisfies the conjunction of "*A*" and "*B*", or "*A & B*", just when it satisfies "*A*" and satisfies "*B*." Our clause for formulas containing quantifiers is a bit more complicated. Consider the formula "(∃*x*)(∃*y*)(*x* is taller than *y*)." According to Tarski, a sequence $<a,b>$ satisfies this formula just when it or (for technical reasons) some other sequence satisfies the simpler formula "*x* is taller than *y*."[16] Supposing that this simpler formula is one of the basic formulas of L2, we look to the first or base clause of our definition to discover the conditions under which it is satisfied by a sequence. If the first member of the sequence is taller than the second member, the sequence satisfies the formula.

As I mentioned above, Tarski's definition of truth is built upon his definition of satisfaction. If *D* is the domain comprising the values of the variables of L2, Tarski's definition of truth for L2 is, in effect, this:

D3: The formula *F* is true in L2 with respect to the domain $D =_{df} F$ is satisfied by all sequences of objects in *D*.

To decide whether a given formula of L2 is true with respect to *D*, we must therefore decide whether it is satisfied by all sequences of *D*-objects. To decide this, we must refer to the details of our definition of satisfaction for L2. If the formula is a simple one, we look to the "base" clause (or one of the base clauses) of the definition; if it is a complex formula, we check the appropriate recursive clauses and work out our answer.

Although Tarski's actual definition of satisfaction (for the languages he considered) involved technicalities that I have not taken account of here, my remarks accurately describe the basic ideas behind his definition. A question we might ask at this point is: "Does Tarski's semantic conception of truth amount to a correspondence theory?" The question is largely terminological, but I should answer no. This answer can be supported by a little reflection on the satisfaction conditions for a simple formula; as we have seen, the satisfaction conditions for complex formulas are to be calculated by reference to the satisfaction conditions for the simplest formulas.

Consider the assertion,

1. The sequence < Tom, Harry > satisfies the formula "*x* is taller than *y*."

This assertion is true just in case Tom is taller than Harry. As this example indicates, the relation of satisfaction is simply the converse of the relation we might express by "is true of," for the assertion 1 amounts to the claim that

2. The formula "x is is taller than y" is true of the sequence < Tom, Harry >.

Clearly, there is no *correspondence* between formula and sequence here—any more than there is a correspondence between the predicate "is red-haired" and Lucille Ball. Lucille satisfies the predicate (the predicate is true of her) because she is red-haired. She doesn't correspond to the predicate any more than the sequence < Tom, Harry > corresponds to the formula "x is taller than y." In both cases the linguistic expression is true of some thing or things in the world because they have (as it were) certain characteristics or are related to one another in a certain way.

In chapter 3 I said that the statement "Snow is white" is true just because snow is white; there is no need, I said, to introduce some object, let alone some fact, to which the statement must corrrespond if it is true. The semantic conception of truth in effect spells out this idea for certain languages having the structure I described a few pages back. There is no doubt that a language such as English does not possess the structure that Tarski's definition requires, for it certainly contains the self-referential sentence "This sentence is false." On the other hand, there is no doubt that, when suitably "regimented," a large part of English possesses that structure. Thus, although Tarski's definition was specifically worked out for a certain formalized language, its underlying ideas can be applied to philosophical disputes about truth—disputes that arise in connection with the less-disciplined language of everyday life.

Truth and Meaning

One of my principal reasons for discussing the semantic conception of truth was to prepare the way for a discussion of a widely accepted theory of meaning that, if correct, would apparently rule out the use I made, in the last chapter, of temporal connectives and adverbial modifiers. This theory of meaning is a truth-conditional theory, and its basic structure is patterned on a Tarskian truth definition. Having explained the key features of such a definition, I am now in a position to discuss the theory. I shall first explain the intuitive basis for it, then develop a sophisticated version of it that has been proposed by Donald Davidson, and finally comment on its metaphysical significance. In a subsequent section I shall offer some general remarks on what might be called the "metaphysics" of truth.

The basic idea underlying a truth-conditional theory is this: We understand the meaning of a sentence when we know the conditions under which it is true, and we know the meaning of a word or phrase when we know how it contributes to the meaning of sentences whose truth conditions we understand. Although this basic idea is, as we shall see, less straightforward than many philosophers realize, a related idea is commonly assumed by logicians when they introduce logical symbolism. As I explained in chapter 2, the E-quantifier is generally interpreted by stating the conditions under which formulas containing it may be considered true, and a logical connective such as "&" is interpreted by showing how the truth value of formulas containing it depend on the values of the simpler formulas that it connects. The idea that the meaning of every word, phrase, or sentence can be given by reference to truth seems to be a generalization of the logician's idea. The generalization is problematic—but more on this later.

The notion of a truth condition is, of course, directly applicable only to declarative sentences, but imperatives and interrogatives seem to have values that are analogous to truth and falsity. An imperative is either obeyed or not obeyed; an interrogative has either an affirmative or a negative answer. Philosophers who accept the truth-conditional theory might therefore contend that we understand the meaning of an imperative when we know its performance conditions and that we know the meaning of an interrogative when we know its affirmation conditions. The formal similarity of these conditions to truth can be seen by the following formulas:

1. The imperative "Jones, do A!" is obeyed just when Jones does A.
2. The interrogative "Did Jones do A?" has an affirmative answer just when Jones did A.

If, as a general matter, nondeclarative sentences have semantic values that are formally similar to truth and falsity, a general theory of meaning that includes them might well have the formal structure of a Tarskian truth definition.

Another idea basic to the truth-conditional theory of meaning concerns the infinity of sentences that any natural language contains. We could no doubt learn the meaning of many simple sentences at our mother's knee, but we could understand the meaning of the countless compound sentences our language contains only by internalizing rules (or principles) of sentence composition. Such rules seem to be neatly captured by a Tarskian truth-definition, for such a definition is recursive in structure, providing (as we saw) a step-by-step procedure by which we can calculate the truth or satisfaction conditions of an infinity of formulas by reference to the semantic values of a finite list of basic formulas. This fact makes it tempting to suppose that a general theory of meaning might have the basic structure of a Tarskian truth definition.[17]

This supposition involves a certain difficulty, however. To see the difficulty, imagine that we are concerned with a very simple object language lacking quantifiers. As I pointed out in connection with the minilanguage L1 (see p. 138), we can define a truth predicate for a language of this kind without speaking of satisfaction conditions: we can speak directly of truth conditions. Thus, if the language contains the truth-functional compound "$P \& Q$," we can specify a truth condition that illuminates the meaning of the compound by saying that "$P \& Q$" is true just when the ingredient formulas, "P" and "Q", are both true. The difficulty, however, is this: When we are concerned with a basic formula of the language—that is, a formula not containing a simpler formula as an ingredient—Tarski's procedure requires us to specify the relevant truth condition by writing in our "translation" of that formula. (I did just this in the first clause of my definition D2 on p. 138.) Yet a truth condition provided by a "translation" is necessarily *based on* an interpretation of a formula's meaning; it does not itself justify, or provide the basis for, such an interpretation.

Davidson, who uses Tarski's definition as a framework for his theory of meaning, is fully aware of this difficulty, and he meets it by "inverting" the order of Tarski's procedure.[18] Instead of starting out with acceptable translations for object language sentences and working out a satisfactory truth definition for those sentences, Davidson recommends the following procedure: we first work out a truth definition; we then test it as an empirical theory by deducing consequences from it that we can verify by the behavior of those who use the language; and finally, if our definition-theory withstands the tests, we obtain the translations (or interpretations) we are after. Since Davidson is an outstanding advocate today of a truth-conditional theory of meaning, I want to describe his approach in some detail; it turns out to be surprisingly complicated.

Davidson on Interpretation

Davidson's initial description of the process by which a truth definition can be worked out is essentially this. To begin with, we observe the behavior and circumstances of the people whose speech we wish to interpret and, on the basis of these observations, we develop provisional *T*-sentences for a large class of their utterances. A *T*-sentence, for Davidson, is (on first approximation) a sentence of the form

s is true if and only if p,

where "s" is a structure-revealing description of a sentence and "p" the statement of a truth condition for s. We initially support such *T*-sentences by relying on a "principle of charity." Assuming, charitably, that most of the sentences to which a speaker assents are true, we attempt to identify conditions that obtain just when he or she assents (or would assent) to them. If, for example, Karl assents to "Es regnet" when and only when it is raining, a plausible *T*-sentence for Karl's idiolect would be:

"Es regnet" is true (for Karl) if and only if it is raining.

Having assembled a large class of provisional T-sentences, we then proceed to construct a truth-definition in Tarski's style that entails those sentences. What we do here accords with the description I gave of a Tarskian definition in the last section (see p. 140). We split the speakers' sentences into recurring parts—into names, predicates, variables, quantifiers, and connectives. We then specify satisfaction conditions for basic formulas containing variables, and we work out appropriate recursive clauses by which to describe satisfaction conditions for derivative formulas. Our next step is to test our truth definition by deducing further *T*-sentences from it, which we attempt to verify in the way we verified our original *T*-sentences. If our definition stands up to test, we then accept it, at least provisionally. If it entails the *T*-sentence

S is true if and only if A,

we interpret the sentence as having the force of

S means that A.

Such a formula "gives the meaning" of a *sentence*; if we are interested in the meaning of a word or sentential part, we look to specific clauses of our truth definition. If we see, for example, that a sequence $<a \ . \ . \ .>$ satisfies a sentential functional "x is F" if and only if the thing a is a dog, we can interpret the predicate "is F" as referring to dogs or as meaning "is a dog."

According to Davidson, "a theory of truth will yield interpretations only if its *T*-sentences state truth conditions in terms that may be treated as 'giving the meaning' of the object language sentences." The problem is, he admits, "to find constraints on a theory strong enough to guarantee that it can be used for interpretation."[19] As we shall see, the plausibility of Davidson's theory depends very largely on his ability to solve this problem.

To appreciate the significance of Davidson's problem, suppose that we have identified what we take to be a sentence of a speaker, Karl, and that we have convinced ourselves that Karl believes it to be true. Our task is to find a *T*-sentence that formulates a plausible truth condition for it. The sentence Karl utters is "Es regnet." Assuming, with Davidson, that Karl's belief provides prima facie evidence that the sentence is true, our aim is to formulate "the conditions" that obtain when Karl has this belief. The trouble is, all sorts of conditions obtain when Karl has this belief or produces his utterance. We want to say that Karl's "Es regnet" is true just when it is raining, but this conception of the *relevant* truth conditions has to be justified, for there are countless other possibilities.

Thus, even if it is always raining when Karl says "Es regnet," he produces his utterance under those conditions; he accepts it as true under those conditions; and (to begin with more remote possibilities) the relative humidity of the air near him falls within a certain range in those conditions. A long list of possible truth conditions could, therefore, be given for Karl's utterance. One could say, for example:

1. Karl's "Es regnet" is true if and only if Karl believes it is raining.
2. Karl's "Es regnet" is true if and only if the relative humidity of the air near Karl is within the interval *XYZ*.
3. Karl's "Es regnet" is true if and only if it is zaining near Karl, where "zaining" applies to a region just in case it rains if Karl is there and doesn't rain if Karl is not there.

The problem, then, is to select *a* truth condition that provides a reasonable interpretation of Karl's utterance. If we merely specify some condition that obtains when and only when Karl's utterance is true, any of the above conditions might be acceptable. Yet none of them provides an intuitively acceptable *interpretation* of his utterance: none gives its meaning.

Davidson has offered a number of suggestions for resolving the problem. One suggestion is that the task of formulating truth conditions for a subject's utterances should be carried out "systematically," the aim being to produce a simultaneous pairing of all true utterances of the subject with true sentences of our own.[20] Such a pairing should reflect appropriate connections between individual sentences. If, as in the *T*-sentence 1 above, we offered our "Karl believes it is raining" as stating a truth condition for Karl's "Es regent," we should expect to find some other utterance by Karl whose truth condition is better represented by our "It is raining." Yet no such utterance is apt to be available. Another suggestion is that a theory of meaning or interpretation is best formulated for a community of speakers. This suggestion is helpful because many interpretations compatible with the behavior of a single person will fail when extended to the entire community. Thus, if Karl suffers sinus headaches when and only when it is raining in his vicinity, a candidate *T*-sentence such as

"Es regnet" is true (for Karl) just when Karl has a sinus headache

might seem as plausible as one having "it is raining" on the right-hand side. Yet the more general *T*-sentence

"Es regnet" is true for a speaker *S* in Karl's community just when *S* has a sinus headache

might easily be refuted while its rival with the clause "it is raining near *S*" stubbornly stands up to test.

Helpful as these qualifications are, they are not sufficient by themselves to render Davidson's theory credible. One difficulty that eludes them was recently pointed out by Hilary Putnam.[21] In the appendix to his *Reason, Truth, and History*, Putnam proved a theorem showing that merely "by fixing the truth-conditions for whole sentences," we cannot expect to obtain suitable interpretations. He illustrated the content of his theorem by a specific case in which the predicates "is a cat" and "is a mat" are each given two radically different interpretations. Interpreted one way, they refer to cats and mats; interpeted the other way, they refer to cherries and trees in the real world and to other things in various possible worlds. Using asterisks to mark the predicates when interpreted exotically, Putnam proved that "A cat is on a mat" and "A cat∗ is on a mat∗" have the same truth value in all possible worlds. His implied conclusion was that, if we merely attend to conditions that happen to obtain in the world or in any possible world, we shall have no basis for assigning them different interpretations. Yet from an intuitive point of view, they are utterly different in meaning.

As it happens, Davidson has an effective reply to Putnam. In an article appearing in 1974 Davidson observed that, if we attend to the indexical and demonstrative elements of a sentence, we can "sharply delimit" the possible interpretations for it.[22] As he emphasized, a plausible interpretation for "Dass ist weiss" must be given by a *T*-sentence having "something like" the form of:

> For all speakers of German x and all times t, "Dass ist weiss" is true spoken by x at t if and only if the object demonstrated by x at t is white.

If T-sentences may assume this form, which is more complicated than the simple form I have considered thus far, Davidson can reasonably contend that a plausible interpetation for "A cat∗ is on a mat∗" could agree with that of "A cat is on a mat" only if the predicate "is a cat∗" is satisfied by the objects that satisfy "is a cat." But this is certainly not true. If I "demonstrate" a certain cat in saying "It is a cat," that cat must, if I speak the truth, satisfy the predicate I use. Yet if, as Putnam stipulates, the exotic predicate "is a cat∗" applies to cherries in our world, then the cat satisfying my predicate does not satisfy Putnam's exotic predicate.

A defender of Putnam might reply that the notion of demonstration has to be interpreted too, so that one who says "That's a cat∗" might be "demonstrating" a cherry on some tree. But this reply misses the point. The notion of demonstration relevant to Davidson's T-sentence belongs to the interpreter, not the speaker. The speaker does, indeed, do the demonstrating, but he does so in the interpreter's sense of the word—that is, he does what the interpreter describes as demonstrating. If Putnam holds a cat in his hands and says, pointing to it, "This is a cat∗," an interpreter like Davidson would never agree that Putnam is "demonstrating" a cherry on some tree that is not even in view.

Although these considerations do, if I am right, provide a plausible means of defending Davidson against Putnam's objection, they put Davidson's program of developing a truth theory in a new light. For one thing, they make it clear that the notion of demonstration is as fundamental to his theory as that of truth. His T-sentences do, of course, contain the world "true," and his truth definition is based upon them. But those sentences also contain, in most if not all cases, demonstrative or indexical elements, the latter including pronouns, tenses, and the like. Davidson might want to insist that the "demonstrates" occurring in such T-sentences is not, strictly speaking, a semantical primitive as "true" is, but it is still fundamental to his theory. In fact, it is no less fundamental than "is true" is.

Another point emerging here is that T-sentences, at least in the revised form, cannot be worked out and confirmed independently of a truth definition: the construction of both goes hand in hand. A provisional truth definition, or a fragment of such a definition, is needed to segment utterances into predicates, singular terms (variable and otherwise), connectives, and quantifiers. To be sure, such a definition is tested by reference to the T-sentences derivable from it, but the structure of the utterances mentioned in those sentences is crucially important in testing them. This fact stands out in the reply I made (on Davidson's behalf) to Putnam. The truth conditions for "A cat is on a mat" are not independent of the truth conditions for utterances in which cats are demonstrated. Thus, we must conceive of Davidson's program as one in which T-sentences are to be developed and revised as a truth definition (or theory) is developed and revised. The segmentation of utterances and the systemic relations between utterances—both explicitly taken account of by the growing truth theory—permits an increasingly fine-grained sifting of the behavioral and other evidence pertinent to evaluating *T*-sentences. It is the evidence obtained in this way that allows us to distinguish the *truth conditions* of many sentences that may, like the two Putnam discusses, have the same *truth values* even in "all possible worlds."

The Power of Charity

The qualifications I have identified thus far go a long way toward rendering Davidson's truth-conditional approach credible, but they do not go all the way. Some remaining problems can be met, however, by an extension Davidson makes of his original principle of charity. In its original, simple form the principle requires us to assume that "most" of the sentences believed true by a speaker are true; the extended principle requires us to assume that the beliefs of others are not "radically different' from our own beliefs.[23]

To see how the extended principle might be applied, consider the truism that the moon is round. If we suppose that Karl holds this belief, we shall also suppose that some utterance in his repertoire is true just in case the moon is round. We shall also suppose that, if Karl's "Dass ist der Mond" is true just when the thing he demonstrates is the moon, a whole class of interpretations for his "Dass is rund" is thereby ruled out. In particular, if in making this utterance he demonstrates the moon, we cannot interpret his utterance as meaning that the object he thus demonstrates is square—or (for that matter) is alive, made of green cheese, or filled with air.

If we always interpret another's utterances in a way that preserves such truisms, we can avoid a problem that arises in connection with coextensive predicates. Such predicates apply, as it happens, to the same things, though they may differ dramatically in meaning. They pose a problem for interpretation because they yield incompatible *T*-sentences that are equally consistent with what we can observe when an utterance is made. Recall one of the candidate *T*-sentences that I mentioned earlier:

Karl's "Es regnet" is true if and only if it zains near Karl,

where "zains" applies to a region just in case it rains there if Karl is present but doesn't rain there if Karl is not present. As I pointed out, this *T*-sentence is a possible rival to one offering the presence of rain as a truth condition, for the bizarre predicate "zains" does, as it happens, truly describe the conditions in which Karl makes his utterance.[24] If, however, we are to identify truth conditions in accordance with Davidson's extended principle of charity, we can disallow such *T*-sentences on the ground that a belief in zaining is a philosopher's invention—not a belief that is widely held in our community or in any other community we know of.

As I pointed out in connection with Karl and the moon, the extended principle of charity often has the effect that, if we interpret an utterance *U* in a certain way, we must disallow various interpretations of related utterances. This effect allows us to dispose of further problems involving coextensive predicates. Consider "creature with a heart" and "creature with lungs." Although these predicates have very different meanings, they are, as it happens, coextensive. Thus, if a speaker demonstrates an animal to which one is applicable, he thereby demonstrates an animal to which the other is applicable; as a result, two *T*-sentences that (in the context of a truth theory) assign significantly different interpretations for the utterance *U* are available. We cannot choose between such *T*-sentences on the ground that either, taken by itself, would be out of line with beliefs we actually have, but the extended principle of charity can nevertheless provide a basis for choosing between them.

The idea is this. Our beliefs about hearts are different from our beliefs about lungs. These different beliefs require us to assign different satisfaction conditions to the predicates "is a heart" and "is a lung." A thing satisfies the predicate "is a heart" only if, for example, it is a pumper of blood, but a thing of this kind does not satisfy the predicate "is a lung." Since these simple predicates are satisfied by different objects, they are semantically distinct and, thus, have different interpretations. Since the complex predicates "is a creature with a heart" and "is a creature with lungs" are built up from core predicates that have different interpretations, they too must have different interpretations even though they are, as it happens, coextensive.

As these last two paragraphs show, the revised principle of charity provides a surprisingly sensitive means of assigning truth conditions to a speaker's utterance. When Davidson introduced the principle, he said that we should assume that a speaker's beliefs do not "differ radically" from our own. In saying this Davidson was no doubt offering a mere rule of thumb to which numerous qualifications are appropriate. For one thing, "our beliefs" must not, as a general rule, refer to beliefs that are peculiar to us as individuals; it should refer to beliefs commonly held in our linguistic community. I may believe that cats are despicable creatures, but this is an anomalous belief and it would be absurd to presuppose it in interpreting the speech of others. Another qualification Davidson would have to allow concerns the likely sophistication of a speech community. If a group of speakers lacked a sophisticated technology, it would be unwise to suppose that an utterance prompted by the sight of a mammalian hair should be interpreted along the lines of "That's a polypeptide helix."

This last example deserves a little more discussion. Michael Dummett has argued that truth-conditional theories of meaning ultimately break down because the truth conditions for many sentences are, as he put it, "recognition transcendent."[25] Although Davidson does not pretend to supply what Dummett expects from a theory of meaning,[26] Dummett's objection can be cast in a form relevant to Davidson's theory by saying that the truth conditions for many sentences cannot be assigned merely on the basis of what an interpreter can experience or recognize when those sentences are uttered. Expressed in this form, Dummett's objection can, however, be met by the sort of consideration that I have been discussing. The key idea is that the truth conditions for some utterances must be worked out on the basis of other utterances whose truth conditions are more easily identified by observation.

Utterances expressing theoretical beliefs are supported, generally speaking, by utterances expressing what Dummett would call their "verification conditions." As interpreters, we have to make conjectures about the beliefs that might reasonably be supported by such verificatory utterances. Our conjectures here can also be supported by drawings or diagrams the speaker might produce when queried about some utterance and by the technical machinery he might use in connection with it. The task of interpreting such utterances is difficult, but the basic strategy for carrying it out is relatively straightforward. There is, in any case, nothing in Davidson's program requiring us to suppose that the truth conditions for an utterance must be open to view.

I must confess that, when I began writing this section, I was convinced that a truth-conditional theory of the sort Davidson describes is fundamentally inadequate. I now see that I greatly underestimated the role of background considerations such as the extended principle of charity in working out the interpretations supplied by *T*-sentences. I was willing to grant that a *T*-sentence could "give the meaning" of an utterance if the truth conditions it specifies are given by a sentence that is a good translation of the utterance or that, as John Foster put it, demarcates, "within the total range of possible circumstances, that subset with which the [utterance] accords."[27] But I could not see how a *T*-sentence of this kind could possibly be obtained and justified by Davidson's approach. I must now concede that if a truth theory is worked out and tested in the way I have described, it can, as Davidson said in reply to Foster, "be projected to unobserved and counterfactual cases." The effect of such projection is that a *T*-sentence derivable from a well-confirmed truth theory conveys the information, to a knowledgeable interpreter, that the utterance it concerns does not just happen true under the specified conditions but *must* be true under those conditions.

In making these irenic remarks I do not mean to imply that I regard Davidson's theory as a definite success. My claim is merely that, properly understood, it eludes the objections I had and have heard others express. One difficulty in appreciating its merits is that, owing to its truth-theory form, it conveys more information pertinent to the meaning or interpretation of utterances than it explicitly sets forth. I want to deal with this point in the next couple of sections. I shall eventually argue that Davidson's theory is actually flexible enough to accommodate the use I made, in the last chapter, of temporal connectives.

Meaning and Indeterminacy

Although "the" theory of meaning is a controversial subject nowadays, some of the alternatives currently debated are actually concerned with different, though related, subjects. As I have explained, Davidson's theory is concerned with "interpretation"; his aim is to formulate a theory that, if known by an interpreter, permits a satisfactory interpretation of a class of utterances. Michael

Dummett's theory, by contrast, is concerned with what a person who understands a language thereby knows or comprehends. Another kind of theory, closely related to Dummett's, is primarily concerned neither with interpretation nor with understanding, but with specifying what, from the point of view of the speaker, the meaning or significance of an utterance consists in.

To see the point in developing a theory of this third kind, we might note some obvious points about language not explicitly discussed by Davidson. To begin with, intelligent people who have mastered a certain portion of a language or dialect can proceed to introduce many new expressions on the basis of those they already understand. They do this when they give definitions. People who can give definitions can also understand them when they are given by others and, if they have learned to read, they can increase their vocabulary by reading books and consulting dictionaries. This is not all, however. A partial understanding of a language or dialect also enables a speaker to clarify the import of words already in use. Such clarification cannot always be accomplished by giving a definition, and it usually cannot be achieved by specifying a truth condition. Fortunately, another procedure is available.

In 1905 Peirce remarked that, when people use words with a "determinate" meaning, "the character of their meaning consists in the implications and nonimplications of their words.[28] He added that when honest people, not joking, want to make the meaning of their words determinate, "so that there shall be no latitude of interpretation," they try to "fix what is implied and not implied by them."[29] Suppose a friend or neighbor says "Bears, moose, and deer have a right to live unmolested by hunters." If we were to ask what this statement means, we would simply laugh at the pronouncement: "What I have said is true just in case bears, moose, and deer have a right to live unmolested by hunters." Clearly, we want some explanation of the speaker's meaning, and we want it given in words that we can understand. Speakers who cannot express their claim in another way can at least tell us what follows if their claim is true and also, if possible, what (of relevance) does not follow. If the speaker concerned with animal rights merely added, "Well, it is wrong for hunters to molest wild animals," we should probably agree that we have some understanding of the statement in question. In fact, if, unable to produce a paraphrase, the speaker were able to outline everything that we could reasonably and nontrivially infer from that statement, we should probably feel that we understand it as well as it can be understood.

When I speak of what can be nontrivially inferred from a statement, I am speaking of inferences that are warranted by the statement's meaning, not by its mere logical form.[30] If I am in doubt about the meaning of "That is a pig," I shall not be enlightened if I am merely told that I can infer the following from it: "Either that is a pig or a giraffe," "Something is a pig," and "Either it is raining or it is not." The nontrivial consequences that help us to understand a statement's meaning are owing to its content; they are warranted by the non-logical expressions occurring in it. At the beginning of the chapter I used the term "material" to describe such consequences. Depending on the speaker, the material consequences of "That is a pig" might be "That is an animal," 'That is a domesticated swine," 'That is a creature whose flesh is called pork." I had this kind of consequence in mind in the first section of this chapter when I said that "*a* is blue, or at least bluish" is warranted by the meaning of "*a* is bluer than *b*."

J. L. Austin once expressed serious doubt that "That's a pig" has any distinctive implications; he claimed that "We learn the word 'pig,' as we learn the vast majority of words for ordinary things, ostensively—by being told, in the presence of the animal, '*That* is a pig'. . . . "[31] It is true that we do "learn" many ordinary words this way, but this learning takes place only because we already know a lot about the language we are learning and can reasonably assume, say, that our teacher is pointing to an animal rather than to a certain undetached pig-part, as Quine might say.[32] Although our understanding of many familiar words involves the ability to apply them to appropriate objects, a propensity to respond with the right noise in the presence of the right objects is not sufficient for understanding a word's meaning. Parroting does not show understanding, nor does a series of lucky guesses. If we really understand a sentence whose meaning, or significance, is at all determinate, we must have some idea of what is inferable from it. I will concede, as I must, that not everything reasonably inferred from a statement is entailed by it; my claim is simply that some of the things thus inferred are entailed by it, and some of these things partially unpack its meaning.

Since few words are actually used with a clear, determinate meaning, it is not always possible to say whether a given inference is or is not warranted by a statement's meaning. Yet if we do attach even a relatively determinate meaning to some statement we make, we must be able to identify at least some inferences that partly unpack that meaning. To deny that any statement is ever sufficiently determinate in meaning to justify such an inference is tantamount to denying that a statement's meaning is a sufficiently definite or determinate thing, even ideally, to provide the subject matter of any significant theory.

The sort of meaning I have described might be called "speaker's meaning," for it is something that self-conscious speakers commit themselves to, and mean to convey, in saying something. It is also something that such speakers may wish to clarify for other people who share their dialect. By contrast, the sort of meaning of principal concern to Davidson might be called "hearer's" or "interpreter's" meaning, for it is given by *T*-sentences that, because they are entailed by a truth theory constructed in a particular way and confirmed by evidence of a certain kind, can reasonably be understood as providing "interpretations" for the utterances of some speaker or group of speakers.[33] Although these two kinds of meaning are, as I shall show, interrelated, the latter is "indeterminate" in a way that the former is not. This difference requires some elaboration.

As I pointed out in chapter 4, W. V. O. Quine has argued—and, in my judgment, made a compelling case for the idea—that translation is always indeterminate. His idea, abstractly speaking, is that expressions of different languages (or speech communities) can be regarded as good translations of one another only by reference to a scheme of translation that segments both languages into parts (words) and correlates them in a way that satisfies certain constraints. Since two languages can always be segmented and correlated in more than one way that meets the constraints, different schemes of translation are always possible. This outcome supports the idea of translational indeterminacy because it implies that, absolutely speaking, there is no such thing as the right or correct translation of an expression in other terms. Such a translation can be considered right or correct in relation to a given scheme of translation, but alternative schemes supporting different translations are, in principle, equally good.

Davidson accepts the thesis of translational indeterminacy, though he does so for reasons somewhat different from Quine's. Davidson appears to hold that the indeterminacy is a consequence of the fact that our interpretation of people's speech is bound up, in a systematic way, with assumptions about their beliefs as well as their meanings and that no single set of assumptions is uniquely supported by the available evidence. Thus, if a man says "There's a hippopotamus in the refrigerator," we can conclude either that he uses words as we do but has some weird beliefs, or that he shares our beliefs but uses words such as "hippopotamus" with a highly unusual meaning.[34] Further evidence may allow us to reject one conclusion in favor of another in a simple case like this, but because our interpretation of one utterance will impose constraints on the interpretation we can place on other utterances, we must base any systematic interpretation of another's speech (or language) on interpretive assumptions to which there are, in principle, equally reasonable alternatives.

Viewed this way, the indeterminacy Davidson attributes to interpretation seems to be based on a problem about verification. For reasons I shall give in a moment, I think the indeterminacy has a deeper, more ontological source—as it has in Quine's account.[35] However this may be, the indeterminacy Davidson finds in interpretation does not expose a corresponding indeterminacy in what I have called a speaker's meaning. The indeterminacy of interpretation is at least a two-person, or two-language, affair; it arises from the variety of ways in which a speaker's words may be correlated with those of an interpreter. A speaker's meaning may be indeterminate in various respects, but this indeterminacy is owing to a lack of clarity about what the speaker's words do or do not (as he understands them) imply. It has nothing to do with the relation of those words to the expressions of some other language, idiolect, or dialect.

In my initial account of Davidson's theory of interpretation I remarked that the notion of demonstration is as fundamental to his theory as the notion of truth. We can now see that the notion of a community belief is equally fundamental to it. These fundamental notions raise a problem with Davidson's theory, and I want to say something about it before proceeding to other topics on my agenda.

Suppose we are concerned to interpret the utterances of a group of people living in a remote area hitherto unvisited by Europeans. If, relying on an extended principle of charity, we interpret utterances of "Gavagai" as true just when the speaker demonstrates a rabbit, we are crediting these people with an ontology similar to ours—one containing rabbits rather than, say, rabbit-stages.

If, furthermore, we disallow interpretations of related utterances that do not cohere with our humdrum beliefs about rabbits, we are in effect crediting these people with "most of our beliefs" about such things. But is this really justifiable? Aren't we *arbitrarily* projecting our ontology and our "ideology" (as Quine calls it) onto the utterances of these remote people and then calling the result "an interpretation of their speech"?

The issues raised here are extraordinarily difficult, and I cannot hope to resolve them to every reader's satisfaction. I can, however, make a few remarks that may be helpful. For one thing, the interpretations we offer are not entirely arbitrary because they are subject to some factual constraints. Thus, if we interpret an utterance as true just when a rabbit is present, we shall have to abandon that interpretation if, later on, we find people confidently uttering it in the absence of furry animals with long ears. For another thing, if an interpretation is theory-laden in the sense that it is applicable to a speaker's utterance only if the speaker knows a certain amount of mathematics, then in the absence of information indicating that such knowledge is in hand (such as the presence of a sophisticated technology) it would be absurd to offer such an interpretation. Finally, general theories applicable to human beings such as evolutionary theory, cognitive psychology, and perhaps even sociobiology may induce us to prefer some interpretations to others on the ground that certain aspects of reality play a particularly important role in the life of any human animal.[36]

In spite of these factual constraints, it remains true that different interpretive schemes will be compatible with any observational data we can assemble. Thus, an element of interpretive arbitrariness seems inevitable. We will, no doubt, prefer the simplest interpretive scheme that accords with our data, but the simplest scheme (if there is one) need not thereby be viewed as the truest to the facts. On the contrary, if "the facts" are supposed to be something other than the data we have or can have, then it is doubtful whether there are such things. The aim of an interpretive scheme is to provide a systematic means of correlating utterances of the interpreter with utterances of the speaker in such a way that the interpreter knows what to expect, in the world and in subsequent behavior (verbal and otherwise), when an arbitrary utterance is made. If alternative interpretive schemes satisfy this aim equally well, there is, perhaps, nothing to choose between them: they are equally satisfactory. This, at any rate, is the position Quine takes on the subject of translational indeterminacy.

Interpretation and Speaker's Meaning

When I discussed Davidson's theory, I explained that, according to him, a *T*-sentence can be understood as "giving the meaning" of an utterance only to someone who knows that the *T*-sentence is entailed by a well-confirmed truth theory that was constructed in a particular way. I also explained that, to be constructed in the way Davidson specified, a theory must not only possess the logical structure of Tarskian truth definition but must also comply with Davidson's extended principle of charity. I remarked that these requirements make Davidson's view plausible because they place powerful constraints on the truth conditions that can be assigned to utterances. In the last section I pointed out that these constraints involve an element of arbitrariness, which is perhaps inevitable with any interpretive system. I now want to relate Davidson's theory of interpretation to the remarks I made earlier about speaker's meaning.

When we construct a truth-definition, we first identify the vocabulary of the language—the singular terms, the predicates, and the logical symbols. We then specify truth or satisfaction conditions for the simplest formulas, and we show, in our recursive clauses, how the truth or satisfaction conditions for complex formulas containing logical symbols are to be worked out by reference to the truth or satisfaction conditions of the simpler formulas contained within them. A definition constructed this way imposes formal constraints on interpretation because if, for example, we interpret a formula "Kab" as meaning that (or true just when) A & B, we cannot interpret the subformula "a" contained in "Kab" in a way inconsistent with A or B. Such a definition also shows us the logical properties of identifiable words or formulas. Thus, if "Kab" is true just when A & B, and "a" is true just when A, we can easily prove, on the basis of logical principles *we* accept, that "Kab" logically implies "a". We can also *see* that the symbol "K" has the logical properties of a conjunction.

It is important to note that, just as the logical structure of a Tarskian truth definition shows us that various formulas of the object language are logically related in particular ways, the extended principle of charity shows us that various formulas are related in meaning. Suppose that we regard "Anything colored is extended, or spread out in space" as a humdrum belief. If our interpretation of someone's language or dialect is founded on this belief (among others), then if we interpret an utterance U as meaning that a certain object is colored red and an utterance U* as meaning that the same object is extended, we shall conclude not only that U is true only if $U*$ is true, but also that U and $U*$ are related in meaning. This meaning-relation between U and $U*$ will be *shown* by the interpretations we give them. To become aware of the relation we need only consider what we mean when we use the words appearing in the interpretations.

This last point brings out an interesting connection between the notion of speaker's meaning and Davidson's theory of interpretation. Suppose I were to clarify my view (or Peirce's view) by saying that the implications and nonimplications that constitute the speaker's meaning of an utterance U are determined by the truisms or humdrum beliefs that are associated with the speaker's utterance of U. In this case Peirce's view would be perfectly consistent with Davidson's theory. Peirce could, in fact, allow that a theory of interpretation could be provided by a truth-theory constructed according to Davidson's specifications. He would have to admit, of course, that such a theory does not *say* what the speaker's meaning of individual utterances consists in, but this can be known, or reconstructed, by any intelligent person who knows the theory, knows how it was worked out, and knows what evidence supports it. As Davidson himself acknowledged, this knowledge must even be in hand if a T-sentence is to be understood as providing an interpretation for the utterance it concerns.[37]

If the utterances in question are not understood as having what Peirce called a "determinate" meaning, it is not clear that Peirce would actually reject this rapprochement with Davidson. I certainly wouldn't reject it. On the other hand, I am convinced that not all aspects of an utterance's meaning are indeterminate in this way. If even an ordinary person says that the cat is on the mat, it is not just a vaguely specified set of humdrum beliefs that warrant the conclusion that the mat is under the cat. One might suggest that such a conclusion is warranted by an especially strong belief, one that might be expressed by saying that, if the cat is on the mat, the mat *must* be under the cat. But this suggestion is not very helpful. As I see it, we are not concerned here with a mere matter of fact; we are concerned with a "relation of ideas." When I say "The cat is on the mat," I make an assertion that is determinate in some respects but not in others. It is determinate insofar as it includes the idea of the mat being under the cat.

Interpretation and Temporal Connectives

Whether I am right or wrong in supposing that some implications of an utterance are warranted by its meaning rather than by some class of beliefs, I think that my use of temporal connectives such as "after" in the last chapter is in no way rendered doubtful by a truth-conditional conception of meaning. Since one of my principal aims in discussing Davidson's theory was to defend my use of such connectives against likely objections, I want to round out this section by commenting on them.

As I explained early in the chapter, philosophers who, like Davidson, want to define a truth predicate for a language containing temporal connectives generally follow Gottlob Frege's example and interpret statements like "Nero fiddled while Rome burned" by referring to moments of time—as in "$(\exists t)$(Nero fiddled at t & Rome burned at t)." This strategy makes it possible to fit such statements very neatly into a Tarskian truth definition and to justify certain intuitively valid inferences involving them on a formal basis. It has the metaphysical drawback, however, of referring to unanalyzed moments of time and, possibly, to a domain of real numbers associated with such moments.[38] The question is, therefore: "If we assume (for the sake of argument) that a truth-conditional theory of interpretation is ultimately satisfactory, must we then adopt Frege's interpretation of statements containing temporal connectives?" As I see it, the answer is no.

The first thing to note here is that there is nothing in the logical structure of a Tarskian truth definition that requires us to treat temporal connectives as Frege did. According to Tarski, the satisfaction conditions for complex formulas containing *logical* symbols must be a function (logically speaking) of the satisfaction conditions for simpler formulas. Thus, the following would be a clause in a recursive definition for a truth predicate applicable to a large fragment of English:

> The sequence s satisfies "p & q" if and only if s satisfies "p" and s satisfies "q".

But although a formula like "p after q" is complex, it does not contain any logical symbols, and Tarski's procedure does not require us to specify its truth conditions as a logical function of simpler formulas.

A philosopher working out a theory of interpretation along the lines described by Davidson would, of course, insist that an acceptable interpretation for an utterance such as "John wept after Mary left" must be systematically related to acceptable interpretations for the simpler utterances "John wept" and "Mary left." The point is correct, but the systematic relation need not be specified in logical terms; it can be represented as a nonformal constraint on interpretation. Recall the truism that the moon is round. As I explained, if we interpret Karl's "Dass ist der Mond" as true just when the object he demonstrates is the moon, then if we credit him as sharing our humdrum beliefs about the moon, we cannot interpret an utterance in which he also demonstrates the moon as true just in case the moon is square. The same idea, essentially, can be put to work in interpreting the utterance about Mary's leaving and John's weeping. The speaker's assumed humdrum beliefs about things done in a certain *temporal order* will constrain the interpretations we place on utterances containing what (according to our segmentation of his or her dialect) are temporal expressions— that is, tensed verbs, temporal connectives, and the like.

It might be objected that we can clearly discern an abstract pattern in utterances containing "after" and that this pattern, or part of it, is represented in schematic formulas such as "If P after Q, then P and Q"—all of whose instances are necessarily true. Since "If John wept after Mary left, then John wept and Mary left" is necessarily true, we ought to be able to prove it by a sequence of logically valid inferences. We could do this if we interpreted "after" as Frege did, but we cannot do it if we adopt the interpretive strategy I described in the preceding paragraph. Therefore, Frege's strategy is clearly the preferred one.

It is true that there are advantages to Frege's strategy, but they are certainly not decisive, particularly in a metaphysical discussion in which the analysis of time is a primary concern. On the other hand, we can also discern abstract patterns in other classes of utterance that can be represented by schematic formulas whose instances are "necessarily true," yet we do not suppose that such instances can be proved to be true by purely logical means. Consider the schematic formula "If a is on b, then b is under a." Although an instance of this formula—"If the cat is on the mat, then the mat is under the cat"—is no less "necessary" than an instance of the schematic formula containing "after," we should not expect to demonstate its truth by purely logical means.

Instances of the schematic forms in point here have traditionally been considered analytically true, and empiricists have always insisted that analytical truths are invariably necessary truths. I myself do not object to calling such truths "analytic"— particularly if, like Peirce but unlike Frege, we do not suppose that the notion of analytic truth presupposes (and is properly clarified by reference to) some notion of synonymy.[39] In fact, if we hold that the primitive "necessary truth" of schematic statements such as "If a is on b, then b is under a" is explained by their role in showing (rather than saying) what the meaning, at least in part, of certain words consists in, then we can regard synonymy as a derivative notion in the theory of meaning.[40] This would not, I take it, be acceptable to a philosopher like Davidson, who does not draw a distinction between analytic and synthetic truth. He would have to say, if he is prepared to talk of a speaker's meaning, that it is not clearly distinguishable from the truisms or humdrum beliefs that a speaker associates with an utterance. As a consequence of this, he could offer no compelling reason to suppose that the schematic statement "If P after Q, then P & Q" is anything other than a truism that imposes an important constraint on our interpretation of utterances containing temporal expressions.

At the beginning of this chapter I called attention to a number of "implications" whose validity philosophers like Davidson have attempted to account for. Some of the statements involved in these cases are distinguished by the presence of adverbs, as in the "implication" between "Jones buttered the toast in the kitchen" and "Jones buttered the toast." If we are really convinced, before having a theory that accounts for them, that these implications are "valid" in the minimal sense that they are instances of argument forms all of whose instances have true conclusions if they have true premises, then we cannot be sure that they can be shown to be *formally* valid. I conceded at the outset that these implications are genuine, but I claimed that they are, in my opinion, "materially" rather than formally valid. I believe that my opinion is supported by the claims I have made in these last two sections. I would account for their validity by saying that the conclusion helps to unpack the meaning of the premise, indicating part of what we commit ourselves to in affirming it.

A philosopher who can accept my claim that such "implications" are not logically (= formally) valid but who is reluctant to speak of material validity might appeal to a weaker notion of implication. The notion I have in mind can be clarified by reference to Davidson's theory of interpretation. If we assign truth conditions or interpretations to utterances on the assumption that certain humdrum beliefs are true and held by the relevant speakers, our theory of interpretation will allow us to prove that, given the truth of the assumed beliefs, certain utterances must be true if certain others are. Suppose, for example, that we interpret an utterance U as meaning that Mary laughed after John laughed. If we also interpret U' as meaning that Mary laughed, we can then prove, on the assumption that whatever is done after something is done is done, that U' is true if U is true. The weaker notion of implication lurking in the background here is that of relative implication. Though weaker than ordinary implication, the notion is just as precise: B implies C relative to A just when the conjunction of A and B logically implies C. If we think of A in this schema as the conjunction of humdrum beliefs assumed by a theory of interpretation, we can think of the implication between U and U' as relative implication.

Truth and Metaphysics

I want to end this chapter with some general remarks on what might be called the metaphysics of truth. As I mentioned when I criticized Hilary Putnam's objections to metaphysical realism, there is an inescapable element of truth in the traditional correspondence theory. However arbitrary our ideas or claims may be, if they allow us to single out objects in reality, reality must contain those objects—just as it contains the patterns we can discern in a tree or cloud. Philosophers such as Russell tried to accommodate this point by saying that true statements "correspond" to elements in reality, but since statements contain both subjects and predicates, those elements in reality were generally regarded as "facts" rather than things. Yet facts, ordinarily understood, are *about* natural objects; they are not themselves such things. If a correspondence theory is to do its intended job, it must be freed from this dependence on facts.

In chapter 3 I mentioned that Wilfred Sellars has found a solution to this problem. According to him, singular statements containing proper names can be regarded as representations or conceptual pictures of objects rather than facts; and when they are true, they picture the relevant objects as they really are. Suppose that "Tom is tall" is such a statement. The object pictured by this statement is the person Tom, and he is pictured *as tall*—just as he would be pictured in an iconic language by a sentence consisting of the name "Tom" printed in tall letters. In my discussion of universals, I argued that predicates, at the fundamental level, are used to characterize objects—to say what they are like—rather than to introduce new objects. Sellars has observed that this characterizing job could be done in a metaphysically less misleading way by referring expressions formed in a certain way. Our actual language is less perspicuous than this because, although the "tall" in "Tom is tall" is really used to characterize Tom— to represent *him* as tall—it looks as if it introduces a new object in relation to Tom, so that the sentence as a whole represents something complex, a "fact." This illusion would not arise if the sentence consisted of a tall name.

Although Sellars's conception of picturing is ideally suited to clarify the sense in which true singular (or basic) statements "correspond" to the world, it does not seem applicable to true statements of other kinds. If, as I have argued in preceding chapters, the world is a system of fundamental objects, statements about derivative objects such as corporations or aggregates should not be viewed as conceptual pictures of existing objects. How, then, should we understand their truth? And what should we say about truth-functional compounds, quantified statements, and statements containing temporal connectives?

If the reductionist ontology that I have defended in earlier chapters is accepted, the strategy for dealing with statements about nonfundamental objects is straightforward. Since statements ostensibly referring to such things are contextually definable by statements about fundamental objects, they are true just when the latter statements are true. These latter statements are not apt to be singular statements, however. Suppose they are truth-functional compounds of singular statements. In this case we can adapt a Tarskian strategy. If P and Q are singular statements, we can say that the conjunction of P and Q is true just when both conjuncts correctly picture the world, and that the disjunction of P and Q is true just when either P or Q correctly pictures the world. As for the negation of a basic statement P, we can say that it is true just in case P does *not* correctly picture the world.

The truth of quantified statements can be understood in two ways. Suppose we are concerned with a simple formula bound by a universal quantifier. One approach is to say that such a statement is true just when all substitution instances of the relevant propositional function picture the world, the totality of these instances being specified by a standard procedure for enlarging our stock of proper names. The other approach is basically similar, although it does not require us to interpret our quantifiers substitutionally. Instead of considering the replacement of the variables in a propositional function by names of real objects, we can consider various ways in which objects can be assigned to those variables. Since, as Michael Dummett has observed, a free variable under a given assignment of this kind "behaves exactly if it were a singular term [or proper name] having the assigned object as its referent,"[41] we can say that a quantified formula is true just when the relevant propositional function correctly pictures the world under all assignments of objects to its free variables.

Although I cannot discuss the truth (or correspondence) conditions of every kind of statement, I do want to say something about the truth of temporal compounds such as "Nero fiddled while Rome burned." The key idea is this: If P and Q are basic statements, then "P while Q" is true just in case P correctly pictures the world *when* Q correctly pictures it. Saying this may sound exceeding trivial, but it actually calls attention to a vitally important fact about our conceptual picture of the world. Metaphysically speaking, this picture is not a static construction of timeless propositions but a constantly changing system of verbal tokens that, by virtue of their indexical character, represent objects in relation to ourselves. Each change in our perspective ideally requires a new display— with, say, "Nero fiddled" replacing "Nero is fiddling" and "Tom is there" replacing "Tom is here"—and the series of these displays should be understood as arranged in a temporal order corresponding to the changing character of the world. If instants are as fictitious as abstract propositions, it is highly misleading to speak of our assertions as true at this or that instant of time. To speak in a way that is metaphysically perspicuous, we should say, rather, that the basic assertions in a given display picture the world when, after, or before this or that thing does or did do this or that.

Chapter 8
APPEARANCE AND REALITY

A STANDARD CONTENTION in metaphysics is that the world is really different from what it appears to be. I have already discussed some highly general arguments for this contention—specifically, arguments purporting to show that, owing to the nature of time and change, the world cannot really contain the persisting things (the continuants) that it seems to contain. In this chapter I shall be concerned with arguments of a less general kind. The ones I shall now discuss are based on facts about perception, and they purport to show that the world we are aware of in perception is not an independent reality but an appearance, or system of appearances, that depends on the way our minds respond to sensory stimulation.

The Immediate Objects of Perception

According to David Hume, "the slightest philosophy" is sufficient to teach us that what we actually perceive is never the external world itself but merely certain "images" or subjective effects that are, presumably, evoked in our consciousness by the impact of the world on our sense organs. Hume supported this claim by the following observations:

> The table which we see seems to diminish as we remove further from it, but the real table which exists independent of us suffers no alteration: it was therefore nothing but its image which was present to the mind. These are obvious dictates of reason; and no man who reflects ever doubted that the existences which we consider when we say *this house* or *that tree* are nothing but perceptions in the mind and fleeting copies or representations of other existences, which remain uniform and independent.[1]

If the terms "this house" and "that tree" apply to things that are literally before our minds on various occasions, then since what is literally before our minds in perception are images or representations, the referents of "this house" and "that tree" must really be images or representations, however strange it may sound to say such a thing.

Hume's argument has been criticized on the ground that the table we see does not actually diminish as we move away from it: the table we move away from, which cannot then be an image, merely seems to diminish, and this apparently diminishing real table is what we actually see.[2] Although Hume's argument is unsatisfactory, his basic point remains plausible if, instead of thinking of a visible object's size, we think of its color. Imagine that you are looking at a painting with a large splotch of red at its center. If you look closely at the splotch, you will be aware of a red expanse and, if the light is good, you will be aware of it *as* red. Your companion, we may suppose, is also looking at the red splotch but, unlike you, she has defective vision: she says that the splotch she sees is indistinguishable in color from the canvas to her left, which is painted a uniform shade of brown. Those who would dispose of Hume's claim by insisting that the table you see does not really change in size, though it may seem to become smaller, would no doubt claim that you and your friend actually see the very same splotch of red, though it may look different to the two of you. But this claim seems to ignore an important question of great metaphysical interest.

The question of metaphysical interest is this: "When your friend looks at the red splotch, doesn't she actually see something that is, for her, indistinguishable in color from what she sees when she looks at the brown painting?" The answer seems an obvious yes. Your friend's response might make you wonder whether, if you could see the red splotch and the brown painting with her eyes, you would see them to be brown or red or some other color. But suppose she tells you that her vision has only recently become defective, and that reds now look brown to her: redness has simply disappeared from her life. If she is honest about this, it seems reasonable to say that when she looks at the red splotch, she sees something that is, in some sense, brown—and this something, since it is not red, cannot be the splotch on the canvas. It would appear to be what Hume called an image.

I have said that the expanse your friend sees is "in some sense brown." The qualification is important, because as we ordinarily use the term "brown" in application to things such as paintings, a thing can be brown without looking brown. Even to a normal observer, a brown thing can look black, reddish, or even purple—depending on the light under which it is viewed. When I say that your friend is aware of something brown when she looks at the red splotch, I am not claiming that the thing is brown in the ordinary sense just described. I am claiming that it is brown in some sense—and this seems reasonable because, if she is asked to describe the expanse she sees, she will naturally say that it is, to her, indistinguishable in color from the brown painting she sees to her left.

If you are not convinced that your friend sees something that is, in some sense, brown, consider what you see when you look at the splotch. You see the splotch *as red*; you are visually aware of its redness. It is fair to say that, in seeing the splotch, you are having a distinctive sensory experience, the experience of seeing red. It is also fair to say that you could have this kind of experience when no physically red splotch is before you; such an experience could be produced by psychedelic drugs or by electronic stimulation of your brain. If this kind of experience were artificially produced in you, you would be aware of something that you would naturally describe as red, but the something would not be an object external to you in space. What you would be aware of in this case is comparable to what your friend was aware of when she viewed the red splotch, which "looked brown" to her. Nothing in your external environment would actually be red just as nothing in the red splotch was actually brown. Yet you would be aware of something in some sense red just as she was aware of something in some sense brown.

In the seventeenth century John Locke introduced a distinction between the primary and the secondary qualities of physical bodies.[3] Among secondary qualities Locke included colors, odors, tastes, and sounds; among primary qualities he included shape, size, motion, and solidity. Like most philosophers of his time, Locke thought that physical objects had secondary qualities only in a manner of speaking; they could be truly described as colored or fragrant, but as so described their color or fragrance would consist in a "power" to cause appropriate "ideas" in suitably placed observers, these ideas being colored or fragrant in the naive sense. Locke's view sounds ludicrous if we think of his "ideas" as we might think of ideas today. But Locke used "idea" as a catchall term representing anything before a conscious mind. If we have an afterimage, or see an object as colored, Locke would say that we have a colored idea. His point might be better put by saying that the colored expanses we are aware of when we look at paintings are not really the surfaces of those paintings; paintings actually consist of enormous numbers of colorless particles, aggregates of which assume the approximate shapes that we believe external things possess.

Locke's chief reason for regarding secondary qualities as only in a manner of speaking qualities of external objects was that this view was required by the "corpuscularian philosophy" of his time.[4] According to this philosophy, we see external objects only as a result of changes that such objects, taken as systems of minute corpuscles, indirectly produce in our consciousness. The idea was that corpuscles of light are reflected from the surfaces of external things and, rearranged by the impact, interact with the corpuscles of our sense organs, ultimately producing the ideas or experiences of seeing colors, smelling smells, hearing sounds, and so on. As Nicholas Malebranche, a contemporary of Locke, remarked, when "we see the sun, the stars, and an infinity of objects outside of us . . . it is not likely that the soul leaves the body and, as it were, goes for a walk in the heavens there to contemplate these objects."[5] What actually happens in perception is that we receive stimulation from without.

The basic structure of Locke's view of perception still seems correct. To see a distant object we must receive information from it; our sense organs are receptors of signals, not transmitters. The point is obvious, but it is obscured by familiar ways of thinking about perception. When Superman is depicted in comic books as using his X-ray vision to see criminals lurking behind stone walls, the X rays are transmitted by his eyes and penetrate the wall, but they do not return with any information. Superman should, therefore, be blind: he must receive information if he is to see anything external to him. A theoretically more satisfactory depiction of Superman's fancied powers would show him to possess analogues of radar screens by which to intercept the radiation he bounces off external objects. It is only be possessing such receptors that we could reasonably suppose him to be seeing anything at all.

Given the structure of an acceptable view of visual perception, we seem compelled to acknowledge that the colors we see result from our reception of signals originating outside us and that the character of these colors is as much dependent on the nature of our physiology as on the structure of the surfaces from which the signals originate. But if we must acknowledge this fact, we can hardly dispute Locke's claim that the colors we see do not literally belong to external objects. This outcome supports the view we took of the two observers of the paintings. If you and your friend are aware of different colored expanses when you look at the painting with the so-called red splotch as its center, the expanses you see do not seem to belong, in a literal way, to the surface of the same painting. We can, of course, insist that the painting really has a red splotch at its center, but insisting on this point, if one is reasonable, amounts to insisting that the center of the painting really is red in something like Locke's "power" sense of the term.

Berkeley's Criticism of Locke

Locke's claim that secondary qualities are not literally possessed by external objects created what might be called the Pandora's Box of modern philosophy. George Berkeley soon opened the box by arguing that if secondary qualities exist only "in the mind" of the observer, the same must be true of primary qualities.[6] Perhaps Berkeley's most important argument for this claim is based on the idea that primary qualities, at least as Locke understood them, cannot possibly be "separated" from secondary qualities. To see the point of Berkeley's idea we need only observe that no thing could possibly possess only geometrical and kinematic properties. A thing's shape is just the terminus, as we might call it, of the thing's content qualities; a colored thing, for example, has a spherical shape just because its color and, perhaps, its tactile hardness *ends* in a spherical way. Take away the thing's nongeometrical qualities and you take away its geometrical qualities as well.

Although Berkeley's basic idea here is, I believe, sound, the argument he builds upon it is not satisfactory. The geometrical and kinematic properties we ordinarily ascribe to external objects may not be separable from some kind of secondary or (as I have called them) content qualities, but they do appear to be separable from the content qualities that Locke recognized. Thus, even if Berkeley's basic idea is wholly correct, external objects may possess familiar geometrical and kinematic qualities without possessing Locke's secondary qualities of color, sound, smell, taste, or feeling. Of course, if, as Berkeley also contends, the only content qualities of which we have any real conception are Locke's secondary qualities, we shall not be able to say, or even imagine, what the content qualities of external objects are supposed to be. But this does not undermine Locke's claim that external objects do have primary qualities and do not have the secondary qualities we commonly ascribe to them.

Another one of Berkeley's arguments seems to fare somewhat better than the last one. The argument can be put this way. If the colors we directly perceive are mind-dependent and not qualities of an external object, then the same must be true of the shapes and other primary qualities *that we directly perceive*. When we perceive a patch of color, we perceive it as having a certain shape. But if the color is mind-dependent, not in or on an external obejct, then *the shaped thing* that we directly perceive is not, since it is colored, an external object, and the shape that we thus perceive cannot itself belong to an external object. Saying this is compatible with allowing that an external thing, or its facing surface, may possess the *kind* of shape (triangularity, say) that is possessed by the mind-dependent expanse that we do directly perceive. On the other hand, this latter idea is not true as a general matter, for the shapes that different people immediately perceive when, as they say, they are looking at the same external object are not generally the same. If different perceivers are directly aware of different shapes in such a case, perhaps only one of the shapes thus perceived may correspond to the shape of the external object. However this may be, if the shapes we directly perceive, being properties, say, of color expanses, are mind-dependent and not themselves qualities of external objects, then the question can arise, "How can we possibly know that external objects have any primary qualities at all?" Berekeley thought that any attempt to answer this question would lead directly to skepticism, a result that his philosophy was specifically designed to avoid.

When Berkeley criticized Locke's philosophy, he accepted one of Locke's key assumptions—namely, that perceived secondary qualities exist "in the mind" of some observer or conscious being. On the basis of this assumption he argued that, since in his view primary qualities are inseparable from secondary qualities and since the arguments showing that secondary qualities are mind-dependent apply equally to primary qualities, all the qualities we attribute to external qualities are mind-dependent. Since he also held that external objects, as we ordinarily conceive of them, consist entirely of primary and secondary qualities, he concluded that external objects themselves must be mind-dependent, or "exist only in the mind."

Unfortunately, the details of Berkeley's view are not as clear as they could be. Since he believed in the Christian God and did not want to allow that external objects do not exist when we, or some other finite minds, do not perceive them (that is, have the appropriate experiences), he concluded that God is always perceiving them. Berkeley's view on this matter was nicely expressed in a limerick by Ronald Knox:[7]

> There was a young man who said, "God
> Must think it exceedingly odd
> If he finds that this tree
> Continues to be
> When there is no one about in the Quad."

REPLY

Dear Sir:
    Your astonishment's odd:
I am always about in the Quad.
    And that's why the tree
    Will continue to be,
Since observed by

Yours faithfully,

GOD.

Given the claims expressed in this limerick, we might say that Berkeley conceived of an external object such as a tree as a system of "ideas," elements of which occasionally exist in our minds and all of which (or all exemplars of which) exist in God's mind, at least when the object can truly be said to exist. Berkeley's view remains obscure because if, as we should expect, the very same idea (as opposed to the same kind of idea) cannot exist in more than one mind, it is difficult to see how two different minds could ever perceive the same external object. Everything considered, Berkeley was far more effective as a critic than as the creator of a well-worked-out philosophy.

Existence "In the Mind"

Although Berkeley's constructive views on perceptible objects are puzzling and unclear, related views were developed and vigorously defended in the early years of our century. These related views are known as versions of phenomenalism. I shall come to terms with phenomenalism in the next section; in this section I want to lay some necessary groundwork by commenting critically on a key idea Berkeley shared with Locke—the idea that sensible qualities such as color exist only "in the mind" of some observer.

To say that a sensible quality exists "in" some mind is not just to say that it is mind- or observer-dependent. The color we see when we look at a painting may be as dependent on our "minds" (our sense organs and nervous system) as a sensory quality can possibly be, but this does not imply that the color exists *in* our minds. In a famous article, "The Refutation of Idealism," G. E. Moore argued that when we have a visual sensation, we are aware of something colored, but while our awareness is mental, the thing we are aware of need not be mental too.[8] Even if we are convinced that the colors we see do not actually exist on or in external objects, qualifying their surfaces, we are not compelled to conclude that they exist in our minds. For all that we know at this stage of our investigations, they might be associated with changes in our brains. Hobbes seems to have held a view of this kind; he called such entities "phantasms" and said, somewhat surprisingly, that they are "internal motions" of our bodies.[9]

Locke's famous distinction between primary and secondary qualities was based on a distinction drawn earlier by such philosophers as Descartes. As we saw in chapter 5, Descartes thought that human beings are really minds interfused with bodies and that such minds could, and after death would, exist apart from their bodies. Although we did not discuss the point, Descartes also held that while human minds are commonly aware of colors, sounds, smells, and tastes, these qualities do not belong to anything physical: for him as for Locke, the real qualities of physical things are geometrical and kinematic. (The main difference between Descartes and Locke in this regard is that Descartes was not a corpuscularian; he held that physical reality is a material plenum in which objects are differentiated by distinctive motions rather than by spatial gaps.)[10] Since Descartes, like Locke, thought that an act or state of awareness must belong to a conscious subject, he had no doubt that, if a quality of which one is conscious does not qualify a merely physical thing, it must be a mental quality, or "mode," of one's mind.

The conception of a mind common to Descartes, Locke, and Berkeley was vigorously attacked by David Hume. As I explained in chapter 5, Descartes was convinced that he must exist as a thinker even when he could say no more about his nature than that he is a "thing" that thinks. Hume argued that Descartes' conviction on this matter was totally unfounded. If we look inwardly, Hume said, we find that we have no experience of a unitary thing that thinks, and no genuine idea of such a thing either. As he put it in a famous passage:

> When I enter most intimately into what I call *myself*, I always stumble on some particular perception or other, of heat or cold, light or shade, love or hatred, pain or pleasure. I never can catch *myself* at any time without a perception and can never observe anything but the perception. . . . I may venture to affirm of the rest of mankind that they are nothing but a bundle or collection of different perceptions, which succeed each other with an inconceivably rapidity and are in perpetual flux and movement. . . . The mind is a kind of theater where several perceptions successively make their appearance, pass, repass, glide away, and mingle in an infinite variety of postures and situations. There is properly no *simplicity* in it at one time nor *identity* in [all its successive] differences—whatever natural propension we may have to imagine that simplicity and identity. The comparison of the theater must not mislead us. They are the successive perceptions only, which constitute the mind; nor have we the most distant notion of the place where these scenes are represented or of the materials of which it is composed.[11]

The view Hume expresses here has come to be known as the Bundle Theory of the Self. Just as Bertrand Russell argued that physical things are bundles of qualities, Hume argued that even minds must be viewed as bundles. To say, on this view, that a quality exists in a mind is just to say that the quality belongs to some mind-bundle.

In my third chapter I argued that, merely on metaphysical grounds, there is no good reason to suppose that things, as we ordinarily conceive of them, must be understood as bundles of qualities. Hume's criticism of Descartes' view of the soul or self is not based on metaphysical but on empirical considerations, that is, on grounds associated with a certain conception of the sources of empirical knowledge. If we assume, as I think we can, that we are rationally entitled to believe in the existence of numerous things that we cannot perceive, then the fact, if it is a fact, that we cannot perceive our selves cannot prove that we are nothing but bundles of experiences. On the other hand, if we are reasonably convinced that we do exist as unitary subjects of experience, we must have some determinate and defensible conception of such subjects. It is futile to insist that we are things that think if we can't say what sort of things we are or how we know that we are things rather than bundles of things.

When I first presented Locke's view of sensible qualities, I assumed that I am a human being and that human beings are sentient animals who interact with their environment. I also assumed that human animals become aware of their environment by perceiving it. Since, as I argued, we can perceive an external thing only by receiving some signal from it (by being stimulated by it), I could reasonably assume that any quality of which we are immediately aware must be physically dependent on us. But none of this required me to conceive of a person or human being as a disembodied mind, let alone a bundle of experiences. Such a conception might, of course, be forced upon me by further considerations—perhaps by the sort of epistemological considerations that motivated Hume—but until such considerations are fully in hand, I can reasonably hold to the conception I began with.

On the assumption, admittedly provisional, that we are conscious subjects of experience who are constantly stimulated by external objects, we can take the arguments of Locke and Berkeley as showing that the items (for lack of a better word) that we immediately perceive are neither our own bodies nor external bodies. This position does not require us to reject the possibility that, though the qualities of the items we immediately perceive are not themselves the qualities of external objects, external objects have such qualities. But this possibility is very tenuous, and it is not supported by scientific considerations. In fact, it is rendered very dubious by such considerations.

According to the molecular theory of matter, a painting on a wall does not really possess a continuous surface; it is a gappy structure, a system of microparticles. The surface may *appear* colored and continuous—we may perceive it as a homogeneous expanse of color—but this is mere appearance, not reality. As far as the appearance is concerned, this seems to be analyzable in relation to the mind-dependent expanses that we directly experience. It is, again, conceivable that the molecules of the painting's surface jiggle about in a color cloud with a precisely rectangular shape; but if the light reflected from the surface of the painting is reflected from the particles and not the cloud, we shall not have the slightest reason to suppose that such a cloud exists. Parity of reasoning suggests a negative verdict in any case, for it does not seem conceivable (to me, at any rate) that tastes, smells, sounds, and qualities of felt smoothness or roughness, as we immediately perceive them, are also duplicated in the external world.

If we take the principal contentions of contemporary physical science at face value, we shall have to say that the physical world, including our own bodies, consists of complicated systems of microentities interacting in a relativistic space-time-causal system. Philosophers who call themselves "scientific realists" accept this kind of view. I consider myself a scientific realist, though I must admit that such a view raises significant problems about the role of consciousness in the scheme of things and that the epistemological grounds on which it is based require careful justification. I shall comment on these matters later in the chapter. For the moment, I want to say something about three important theories that have dominated philosophical thinking about the nature of reality in the past two hundred years. In one way or another these theories—I have in mind skepticism, phenomenalism, and a form of Kantianism—are all based on the key assumptions of an empiricist epistemology. I shall argue that such assumptions must be improved upon if the thesis of scientific realism is to be satisfactorily defended.

Skepticism and Phenomenalism

The skeptical view I propose to discuss is associated with the name of David Hume. As I have noted, Hume thought that what we are immediately aware of in perception is always an image or impression, not an external thing. He also thought that what we are aware of, when we look inwardly, is not a unitary mind or ego but a mere bundle of experiences. Although he acknowledged, in his famous *Enquiry Concerning Human Understanding*, that we cannot help believing in an external world and in ourselves as persisting unitary beings, he insisted that these natural beliefs cannot be rationally defended.[12]

The basis for Hume's skepticism lay in his conception of our legitimate sources of empirical knowledge. These sources consist, he thought, of perception, memory, and experimental inference, the latter being founded on the relation of cause and effect. Since in perception we are aware only of images ostensibly representing external things, we cannot know by purely perceptual means that our images correspond to any external reality. Memory cannot help us here, because we can remember only what we have perceived or otherwise come to know. As for experimental inference, we can reasonably conclude that a certain event has a particular cause only when we have the experience of a constant conjunction between events of these kinds. But since we can never, in Hume's opinion, experience the alleged external causes of our perceptions, we cannot conclude that such causes even exist. Thus, our natural, instinctive belief in a world external to our consciousness cannot be rationally defended; it is not "founded," Hume says, "on reason or any process of the understanding."[13] The same holds true for our beliefs in the existence of our selves as persistent, unitary things. We have no experience of such things, and we have no basis for inferring their existence.

Empiricists who, like Berkeley, were fully confident that we do perceive material things and know them to be colored, fragrant, and the like, were strongly inclined to defend phenomenalism. Since unitary selves or minds were shown by Hume to be just as dubious as unobservable external things, phenomenalists argued that selves as well as external bodies must be understood as, really, constructs out of sense data—that is, constructs out of the entities that, like immediately perceived color expanses, unquestionably exist.[14] Exploiting Bertrand Russell's work on logical constructions, twentieth-century phenomenalists offered a linguistic version of the theory.[15] According to this version, statements about things such as trees and houses can be shown to be equivalent in meaning to complicated statements about sense data—just as, according to Russell, statements about numbers can be shown to be equivalent in meaning to (or to be definable in terms of) statements about classes and, ultimately, statements about properties. The aim in both cases was fundamentally the same: to show that statements ostensibly about "metaphysical entities" whose existence cannot be ascertained by acceptable principles of evidence can be replaced, for critical purposes, by statements about entities whose existence cannot be reasonably doubted.

To understand the linguistic phenomenalists's procedure, consider Macbeth's hallucinatory experience of seeing a dagger. The statement that a real dagger is before him would be equivalent (on first approximation) to the statement that certain daggerish sense data now exist and that if sense data of other kinds *were* to occur in Macbeth's experience—for example, visual sense data of Macbeth's touching the dagger—then certain other kinds of sense data would ensue in his experience—for example, tactile sense data of something sharp being touched.

The task of showing, even in useful but gappy outline, how external object statements could be translated into statements about sense data turned out to be enormously complicated, and critics argued that it could not possibly be carried out.[16] Perhaps the basic difficulty concerns the idea of a perceiver. We normally assume that people perceive things from various spatial perspectives and that the experiences (or sense data) they have when they perceive an object are dependent both on the surrounding conditions and on their peculiarities as observers. Thus, if Macbeth had numb hands, he would not have daggerish tactile sense data even if he were to succeed in grasping a real dagger. Yet if all reference to perceivers must be eliminated in giving a sense-datum translation for an ordinary physical-object statement, we could never supply such a translation. I might be able to predict the kind of sense data *I* would have if *I* turned my head 180° and squinted *my* eyes while remaining in *my* chair in *my* study. But I have no idea how to construct a pure sense-datum translation—one not limited to my sense data in conditions with which I am familiar—for any physical-object statement whatever.

It is important to realize that the difficulty here is one of principle, and not merely the result of my excusable ignorance. For any empiricist, a good share of our ignorance is inevitable and, in a sense, excusable. Even with the best will in the world and by adhering carefully to approved canons of evidence, I cannot possibly ascertain the shape of every blade of grass in my lawn. Nevertheless, by careful examination I could ascertain the shape of any particular blade of grass I might be interested in, so my ignorance about some blades of grass—those I don't get around to examining—is philosophically excusable, particularly since I have better things to do with my time than examining hundreds of thousands of blades of grass. My ignorance about how to construct the sense-datum statements supposedly corresponding to external-object statements is not of this excusable kind, because to construct them I would have to have information that, on strict empiricist principles, I have no possible way of getting.

A key difficulty is this. Since I have, for example, no access to the mind of Macbeth (supposing him to exist) I have no way of knowing what sense data he would have if he first had sense data of such and such a kind and were, as the vulgar say, in such and such a position in the world. The sense datum equivalent to an external-object statement is supposed to concern the sense data that all observers would have in this or that circumstance, but, as a matter of basic empiricist principle, I can have no knowledge of what goes on in another mind. For me, another mind is just as mysterious as a genuinely external object: I have no access to it. Given this, my difficulty in finding translations in sense-datum terms for ostensibly external-object statements is a difficulty in principle; the task is not one that, if empiricism is a sound theory of knowledge, I could possibly complete. This exhibits a fundamental objection to phenomenalism in the form we are now considering.

Although linguistic phenomenalism has been (so far as I can tell) universally abandoned in the past twenty years, there may still be philosophers who believe that a nonlinguistic version of phenomenalism is defensible. They might argue that, even though the translations required by linguistic phenomenalism cannot, in general, be carried out, it may yet be true that nothing really exists but sense data. If, they might add, sense data come in different bundles corresponding to the so-called minds of different observers, then those bundles may have, over time, a kind of unity and variety that would represent (or be the factual foundation for) the common idea that different observers exist and move about in a world of external objects.

To get an imaginative idea of the kind of nonlinguistic phenomenalism envisaged here, it is helpful to consider the metaphysical view worked out by Leibniz in the seventeenth century.[17] According to Leibniz, the world consists of infinitely many monads, each of which is a psychic entity (or mind of sorts) whose internal states mirror the universe from its own point of view. Leibniz did not believe that either space or time is ultimately real, but he did think that monads (at least the dominant ones that are human souls) have a spatial apprehension of the world and that their internal states occur sequentially, so that they experience things before, after, and while they experience other things. Since the experiences of each monad hang together, overlapping temporally and, at each instant, constituting a unified representation of reality, each monad has a coherent, unified mental history that, considered by itself, is indistinguishable from the mental history of a being that moves around in a spatial world of interacting objects. This mental history is in some respects very deceptive, for monads do not, Leibneiz says, either move or interact: they were so created by God that the point of view of each changes in harmony with the point of view of the others.

It is easy to see how a form of nonlinguistic phenomenalism could be developed from Leibniz's view: One has only to think of each monad as a mere bundle of cohering perceptions, cohering in the sense of being organized into a unitary "point of view" and overlapping in an appropriate temporal sequence. The ultimate objects of the resulting world are thus perceptions or "sense data," just what the nonlinguistic phenomenalist wants. It seems to me that, scientific considerations apart, such a view could conceivably be true, though it sounds pretty fantastic. Of course, if one is moved to embrace phenomenalism because one fears the apparent skeptical consequences of Hume's empiricist principles, one will not find the view defensible. What reason could one possibly give, on Hume's principles, for believing in all those bundles of cohering experiences and in the harmony between the bundles?

Kant's Metaphysics of Experience

A distinctive empiricist claim, which I have not yet commented on, is that any significant idea (or word) must arise from (or be definable by terms referring to) experience. This claim has been used to support phenomenalism, because if we could never experience external objects, we could not have a significant idea of them as irreducibly or genuinely external to us. Obviously, this claim could be used to oppose Leibniz or even phenomenalism if the latter implied that other minds or bundles exist. How could I have a significant idea of something I couldn't conceivably experience, another's idea or image? An interesting metaphysical view that involves a partial rejection of this empiricist claim and also involves what might be called an improved phenomenalism is that of Immanuel Kant.[18] Kant's metaphysical view is as complicated as any ever developed, but certain aspects of it are, fortunately, both clear and illuminating.

A particularly interesting aspect of Kant's metaphysics is his criticism of Hume's Bundle Theory of the Self. Although Kant agreed with Hume that, when we look inwardly, we find no unitary mind or self, he argued that a unitary, active self must nevertheless exist. Consider the experience of hearing a short, familiar tune such as the first few bars of "Three Blind Mice." When we hear the tune, we are aware of it as a unitary thing, though the notes come to us one by one. The fact that we are aware of the tune as a unitary whole shows us, Kant thought, that our minds must be active things that hold our experiences together.[19] When we experience the last note of the tune, the first one has ceased to sound; we are thus remembering it instead of hearing it, and our memory of what we have heard is fused with what we are now hearing. There is an obvious difference, Kant insisted, between a bundle of experiences and the experience of a bundle; and since the bundles we sometimes experience involve successive occurrences, we must have active selves that impose a characteristic unity on the things we experience.

As we saw in chapter 5, Descartes also inferred that he must exist as a conscious thing, but Descartes' inference and his idea of his self both differed from Kant's. In making his inference Descartes tacitly relied on the metaphysical principle that thinking is an activity or "mode" and that activities must belong to things or "substances." For reasons that we discussed, he also thought that the thing to which mental activities belong must be a mental substance, or mind. But Kant did not rely on the metaphysical principle Descartes used, and he did not believe that the self whose existence he inferred could be considered a mental substance. His argument was that the elements of the bundle Hume spoke of had a kind of unity that must result from the unifying activity of some subject, but the only thing he thought we could justifiably claim to know about this subject is that it is a thing, an x, that performs certain functions. Since this x clearly transcends our experience, Kant called it a "transcendental self."[20]

Kant called the domain of our experiences "the phenomenal world" or "the world of appearances." Since our transcendental selves cannot be experienced, they belong to a different domain, the world of "things-in-themselves." Things-in-themselves not only include transcendental selves but other things that are, he thought, largely responsible for the material features of the appearances that we experience. Although the point requires careful qualification, Kant thought that our transcendental selves are "receptive" to stimulation by other things-in-themselves, and that the world of our experience is the result of the organization and interpretation that our transcendental selves place upon the stimulation they receive. In certain respects Kant's view here is the same as Descartes'. Descartes thought that the experiences we have in viewing the world are the result of changes brought about in our souls by the influence of external objects; he also thought that what Locke called the secondary qualities of our experiences do not correspond to occurrent qualities in external objects. Kant differed from Descartes in thinking, first, that our transcendental selves, which are receptive to stimulation from other things-in-themselves, cannot be experienced or known as they are in themselves and, second, that the things-in-themselves that thus stimulate our transcendental selves must remain utterly unknown to us. The only things we can have genuine knowledge of are the appearances of things-in-themselves that we experience.

Kant's view that, theoretically speaking, things-in-themselves are utterly unknowable was based on considerations of two principal kinds. The first considerations are fundamentally empiricist. Since we cannot possibly experience things-in-themselves as they are in themselves, we can have no scientific basis for attributing any particular qualities or features to them; in fact, we cannot have any determinate ideas of them because such ideas can arise only from experience.[21] In view of Kant's utter skepticism about the nature of things-in-themselves, one naturally wonders why he should be so confident that, apart from his own transcendental self, such things even exist. The answer to this is supplied by the other considerations supporting his view that things-in-themselves must be utterly unknown to us. These considerations are implicit in a group of arguments that he called "the Antinomy of Pure Reason."[22] According to these arguments, our reasoning about the world will lead us into contradictions if we do not carefully distinguish the world of appearance from the world of things-in-themselves. To avoid the contradictions we must also acknowledge that our genuine, scientific knowledge extends only to appearances. For reasons based on his theory of morality, Kant thought that we can have certain justifiable beliefs about things-in-themselves, but such beliefs cannot amount to genuine knowledge.

If what I have been calling "determinate" ideas invariably arise from experience, it would appear that, if we can even think of things-in-themselves, we must have nondeterminate ideas. Kant agreed with this.[23] The nondeterminate ideas he recognized appear to be what he called "unschematized categories." Our transcendental selves can organize experience in two basic ways: by fitting it into a space-time framework, and by subsuming it under concepts. To do the latter, our transcendental selves need certain concepts that are not derived from experience; these concepts are "purely formal," having no empirical content. The abstract notion of a logical subject (a subject of attributes) is such a concept, as is the abstract idea of the ground-consequent relation. Our selves have an innate, or unacquired, ability to think according to the patterns, among others, of "x is F" and "if . . . then . . . ." To think according to these patterns is to exercise the abstract concept of a thing in general (a logical subject) and of a ground and consequent. Kant called such abstract, pure ideas "unschematized categories."

Our unschematized categories can be applied to experience by a process of schematization, which gives them determinate content.[24] The idea of a substance is a schematized version of the concept of a logical subject, for a substance is just a continuing logical subject, that is, a persisting thing having empirical features. The concept of causation is also a schematized concept, for it amounts to the notion of a temporal ground and consequent, the temporal ground being the cause and the temporal consequent being the effect. Although Kant sometimes expressed great uneasiness in allowing that we can even think anything definite about the world of things-in-themselves,[25] he presumably allowed that we can conceive of a thing-in-itself as an unknown logical subject that no doubt stands in unknown ground-consequent relations to other things-in-themselves. He would have had to add that some of these unknown logical subjects, namely transcendental selves, organize sensory input in various ways, but the need for saying even this much about things-in-themselves seems to have made him very uncomfortable.

I originally introduced Kant as a philosopher holding an unusual form of phenomenalism. Although he said that the objects of experience are appearances in a transcendental sense—that is, they are, as objects, appearances of things-in-themselves—he also made it clear that certain experiences are (or involve) appearances of things in a nontranscendental sense. Suppose you have the experience of seeing something red. If you begin to think about what you see, you might decide that you are seeing part of the surface of a red balloon. As an object of experience, a red balloon is, Kant seems to say, a system of actual and possible perceptible entities, and the red expanse that you experience is an appearance of the balloon in the sense that it belongs to the system. The system, however, is itself an appearance in a different sense: it is a transcendental appearance of a thing-in-itself. Thus, Kant offers a phenomenalist account of empirical objects (objects of experience), but he evidently regards each such object (or system) as a transcendental appearance of something nonphenomenal.

Readers of Kant sometimes fail to recognize his phenomenalism because in the second edition of his famous *Critique of Pure Reason* he included a section called "The Refutation of Idealism," which can be read, incorrectly, as a refutation of phenomenalism.[26] But Kant's chief point in this section was that, if we speak of the world in an empirically significant way, we shall have to allow that it includes other people and external objects as well as ourselves. Thus, insofar as I can refer to myself in determinate, empirically significant terms, I am referring to myself as an object of my own experience—as something experienced by my transcendental self. Yet the objects of my experience also include other people as well as such things as trees and stone walls. What I thus experience is, in the transcendental sense, "ideal"—and this is true of me, my empirical self, as well.

As objects of knowledge and experience, I and others have a comparable status: they are every bit as real, empirically speaking, as I am, and trees and stone walls are as irreducibly real as we both are. Of course, taken as systems of experienceable data, these empirically real things are all transcendental appearances—appearances to my transcendental self, at least. Yet I have no experience, and thus no empirical knowledge, of my transcendental self, and it is not my transcendental self to whom I refer when I use the pronoun "I" or the name "Bruce Aune." As far as empirically significant concepts are concerned, the objects to which they apply are all "ideal" or "phenomenal" in a transcendental sense; they belong, not to my consciousness as a creature of flesh and blood, but to the consciousness of a transcendentally real thing in itself.

Kant's phenomenalism concerning empirical objects differs from the usual nonlinguistic variety in further respects worth mentioning. If I, as an object of experience, am just a system of actual and possible appearances belonging to *my* transcendental self, then Kant's phenomenalism does not presuppose a knowledge of how other transcendental selves experience the world; it must amount to a phenomenalism arising within the consciousness of each transcendental self—if, indeed, there really is more than one such self. No one transcendental self can know what other such selves are experiencing, but then no one such self can pretend to *know* what is going on with any transcendental self. Thus, certain difficulties that arise for standard nonlinguistic phenomenalism do not arise for Kant. On the other hand, the world of *my* experience, insofar as I am a transcendental subject of experience, would seem to be the world of *one* transcendental consciousness—and so, in a sense, a solipsist's world. Insofar as one believes in other minds—other transcendental subjects of experience—one's belief can garner little support from Kant's philosophy.

On the grounds of Kant's own metaphysical assumptions, his transcendental idealism is a pretty dubious doctrine. We may believe that we are something over and above anything presented in our experience, but if we can *know* of ourselves, as subjects of experience, only in the tenuous terms that Kant allows (as bare x's working behind the scenes) this knowledge amounts to very little—as does the knowledge of other things-in-themselves. When Kant discussed the distinction between phenomena and noumena (the latter being things we can think of but not actually know about), he himself emphasized that this "knowledge" is vanishingly small.[27] In view of this, philosophers soon rejected Kant's whole story about things-in-themselves. Some followed Hegel in arguing that reality is wholly spiritual and that our own experience is just a fragment of the whole—a fragment that can, however, evolve or grow, becoming more and more adequate and comprehensive until we "become one with the Absolute," the latter being (roughly) reality itself.[28] Others, such as J. S. Mill,[29] reverted to a more old-fashioned phenomenalism, and still others, like Marx, abandoned the philosophical perplexities that led to Kant's philosophy, espousing a fairly naive realism according to which we are assured of the existence of the external world by virtue of interacting with it.[30] If we are to discover and defend a more satisfactory metaphysical view of experience than Kant's, we shall have to go back to the considerations that prompted Kant's view and try to resolve them in a less problematic way.

Objections to Classical Empiricism

The basic considerations that led us to discuss Kant's metaphysics of experience can be described as follows. To begin with, we are aware in experience of colored expanses, smooth or rough textures, smells, sounds, and so forth. The things we thus experience cannot, it appears, be external objects themselves; they must in some sense be aspects of ourselves. The grounds for this last idea are twofold: If external objects did exist, we could gain information about them only by attending to signals we receive from them; and current theories of matter make it reasonable to suppose that the colors and so forth that we are aware of in experience must be the results of signals received, not external objects themselves. According to these theories, the attributes of external objects are very different from the qualities we encounter in direct experience— in fact, those attributies are highly theoretical, appropriate to swarms of imperceptible particles.

This outcome is highly problematic. According to the empiricist theory of knowledge, there is no rationally acceptable way of defending scientific claims about imperceptible entities. What is more, the empiricist theory of meaning requires us to acknowledge that such claims do not, strictly speaking, make sense, for their ostensible subject matter transcends the limits of any possible experience. Yet if meaningful discourse and genuine knowledge must be restricted to the domain of what we can directly experience, we must either reject both our ordinary and our scientific views of the world as entirely ill-founded or even, strictly speaking, meaningless, or we must try to develop some form of phenomenalism. Yet standard forms of the latter are highly dubious doctrines that can be seen, on examination, to deliver far more than they seem to promise. The same is true, we must now say, of Kant's transcendental idealism.

Obviously, if the outcome we have reached is to be avoided, some of the considerations leading to it must be rejected. Although some philosophers believe that the causal theory of perception—the assumption that we can have perceptual knowledge of external objects only by attending to signals we receive from them—is at fault, I think that this assumption is the soundest of the lot. If X is at a distance from Y, the only way X could conceivably be aware of Y is by attending to some signal coming from Y, whether the signal be conveyed physically or even (as a remote possibility) telepathically. For my part, the dubious assumption that makes all the trouble is the one expressing the empiricist theory of knowledge.

As I have described it, the empiricist theory of knowledge might better be called the "classical" empiricist theory, for not every contemporary philosopher who wants to be considered an empiricist would accept that theory. In the context of the predicament, the classical theory is, in fact, incoherent. We are told that anything we can know about the world must ultimately be based on what *we* can experience; yet the theory ends up taking us, as subjects of experience, completely out of the picture, or at least casting serious doubt on our presence there. This incoherence is certainly a symptom that the classical theory is off the rails from the very beginning.

Before working our way into serious perplexity about ourselves and the world, we had a fairly definite, coherent picture of ourselves as rational animals living in a world of trees and flowers or bricks and mortar. This picture represents what Edmund Husserl called "the natural standpoint" and what Wilfrid Sellars has called "the Manifest Image of man and the world."[31] Instead of quickly abandoning this natural view, as Hume's principle require, we might think of changing it be reinterpreting ourselves and the objects around us in scientific terms—as, at least for the most part, systems of microentities. Conceiving of ourselves in this way is, to some extent, comparable to Kant's strategy in conceiving of his nonphenomenal self as a transcendental object, but it has the advantage of allowing definite knowledge and, what is more, a determinate conception of ourselves. We are not just unknowable x's that process experience in various ways; we are systems of knowable objects in interaction both with themselves and, more or less directly, with the other systems making up our world. It is, of course, the task of theoretical science, and not armchair speculation, to provide a detailed account of what we and other natural things are really like.

Conceiving of ourselves as systems of scientific objects may or may not be fully satisfactory, all things considered, but if we attempt it we shall have to reject two key assumptions of classical empiricism. The first and most fundamental assumption that we shall have to reject is the one limiting significant meaning to expressions referring to objects of direct experience or to constructs that can be resolved into such objects. The second assumption concerns allowable forms of inductive, or "experimental," inference. According to this second assumption, permissible inductive inference is ultimately based on some kind of generalization from experience, and its conclusion can refer only to possible objects of experience—the sort of objects from which the generalization is made. It is obvious that if we are to have genuine knowledge, or at least reasoned opinion, about systems of imperceptible scientific objects, we must not only be able to make significant references to them (as disallowed by the first assumption) but to draw acceptable "experimental" conclusions about them (as disallowed by the second assumption).

A Revision of Classical Empiricism

Even though classical empiricism involves assumptions that must be rejected, it is a commendably critical theory of knowledge, and we can improve upon it only if we have a fairly precise understanding of its key assumptions. Its assumption concerning meaning is reasonably clear by virtue of the preceding discussion, but the assumption concerning experimental inference deserves a little more exposition. Since Hume is the shining example of a classical empiricist, I shall begin by discussing this last assumption as it appears in his philosophy. My ultimate aim in this section is to revise or amend, rather than simply reject, the empiricist theory of knowledge.

According to Hume, all "experimental inference" is ultimately based on the relation of cause and effect.[32] If we infer that a letter that we receive was written by our friend Mary, we shall be making an experimental inference, relying on a causal principle to the effect, perhaps, that the kind of handwriting we see on the letter was caused (or written) by Mary. Here we infer the existence of a cause, which we do not actually observe, from an effect that we do observe (the handwriting on the letter) by virtue of a causal principle that we have learned from experience. Our reasoning here has the structure of this:

> This X occurs.
> X's are caused by Y's (or Y).
> Therefore, a Y (or Y) caused this X.

This kind of reasoning is not distinctively empiricist—in fact, it can be reconstructed as a syllogism—but Hume prescribed an empiricist basis for the causal principles it involves. According to him, such principles are acceptable only when they are based on experience. Although he insisted that we simply accept such principles when we have had the appropriate experiences, other empiricists have argued that there is a further form of inference by which such principles are derived as conclusions. Yet Hume and other classical empiricists are agreed on one crucial point: Causal principles, when acceptable, are based on experience and concern only possible objects of experience.

Hume said that when we experience a "constant conjunction" between occurrences of a kind X and a kind Y, we begin to believe that occurrences of kind X are caused by occurrences of kind Y. Other empiricists claim that from the premise that occurrences of kind X are constantly conjoined with occurrences of kind Y, we draw the conclusion that X's are always conjoined with Y's and that, consequently, X's can be considered causes of Y's. Both agree, however, that when a causal principle is acceptable, the X's and Y's it concerns are the sort of thing we can observe, for we accept such principles, they say, only because of our experience with cases of X and Y. If a certain alleged occurrence is the sort of thing we could not possibly experience (such as the change of state in some invisible, exotic microobject), then we could have no rational basis for accepting any causal principle concerning it.

The kind of inference by which, according to classical empiricists other than Hume, we generalize from our experience has been called "inductive generalization."[33] This form of inference is not restricted to cases in which we accept causal principles. Formulated in a very general, statistical way, the principle involved is this:

> If n/m instances of a large, randomly selected class of things or occurrences of a kind E are observed to have some property P (perhaps the property of being conjoined with something of another kind) and if no evidence to the contrary is available, then probably n/m instances of all E's have the property P.

As I have expressed it, the principle here is extremely vague, for it does not tell us how large the class of E's must be or what contrary evidence might amount to. Hume, who didn't think that we accept generalizations as the result of inference, was content to say that our confidence in a generalization simply increases as we encounter favorable evidence. In his view the process by which we adopt generalizations is nonrational and instinctive: "It does not rest," he said, "on reason or any process of the understanding."[34] Other classical empiricists have disagreed with Hume on this matter. But though they have urged that inductive generalization is a genuine and legitimate form of inference, they have not been able to eliminate the vagueness in the principle that such inferences tacitly involve.

In the late 1940s it was shown by Bertrand Russell[35] and then, independently, by Nelson Goodman[36] that the sort of principle I have tried to formulate is inherently defective, requiring qualifications that Goodman has been trying to supply since that time. However this may be, even an improved version of the principle will not be adequate for all scientific purposes, for it will not permit us to draw conclusions about things that we cannot possibly observe, such as fundamental microentities. To avoid this kind of inadequacy with inductive generalization, a more basic (some would say alternative) form of inductive inference is now generally accepted by empiricists. This other method has been interpreted in different ways by different writers and, depending on the interpretation, has been given a variety of names, such as "the method of hypotheses," "the hypothetico-deductive method," "Bayesian inference," and "inference to the best explanation." In what follows I shall ignore such differences of interpretation and concentrate on common ground.[37]

A fundamental idea behind this other method is that, if we succeed in identifying various hypotheses that, if true, would explain some phenomenon, then we are rationally entitled to accept the best such hypothesis, provided that we do so in an appropriately critical spirit. By ''appropriately critical spirit'' I mean at least this: We accept the hypothesis only until a better one comes along, and we try, in the mean time, to add credibility to it by testing its consequences in further cases. Although empiricists are now generally agreed about the acceptability of the method, they find it every bit as difficult to describe precisely as the older method of inductive generalization. A key point of unclarity concerns the notion of the ''best'' available hypothesis. The most that can be said here, at least in general terms, is that the best hypothesis in a class of rivaling hypotheses H is, other things being equal, the simplest, the richest in explanatory power, and the one that accords best with other hypotheses and theories whose acceptability is at least as great as that of any hypothesis in H.

It seems obvious that the method of hypothesis is our only hope for developing reasoned beliefs about the external world. I have observed several times that, if there are external objects removed from us in space and time, we could expect to learn of their existence only by attending to signals (or information) that we receive from them. But a signal is one thing; its external cause is quite another. To ascertain the cause of the signal, we have to develop theories or explanatory hypotheses about it and then adopt the most satisfactory one—provided, of course, that we do so in an appropriately critical spirit. Since the method of hypotheses is, in fact, the basic method employed in the so-called advanced sciences, we can provisionally accept its results for the nature of the physical world. As we know, the big picture implied by these results is far more intricate than the commonsense picture we started out with.

We can use the method of hypotheses to overcome the limitations of classical empiricism only if we are prepared to reject the restrictive conception of meaning that the theory involves. Obviously, if we hold that statements about unobservables do not, strictly speaking, make sense, it would be utterly pointless to try to confirm such statements by the method of hypotheses. I have already urged that the classical empiricist conception of meaning must be rejected, but it is important to realize that, in spite of crucial defects, it is a very plausible conception that deserves to be amended rather than simply abandoned.

If we stand back and reflect on the empiricist tradition as a whole, we can readily identify the basic considerations underlying the conception of meaning that empiricists have generally espoused. Perhaps the most elementary consideration is that we can define some of the words we use by other words in our vocabulary—as we can define ''bachelor'' by the words ''unmarried, adult, male human being.'' Since even the wisest person has only a limited vocabulary, it is clear that not all our words can (without circularity) be defined this way. The words that we cannot thus define make up the ''primitive terms'' in our vocabulary. To the question ''How can a primitive term possess meaning or apply to the world?'' empiricists have answered ''By association with objects of experience.'' According to standard empiricist doctrine, we learn to apply certain words to things we experience, and the meanings we attach to those words consists in (or is constituted by) mental habits of association that enable us to relate the words to appropriate objects. As for the referential meaning of our nonprimitive vocabulary, this is indirectly owing (empiricists say) to the primitive terms by which we can ultimately define the rest of the words we use. A verbally indefinable word not directly associated with some object of experience is therefore, for empiricists, wholly lacking in experiential content. We may use it to express our feelings, but we cannot allow that it has genuine referential meaning.

Although this restrictive view of referential meaning is not acceptable, it possesses a core of truth that must be preserved by any tenable alternative. According to the conception of speaker's meaning that I presented in the last chapter, the meaning of every expression is partly dependent on its relations to others. Even if a predicate P is primitive for a certain speaker and cannot be explicitly defined by other words in his or her vocabulary, there must some other predicate Q in that vocabulary such that, if P is truly applicable to something x, it follows (nontrivially) that Q is applicable to x or to something else. The idea here is that the speaker's meaning of a predicate is determined by its implications or immediate consequences; and these implications or consequences are conveyed by other predicates available to the speaker. This idea allows us to pinpoint the element of truth in the classical empiricist conception of meaning. Instead of saying that a primitive predicate has empirical content only because it is directly associated with experience, we can say that it has such content only if it is (at least) related, by principles of inference, to other predicates that, individually or collectively, have such an association.

When we change the implications of a word, we change the meaning it has for us. Since every meaningful word has some distinctive implications, it follows that referential meaning (for appropriate speakers) is never a mere function of a word's association with reality. Classical empiricists failed to appreciate this point, and their metaphysical views suffered accordingly. To avoid further error, it is important for us not to make the opposite mistake of supposing that a primitive or undefined expression need possess no connection with experience whatever. Although I should hesitate to offer, in the style of some twentieth-century empiricists, a criterion of cognitive significance, I think we can reasonably insist that an expression can possess referential meaning only if, possibly by virtue of nontrivial inferential relations to other expressions, it has at least some connection with our experience.

The Mental and the Physical

Having put the key assumptions of classical empiricism behind us, we can now return to the metaphysical problems associated with perception that originally concerned us in this chapter. On the basis of considerations emerging from our discussion of Locke and Berkeley, we can take it as established that the colors we see, the sounds we hear, and the odors we smell are not themselves qualities of external bodies (at least in the original, naive sense of the words "color," "sound," and "odor") but, in some way or another, qualities or aspects of ourselves. This reinterpretation of sensible qualities requires a reinterpretation of our terms for our selves; our identities as sensible objects—as creatures of flesh and blood—must be understood in a new way. Instead of thinking of ourselves as transcendental egos or Cartesian spirits, it seems reasonable, as I said, to think of ourselves as, at least in large measure, physical systems comparable in many respect to such compound entities as cats, monkeys, or even trees.

The patent differences between a living human being and a tree, cat, or even ape cannot be ignored in any adequate theoretical account of our selves and our relation to the world. These differences are of lively concern in contemporary metaphysics, and they prompt the so-called mind-body problem in its contemporary form.

One strand of the current mind-body problem concerns "the sensible qualities we immediately perceive." If such qualities must be understood as, in some sense or way, aspects of ourselves, the question immediately arises: "If we are largely physical systems whose brains consist mainly of neurons in their large-scale features, exactly how do sensible qualities fit into the picture?" This question inevitably arises because sensible qualities do not seem to fit together with brains or nervous systems any better than they fit together with tables, chairs, or paintings on walls. On the face of it, brains as well as tables and paintings are systems of colorless, odorless, soundless microentities, and sensible qualities appear to have no place in them. This matter was noted by Leibniz in the seventeenth century when he said:

> Suppose that there be a machine, the structure of which produces thinking, feelings, and perception; imagine this machine enlarged by preserving the same proportions, so that you could enter it as if it were a mill. This being supposed, you might visit its insides; but what would you observe there? Nothing but parts which push and move each other, and never anything that could explain perception.[38]

Leibniz concluded that a conscious, sentient being cannot be a machine; and this conclusion should be tempting to us as well if we think of the fine grain of a human brain, where impulses are carried along a neuron by the movement of potassium and other ions across the fiber walls.

Like Leibniz, Descartes also thought that a human self could not possibly be a physical system (or "machine"), though he did accord this status to cats, dogs, and apes. As I noted in chapter 5, two of Descartes' best-known arguments for his view do not succeed; one was based on the idea that he could imagine himself existing without a body, and the other was based on the idea that a self, considered as a subject of experiences, is indivisible in a way that a physical body is not. But Descartes had two other lines of argument that are worth mentioning. One concerns the intelligence (or rationality) of a human being, and the other concerns our perception of sensible qualities.

In his famous "Discourse on Method" Descartes outlined two key reasons why, in his opinion, a human being cannot reasonably be regarded as a mere machine or mechanical system. The first was that, though a machine could no doubt be designed to emit sounds closely resembling human speech, a machine could not be designed so that it could arrange its speech in novel ways, "in order to reply appropriately to everything that may be said in its presence, as even the lowest type of man can do."[39] The second reason was really a development of the first one; it is that human beings possess a power of invention, so that they can respond intelligently to unforeseen circumstances in a way that a mere machine could not. The latter can respond, Descartes thought, only in ways it was designed to respond; it is inherently lacking in invention or creativity.[40]

Neither of these reasons is impressive today, and even in Descartes' time Spinoza was unimpressed with them, arguing that "no one has . . . determined what the body, without being determined by the mind, can do and what it cannot do."[41] At present there is active research in the field of artificial intelligence, and machines have already been designed that exhibit both selectivity of response and creativity in a way that mimics, at least in a limited degree, the features we associate with our rationality. An artificial brain really comparable to a human one has, of course, not yet been created, but there is no doubt that Descartes' confidence in what a machine (or purely physical system) cannot do is wholly unwarranted: there is no real evidence that it is true. Quite apart from this, not even Descartes could explain why a soul or spirit can do things that a machine cannot do. Thus, Descartes cannot pretend to have a nonmaterialist theory that is clearly preferable to any materialist theory that might be developed.

If we thumb though the literature of experimental psychology, we find no serious attempt to account for human rationality and inventiveness by postulating a spirit or soul. It is conceivable, as I explained at the end of chapter 5, that we might actually possess a spirit or soul, but there appears to be very little scientific interest in such things. As a matter of fact, the very conception of an immaterial spirit is so vague and indeterminate that no coherent theory of a nonphysical source of rationality and inventiveness is even on the horizon. One might believe on religious grounds that we all have or in some sense are spiritual beings, but one's belief here appears to be associated more with a word and a hope than with a hypothesis that is a serious rival to "materialist" ones. If our aim, as students of metaphysics, is to work out the general lines of a view of ourselves that, all things considered, is most reasonable or probable, then we should not feel compelled to account for our undeniable rationality and creativity by postulating some nonmaterial entity that might be called a soul or spirit.

The other Cartesian line of argument supporting the nonphysical character of our selves is, as I said, associated with the existence of sensible qualities. Like Locke and most contemporary thinkers, Descartes was convinced that physical things do not acutally possess the so-called secondary qualities of color, smell, taste, and sound. In his view physical things possess only geometrical and kinematic qualities, these being sufficient, he thought, to produce experiences of seeing colors, hearing sounds, and smelling odors in sentient beings. These experiences of seeing and so forth, not being physical, could not be the properties of a physical thing. Since as temporal occurrences they must be properties or "modes" of some substance, they must be properties of an immaterial substance, which is just what a mind is.

This last line of thought is no more compelling that the first one; it is certainly too weak to stand on its own feet. If we don't have some antecedent reason to postulate a mind or soul, we shall not be rationally compelled to do so by this line of thought. We may have good reason not to attribute sensible qualities to external objects, but this does not require us to suppose that special animate objects—namely, creatures with properly functioning brains—cannot have sensory experiences, or be in sensory states, which somehow involve sensory qualities. As I mentioned earlier, Hobbes took substantially this line when he argued that sensory experiences are simply "internal motions" in the brain of a creature that can think, move, and respond to sensory stimulation. Contemporary materialists take the same line, though they add that the relevant internal motions are purely physical states of a living brain.

It is probably fair to say that, at least in the United States, scientific materialism is the most widely held metaphysical view.[42] Yet one who merely asserts that experiences of seeing colors and the like are physical, without carefully explaining what the term "physical" is supposed to mean, is saying very little of philosophical interest. If "physical," as used by the materialist, means only "not spiritual in the sense of being an attribute of a Cartesian spirit," we can easily allow that such states are physical, but we may remain seriously perplexed about their metaphysical status. This perplexity can be generated by the following considerations.

It is generally assumed that the purely physical properties of an aggregate are "reducible" to the purely physical properties of the elements composing it—in the way that the physical properties of a pile of stones are reducible to the physical properties of the stones. To say, for example, that the pile of stones weighs one ton is to say that the weights of the individual stones add up to one ton. The basis for this assumption, which is more accurately expressed by saying that true statements ostensibly about an aggregate are equivalent to statements (perhaps complex ones) about the elements composing it, is the metaphysical one, mentioned in chapter 1, that an aggregate is nothing over and above the relevant elements arranged in appropriate ways.

If the materialist is to be understood as saying that a living human being is merely an aggregate consisting of the sort of microentities found in inorganic nature, then his doctrine is highly dubious: Nothing currently known about protons, neutrons, or their more exotic constituents implies that, when arranged in certain ways, they will individually or collectively possess the sensible qualities involved in an awareness of red or the smell of a rose. On the contrary, it is entirely possible that there are fundamental entities peculiar to animate beings (perhaps Hobbes' phantasms or the constituents of such things) or that some of the properties of a living brain are *emergent*, that is, not reducible to the properties of the entities composing it.[43] In either case there would be something very special about a living human being—something not reducible to the properties of inorganic elements.

Someone is bound to object that there is nothing really unusual about emergent properties of aggregates, for the properties of many patently physical aggregates have irreducible features. Take ordinary table salt, for instance. Chemically, table salt, if pure, is an aggregate of NaCl molecules; yet the property of saltiness is not reducible to the properties of sodium and chlorine, which are highly noxious to human beings. This kind of example is useless, however. Saltiness, the taste, is a relational property consisting in the effect on a human being (or similar animal) of NaCl. Human beings are aware of saltiness when they taste NaCl, and this awareness exists in human beings, not in the NaCl. But a sensible quality, of which the taste of salt is a special case, is just the sort of thing that would seem to be emergent if a human being is supposed to be a system of purely physical entities.

Since our knowledge of physical reality is still significantly limited, we must allow that it is entirely possible for special "sensible" entities to exist in the organic systems we call brains. This possibility is not taken very seriously by most philosophers today, however. The most popular current view is that sensory experiences are sensory "states" of a physical being, something thought to be an aggregate of more fundamental physical entities. But unless the distinctive qualities of a sensory experience are simply ignored, these sensory states have every appearance of being emergent. To prove otherwise, or even to make a strong case to the contrary, one would have to show that the distinctive features of a sensory experience can be constituted by (reduced to) the distinctive features of purely physical elements. No philosopher has come close to doing this. Thus, a purely materialist or emphatically physicalist conception of a human being is a highly speculative one for which there is very little (if any) evidence. The last word on the part of the mind-body problem concerned with sensible qualities seems to belong to the speculative scientist rather than the philosopher.

In the early pages of this chapter I explained how the view of ourselves and the world that Husserl called "the natural standpoint" is undermined by the theoretical view that has been under development since the seventeenth century. Although metaphysical speculation by philosophers has, over the years, cast doubt on both views, leading to such doctrines as skepticism, idealism, phenomenalism, and Kantianism, I argued that the theoretical-scientific view is wholly defensible if a more up-to-date conception of referential significance and justifiable experimental inference is allowed. Yet if the theoretical view is defensible, the natural standpoint must be rejected as a sound or true view of reality. This is problematic, because the theoretical-scientific view is not yet complete, and the parts we now possess may undergo revision. If we reject Husserl's natural standpoint, will we not be faced with a kind of skepticism?

The answer to this question is, I believe, no. To reject the natural standpoint as providing an ultimately true picture of reality does not require us to reject it entirely; we can reinterpret it as providing a true picture of the way the world *appears* to creatures like us. Consider color again. When we observe an

Albers or Miro painting, we shall perceive it (if we are normal) as colored, as actually having the sensuous color qualities of which we are immediately aware. Metaphysical reflection may convince us that the painting does not really possess the qualities we naturally attribute to it (the colors naively conceived), but there is no doubt that the painting appears to have those qualities. We can interpret this appearance as a relational property of the object—as its "power," in Locke's sense, to produce color experiences in us.

We can adopt a similar strategy in reinterpreting the other qualities of the object as they are conceived by the natural standpoint. The smoothness and lack of perceptible gaps of its surface can likewise be understood as an objective appearance, the appearance it presents (we assume) to standard observers under standard conditions. In adopting this strategy we are, in effect, following Kant's lead, but we shall differ from Kant in holding that external things-in-themselves (such as paintings) are not unknowable, though they are not directly perceivable in the naive sense. As far as we know, things-in-themselves are as theoretical as the physicist tells us they are. The theoretical-scientific account may be incomplete and subject to revision, but it provides the best available view of what the world is *really* like.

Chapter 9
METAPHYSICAL FREEDOM

THUS FAR I have found it reasonable to consider a human being as a largely physical system, one with mental or sensory aspects, but not one involving an immaterial soul or spirit. This view raises problems when we think of ourselves as creatures capable of doing things of our own free will. Actions done this way are said to be metaphysically free, and our alleged capacity to perform them raises problems that are as difficult to resolve as any discussed in previous chapters.

Freedom and Determinism

If we neglect the theological concerns that have raised problems about the possibility of human freedom, we can say that the basic secular problem about free will arises from a clash between two familiar assumptions.[1] The first is the commonsense assumption that our voluntary behavior is, at least in many instances, entirely up to us and that we alone are ultimately responsible for it. The second is the metaphysical assumption that there is a cause or sufficient explanation for everything that happens in nature and that our choices as well as our actions are always the result of some antecedent cause or condition. These two assumptions generate a problem about human freedom because it is hard to see how an action or choice could possibly be free if it is caused—and thus "determined"—by some prior occurrence or condition.

For some philosophers, the only rational response to the problem is to reject the commonsense idea that our voluntary behavior is freely performed. This response is recorded in the limerick:[2]

> There was young man who said "Damn!
> I learn with regret than I am
> A creature that moves
> In predestinate grooves;
> In short, not a bus but a tram!"

Other philosophers, some more sophisticated than the young man, have responded to the problem in the opposite way. Fully confident that they are buses and not trams, they have simply abandoned the metaphysical assumption that every natural occurrence must have a cause or sufficient explanation.

This last response is not just a naive expression of human self-importance; it is as familiar and as carefully considered as a standard opening in chess. As far as we know, the earliest philosopher to make this response was Epicurus, who lived in the fourth century B.C. According to him, the bodies we observe in nature are made up of tiny atoms that, though commonly behaving in regular, lawful ways, are capable of occasional "swerves," which are spontaneous and uncaused.[3] Since he believed that our souls as well as our bodies are made up of such atoms, he thought that their undetermined swerves could account for our occasional acts of genuine freedom. A similar view, very generally speaking, was espoused by Sir Arthur Eddington in our century.[4] According to him, the fundamental laws governing the behavior of basic physical entities are irreducibly statistical, and certain quantum transitions involving those entities are inherently unpredictable and therefore undetermined by antecedent causes or conditions. Like Epicurus, Eddington thought that the fundamental indeterminism in nature left open the possibility of genuine human freedom.

Unfortunately, when we examine the matter carefully we find that the kind of indeterminism espoused by Epicurus and Eddington does not seem to help the case for human freedom. To see this, suppose that, as the result of an undetermined swerve or quantum transition in some atom of my brain, I suddenly fall to my knees and begin singing "The Star-Spangled Banner." Do I thereby act freely? Certainly not: I may be utterly baffled by my strange behavior and fearful of what my body will do next.

A supporter of Epicurus might object to this example on the ground that, to be free, an action must be voluntary or willed and that the bizarre action I have just described is not voluntary at all. But this objection does not really help matters. Suppose that I suddenly do something that I fully mean, will, or intend to do, but that my willing or intending, which sets my body in motion, is as undetermined—as uncaused and spontaneous—as the swerve of an Epicurean atom. My willing or intending might then be just as astonishing to me as my "act" of singing "The Star-Spangled Banner," and it might lead me to fear what I will mean or will to do next. If I frequently found myself willfully or intentionally doing surprising things, I might begin to worry about future attacks of uncaused volitions or motivated actions, and I might reasonably believe that, when such acts occur, I am just as unfree as the most hopeless drug addict, who is driven to seek a fix by (in this case) *caused* wants or urges.

The examples I have just described bring out a point of great importance: The very notion of metaphysical freedom—of doing something of one's own free will—is extremely unclear. It is not as if philosophers who argue about such freedom have a clear idea of their subject and differ mainly on the question of whether voluntary human behavior (or perhaps the human mind or will) is or is not causally determined. On the contrary, a clear conception of human freedom is very difficult to develop, and philosophers who argue about human freedom almost never agree on what freedom is supposed to be. If we are to make any progress with the subject, we shall have to try to make the subject clearer by forming a definite conception of what metaphysical freedom actually amounts to.

Freedom and Unmoved Moving

One recent attempt to clarify the notion of metaphysical freedom can be traced back to the ancient Greek idea of an unmoved mover.[5] In a famous passage in his *Physics* Aristotle said this:

> There are two senses in which we may regard one thing as producing motion in another. Either the mover is ultimately responsible for the motion, or else it is not ultimately responsible but transmits the motion from an ulterior source; and in the former case, either the action of the mover immediately precedes the result or there are intermediate steps. Thus a cane that pushes a stone is itself moved by a hand which is in turn moved by a man; the man himself, however, is not moved by anything further.[6]

When Aristotle says that the man here is "not moved by anything further," he means that there is no other "thing" that moves him. Sometimes a man is moved by another man, as when one wrestler throws another across the ring, but people can sometimes move themselves—and when they do, they operate as unmoved movers. According to the conception of metaphysical freedom espoused by some contemporary philosophers, it is only when people act as unmoved movers that they truly act freely.

Aristotle's notion of an unmoved mover applies to continuants, not to events or processes, which philosophers in the tradition of Hume regard as causes. When Aristotelians describe movers as causes, they are employing a notion of cause that is sometimes termed "agent causation." There is no doubt that in everyday life we do apply the word "cause" to things in the sense of continuants, but we also apply it to events and processes. These two uses of "cause" have stirred up controversy in connection with the problem of freedom, because many philosophers insist that agent causation is reducible to event causation. When we say, according to these philosophers, that a car knocks over a lamppost, we can only mean that the car does something as the result of which the effect occurs. Strictly speaking, the effect (the lamppost's falling over) was produced by an event cause—specifically, the car's hitting the post with sufficient force.[7]

There is no doubt that people are unmoved movers in Aristotle's sense, for they often move such things as canes or chairs without themselves being moved in the way canes or chairs are moved—by being pushed or dragged about, for example. On the other hand, when people act as unmoved movers, the movements they make seem to result from (and thus be the effects of) their wants, beliefs, and choices—and these states or occurrences certainly appear to have causes of their own. Many philosophers who think of themselves as unmoved movers deny this last idea, but Aristotle himself seemed to accept it. In his famous *Nichomachean Ethics* he argued that if we have a certain end or purpose and discover a suitable means of realizing it by an action we can perform here and now, we will choose to perform it, and our action will *result* from our choice.[8]

It may be argued that Aristotle's account of the conditions leading to purposive action is incorrect, but there can be little doubt that people are led to act by their reasons and motives, and that their reasons and motives are normally formed as the result of things that have happened to them. If we accept the view that the operation of agent causes is always reducible to (or explicable by) event causes in the agent, we shall have to allow that the actions of human unmoved movers are "determined" by antecedent causes or conditions. If we are right about this, anyone who is convinced that an action is determined by antecedent causes or conditions will not be able to defend human freedom by appealing to the ancient idea of an unmoved mover.

Is the reducibility thesis correct or not? Should we or should we not agree that, whenever an agent cause produces some effect, the effect must be understood as resulting from some event cause internal to the agent? If the position I took in chapter 6 is sound—the position, namely, that events are not ultimately real in a world of continuants—it might appear that the reducibility thesis is extremely dubious. From the perspective of descriptive metaphysics, the world of common sense is a world of things; and if events are not ultimately real in such a world, even causes are not ultimately real there either. I accept this consequence, but I do not therefore agree that agent causation is ultimately inexplicable or undetermined in a world of things. As I explained, one who denies that events are ultimately real will want to reinterpret the principle that every event has a cause and say that there is a causal explanation for everything that anything does. The thesis of causal determinism may possibly be false, in which case there is not a causal explanation for everything that happens. But the question whether events are, or are not, ultimately real has no bearing on the issue. The thesis of universal determinism (as it may be called) is logically independent of the question whether events are ultimately real or mere fictions.

If I am right here, the reducibility thesis concerning agent causes and event causes is not really crucial for the proper resolution of the free-will issue. The question that is perhaps crucial, at least from the present perspective, is whether there is a causal explanation for everything, whether (more specifically) there is a causal explanation for everything that a human being actually does. At the beginning of this chapter I pointed out that some philosophers regard the principle of universal determinism as self-evident; they regard it as undeniable that there is a sufficient condition (or explanation) for everything that anything does. I also pointed out that other philosophers have denied that such a principle is even true; in their view the fundamental laws of nature are purely statistical, allowing the possibility of undetermined occurrences. Since this last view, if correct, need only imply that certain microevents (or the behavior of certain microentities) are undetermined, not that a human being's action is undetermined or that there is no sufficient explanation for the fact that a person does a certain thing intentionally or voluntarily, a denial of universal determinism is not thereby sufficient to support metaphysical freedom. The fundamental issue concerning metaphysical freedom must be pursued at a deeper level.

Explanations of Purposive Behavior

Regardless of their position on the subject of metaphysical freedom, philosophers uniformly agree that the sort of actions commonly thought to be free are in some way based on the actor's beliefs and motives. With the problem of metaphysical freedom hovering in the background the debate has centered on the question of how, exactly, reasons and motives are related to purposive behavior. Some argue that the relation here is not causal at all; they claim that certain reasons and motives can explain purposive behavior without in any way determining it. Others insist that the relation is causal and that purposive action is just as determined, though in a different way, as the behavior of a leaf fluttering on a branch.[9] To come to terms with the debate about metaphysical freedom in its current form, I must therefore say something about the relation between reasons, motives, and purposive behavior.

When, in ordinary life, we explain why Tom or Mary did a certain thing, we offer what is known as a teleological explanation. We identify the end we suppose they were pursuing and we contend, or at least support the idea, that they believed that, by doing what they did, they would realize their end. Thus, if Tom wished to please Mary on her birthday and thought that she would be pleased if he took her to her favorite French restaurant, he might naturally invite her to have dinner there. Teleological explanations may be extremely complicated, at least when worked out in detail; but they always point to some purpose or purposes that the actor had and, if they are reasonably explicit, identify certain beliefs related to that purpose (or those purposes). Typically, the explanation affirms that the relevant actions resulted from a line of practical reasoning involving the cited purposes and beliefs. The assumption is that the actors behaved as they did *because* they had certain purposes and reasoned that, by acting as they did, they would realize those purposes.

The most natural interpretation of the "because" in this last sentence is a causal one. If the explanation is sound, the actors' behavior is causally explained by the fact that they had the relevant purposes and reasoned their way into doing what they thought would realize those purposes. So understood, their actions resulted from their reasoning in as natural and as lawful a way as that in which the output of a calculating machine results from data processing internal to it. This interpretation is natural because, when a teleological explanation is viewed as a special form of causal explanation, there is no doubt that it provides a perfectly genuine explanation of *why* the actors behaved as they did, and it also fits in nicely with the idea that a human being, as a creature of flesh and blood, is a perfectly natural thing whose behavior, like the behavior of other natural things, is governed and thus explainable by natural regularities or laws.

Although a causal interpretation of the relevant "because" is a natural one to take, some philosophers stubbornly reject it. They allow that a teleological explanation, when sound, tells us why a person did something, but they deny that the explanation shows us that the doing was causally determined by the actor's purposes, beliefs, and practical reasoning. As they see it, when we are given satisfactory teleological explanations for purposive actions, we know why the actors, being reasonable creatures, would decide to act as they did because we know why they saw their actions as something that fulfill their purposes. But their reasoning did not "determine" their choice; they were capable of choosing differently. Had they done so, they would, no doubt, have had a motive for doing so, but the motive would not have made the alternative choice inevitable. A human being is inherently capable, these philosophers say, of choosing or willing freely no matter what advantages he or she may see in a given course of action. A teleological explanation is, therefore, very different from a causal explanation. It allows us to understand what someone saw in a course of action—what purposes and so forth it would satisfy. But it does not show us what determines his or her choice or volition, for a free choice or volition is not determined at all.

Philosophers who hold this last view of teleological explanations are usually called "libertarians"; they are given this name because they believe in metaphysical freedom and think that such freedom is incompatible with any kind of causal determinism. I shall comment critically on the libertarian position in the section to follow. Here I shall simply observe that, in my view, the causal interpretation of teleological explanations is the correct one. Our purposive behavior *results* from our practical reasoning, the reasoning by which we make choices on the basis of our purposes and beliefs. This reasoning may be good or bad, valid or invalid, but it is governed by mental habits (or "dispositions") that are firmly rooted in the causal order.[10]

The Libertarian Position

If we ask why libertarians are convinced that our choices or volitions do not result from a causal process of reasoning, we do not receive a very satisfactory answer. Like Samuel Johnson, some libertarians simply insist, "Sir, we *know* we are free," and then add that being free requires not acting (or choosing) as the result of causal antecedents. This response is not satisfactory because, if being free requires causal indeterminism, we cannot reasonably claim to *know* that we are free at all. Wittgenstein is reported to have made a remark to this effect: "See those leaves being blown about by the wind? If they were conscious, they might be thinking, 'Now I'll go this way; now I'll go that way.'" They might think that it is entirely up to them which way they will go—that their movements are in no way determined by the wind. But they would be wrong, no matter how strongly they are convinced to the contrary."[11] Obviously, something similar could be true of the libertarians. Their conviction that their wills, their choices or decisions, are undetermined by their purposes or beliefs (or the reasoning in which those purposes and beliefs are reflected) could simply be wrong, a mere illusion.

Another answer was offered, in effect, by Kant.[12] According to him, it is at least possible that, as things-in-themselves, we have a power of free (undetermined) choice. Although we cannot really know whether this possibility is actual—whether we truly have such a power—we must assume that it is actual if we are to make sense of morality. Common morality requires us to do certain things whether we want to or not. Yet the idea that we ought to do a certain thing would not make sense (it would be contrary to reason) if it were not possible for us to do it: *ought* implies *can*. Since we cannot reasonably deny that we have certain obligations, we must assume that we are free to carry them out, whether we can actually claim to know that we are free or not.

Although Kant's claims about freedom are based partly on his metaphysically objectionable view of things-in-themselves, those claims involve important elements of truth. For one thing, even staunch determinists will have to agree that their determinism is founded partly on conjecture, not certain knowledge. Their belief that voluntary actions are caused (or "determined") by purposes and the like may be more plausible than the libertarian's alternative, but it is certainly not self-evident and it may possibly be mistaken. For another thing, it does seem reasonable to suppose that, if you ought morally to do a certain thing, then you must be able, in some sense, to do it. Thus, Kant's approach to freedom involves reasonable, perhaps even undeniable, elements. Nevertheless, the sound points in Kant's approach are not sufficient to render the libertarian view acceptable. As we shall see, a strong case can be made for the idea that the sense in which we must be *able* to do what we ought to do is a practical one not implying that our actions are undetermined in the way claimed by libertarians.

The libertarian view that our choices and therefore our actions are not determined by our beliefs and purposes has little to commend it, therefore, apart from the stubborn conviction that we really are free and that we would not be free if our choices were determined by anything else. As a first step in developing some of the key considerations that can be urged against this conception of freedom—a conception that Hume called "the freedom of indifference"[13]—we should observe just how peculiar the view really is. According to the libertarian, my mental state (my purposes, beliefs, and so forth) at the time I freely do something *A* does not determine my choice or action because it is possible for me, being in that state, to do (or choose to do) something else. This is a peculiar, puzzling idea because my motivational state at a given time may favor my doing *A* and nothing else. If, in that state, I were to do (or choose to do) something other than *A*, my choice would be unmotivated, and I would not be acting for a purpose. But a purposeless act or choice could hardly be voluntary; it would be utterly aimless. Yet the libertarian asks us to believe that my freedom in doing (or choosing to do) *A* in such a case depends on the possibility of my *purposelessly* doing something else instead. It is no wonder that David Hume called this peculiar conception of freedom "the freedom of indifference."

A more fundamental difficulty with the libertarian's view is that, convictions about being metaphysically free aside, the scientifically most plausible conception of human beings is that they are complicated organic systems whose ability to think and act is a function of their nervous systems, these systems being constituted by aggregates of physical entities that obey the laws of physics. As we have seen, human brains may involve sensory qualia in one way or another; but such brains still seem to be largely physical systems whose behavior is no less predictable, or lawful, than the behavior of the microentities in a frog, swamp, or atomic explosion. Since the libertarian's view seems to rest mainly on a stubborn subjective conviction rather than one reasoned argument, the alternative, scientifically more orthodox view, though certainly not self-evident, is clearly preferable and should be accepted if we are concerned to base our view of a human being on plausible reasoning rather than on faith or feeling.

The Reconciler Position

The libertarians' chief opponents, among those who defend some form of human freedom, are usually called "reconcilers." Like the libertarians, the reconcilers generally believe that one who acts freely must be *capable* of doing otherwise, but they do not contend that this capacity to do otherwise could be exercised by purposeless, or "indifferent," actions. They are called reconcilers because they seek to reconcile their belief in human freedom with a belief in determinism—with the belief, that is, that our free actions as well as our reasons and motives have causal antecedents.

Perhaps the earliest expression of a reconciler view can be found in the writings of Thomas Hobbes. According to him:

> Whenever we say that someone hath free-will to do this or that, or not to do it, it must always be understood with this necessary condition: *if he wills.* For to talk of having free-will to do this or that whether one wills or not is absurd.[14]

The key idea here, which has been developed more fully by recent reconcilers, is that the sense in which we must be capable of doing other than what we freely do is a conditional one: we can do differently in this sense when and only when we would do differently *if* we willed to do so.[15] As reconcilers view the matter, it is largely because libertarians overlook the necessary condition Hobbes speaks of that they end up requiring motiveless acts as alternatives to the actions people freely perform. Yet a conditional interpretation of the relevant capacity does not require indeterminism. My action might be determined, or caused, by the reasons and motives that I now have, but I am capable of doing otherwise in the conditional sense that, had I willed (wanted, had the purpose) to do otherwise, I would have done otherwise: nothing in the circumstances would have prevented me from realizing some other purpose.

Although libertarians and reconcilers generally agree that a reasonable conception of doing something freely requires that the actor be able, in some sense or other, to do otherwise, the idea is really very doubtful. This can be seen from the following thought-experiment.[16] Suppose that Dr. X invents a machine capable of producing volitions (choices or motivating desires) in people by stimulating certain areas of their brains. Suppose also that Dr. X has a subject, Smith, in his laboratory and wants to convince a colleague that Smith, when he awakens from a drug-induced nap, will certainly eat the apple placed before him. He will do so, Dr. X says, either freely or unfreely. Smith is connected to the remarkable new machine. If, when he awakens, he has no wish to eat the apple, he will be made to eat it by the machine: the machine will induce a determining desire to eat it, and he will then eat it, intending to do so. Smith then wakes from his sleep, sees the apple, and decides to eat it; the machine is never activated. It is natural to say that Smith freely eats the apple because his action, being in no way interfered with, is just as free as any other action of his ever was. Thus, I should say that if humans are ever capable of doing things freely, Smith freely eats the apple. Yet in a fundamental sense Smith could not do otherwise: he would eat the apple one way or another, and he would do so intentionally.

I think this example succeeds in bringing out a point that deserves to be accepted: If actions are ever free, they are so by virtue of their own characteristics, not partly by virtue of something else that the actor might do in the circumstances. Not only is the plausibility of this point illustrated by the example of Smith and Dr. X, but, once we have it firmly in mind, we can see that it is plausible on general grounds. Consider this. If Smith's freedom in doing one thing depends on his ability to do something else, then this other action will be done freely or not done freely. If it must be done freely, then the freedom of one action will depend on the possibility of the actor doing something else freely, and so on indefinitely. This is absurd, because to decide whether one action has a certain property, we shall have to decide whether another possible action has the very same property—and there is either no end to this or we move in circles. The other alternative is equally absurd, because then the freedom of an action will depend on the possible occurrence of an unfree action—of something as irrelevant to freedom as the jerky movements of a mechanical duck. Thus, on general grounds as well as on grounds of specific examples, the doctrine that the freedom of one action depends on the character of other possible actions seems extremely dubious.

In a famous passage John Locke described an example somewhat similar to that of Smith and Dr. X, though the conclusion Locke drew is apparently different from mine. Here is Locke's example:

> Suppose a person be carried, whilst fast asleep, into a room where is a person he longs to see and speak with; and be there locked fast in, beyond his power to get out: he awakes, and is glad to find himself in so desirable company, which he stays willingly in, i.e. prefers his stay to going away. I ask, is not his stay voluntary? I think nobody will doubt it; and yet, being locked fast in, he is not at liberty not to stay, he has not freedom to be gone.[17]

If the question here is "Does the man stay in the room of his own free will?" my answer is yes: he stays there freely, though he is not free to leave. In giving this answer I am not disputing Locke's claim that the man's freedom is limited by his being locked in the room; I am saying that the man's action—roughly, his staying in the room—is free. There is no inconsistency in my position here, for the freedom of a person is one thing and the freedom of a certain action is something entirely different. Had the man in Locke's example resented his predicament and struggled to break free, he would not have remained in the room of his own free will. As it was, he stayed there *because* he wanted to.

To avoid an objection that is apt to arise here, I should add a word about what might be called "overdetermination." Suppose Tom and Mary are having a chat in a small room. Both are becoming warm, but neither says anything about it. Finally, Tom gets up and opens the window. If we ask "Why is the window open?" a reasonable answer is "Because Tom opened it." As it happens, Mary was on the point of opening it when Tom stood up; so if Tom didn't open it, Mary would have done so. But this does not imply that Mary's attitude to the window—or the fact that, if Tom had not opened it, Mary would have done so— partly explains why it is open. Now think of Locke's example. His man willingly stayed in the room; he wanted to be there and made no effort to leave. In view of this it is fair to say that he stayed there *because* he wanted to. It is true that he could not have left had he tried to do so. But this fact does not imply that it is wrong to say that he stayed there *because* he wanted to stay there. To this I might add: The fact that he could not have got out does not imply that it is wrong, or unreasonable, to say that he stayed there of his own free will.

These last remarks leave no doubt that, in my view, a reasonable conception of human freedom is quite compatible with the idea that our voluntary actions are causal consequences of our motivational state and that the components of our motivational state (our purposes and beliefs) also possess causal antecedents. As we have seen, the idea that our free actions are "determined" is easily combined with Aristotle's conception of an unmoved mover, a conception that is naturally applied to normal human beings. To express the conception of freedom involved here in more up-to-date terms, we might say that people do things freely when they do them voluntarily, not being forced to do them by some other person or thing—as the cane or chair is forced to move by the person moving it. I cannot deny that this conception of metaphysical freedom must be qualified in certain ways if it is to be fully acceptable; in fact, I will offer some qualification in a later section. But the necessary qualifications will not render such freedom incompatible with the view, which may or may not be true, that all natural occurrences, voluntary human behavior included, are causally determined by antecedent conditions.

Freedom and Morality

Thus far I have been concerned with purely metaphysical issues relating to human freedom, but the dispute between libertarians and others is also carried out in the context of moral philosophy. To bring out some of the basic issues in this other area of dispute, I want to begin with some moral objections that a libertarian is bound to raise with the conception of freedom that I favor and have briefly described.

According to both libertarians and reconcilers, people can reasonably be held responsible only for things they freely do or for things that are foreseeable consequences of what they freely do. An action for which we are morally responsible is one for which we are appropriately blamed and, if it is seriously wrong, even punished; but it is clearly immoral (as well as decidedly stupid) to punish people for things they cannot help doing. Since I have argued that one who acts freely need not be capable of doing otherwise, am I not open to the charge that my conception of freedom should be rejected on moral grounds alone?

My answer, of course, is no. My conception of freedom is not morally objectionable—but my answer here does involve, I must admit, a certain conception of morality, one that accords with the reconciler position. Although I have rejected the reconciler's idea that one who acts freely must always be capable of doing otherwise in a conditional sense, I have not denied that one who acts freely is *normally* capable of doing otherwise—and I am prepared to allow that the reconciler's conception of moral responsibility, which rests on this latter idea, is, on the whole, correct, requiring qualification rather than outright rejection. To bring my conception into line with the demands of a reasonable morality, I shall therefore begin by describing the reconciler's characteristic approach to the notion of a morally responsible action.

In sharp opposition to libertarians, reconcilers insist that punishable actions *ought* to be regarded as causally determined. If, in their view, an action were not determined by the actor's motivational state, it would be pointless, even immoral, to blame him or her for performing it. According to them, blame (let alone punishment) is morally acceptable only when it has an appropriate effect on the agent—only if it helps, or can be expected to help, induce new purposes that will result in better behavior. We do not, generally speaking, punish people for nonvoluntary actions (things they don't mean to do) because the whole point in punishing offenders is to change their purposes or aims, to induce morally preferable ones; and actions not done on culpable aims do not deserve to be corrected. If we could not reasonably say that morally objectionable aims result from bad motives that can be influenced by blame or punishment, we should be blaming or punishing an offender out of a primitive desire for vengeance—something no morally sensitive person could possibly condone.

These last considerations relate to the subject of being *able* to do what one *ought* to do in the following way: To be able to do what one ought to do, one's nature and circumstances must be such that, if one willed or chose to do what one ought to do in those circumstances, one would succeed in doing so. The aim of punishment, according to the reconciler, is to bring it about, at least ideally, that one who acts wrongly will choose to do the right thing in future cases. Since this aim can be accomplished only by influencing the will of the offender and, from his or her example, the potential offender, punishment is fundamentally different from mere abuse. People who are punished must know why they are being punished; they must be shown that they are being punished *because* they did (or chose to do) something that is wrong. Blame or censure is, in effect, a mild form of punishment whose purpose is exactly the same as that of severe punishment: to influence the will in a morally appropriate way. If our wills could not be *affected* or *changed* by punishment, the institution would be pointless or even barbaric.

Although compelling to reconcilers, these last considerations are not convincing to libertarians. There are two basic reasons for this. The first is that, in spite of what I have argued, libertarians hold firmly to the idea that people act freely only when they can do otherwise, and they insist that the sense in which such people must be able to do otherwise is a nonconditional or categorical one.[18] To be able to do otherwise *if* one so wills or chooses is not enough for genuine freedom because such willing or choosing is not really in one's power (they say) if it is determined by antecedent conditions—even if those conditions consist of one's own purposes and beliefs. Libertarians will allow that punishment may be directed, in part, to improving a person's will, but a will can be influenced, they say, without being determined. As they view the matter, people who have been punished may gain morally preferable purposes, but if they are genuinely free, they must have it in their power to act or not act on those purposes. To give offenders new purposes or motives is not the same as determining them to will or choose in a new way, as if they were some kind of machine.

The second reason for the libertarian's opposition to the reconciler lies in his distinctive view of punishment. I said that libertarians *may* allow that part of the purpose of punishment is to influence the will to better future behavior, but they generally insist that the fundamental aim of punishment is not at all reformative: it is to square moral accounts. This seems to be the traditional Judeo-Christian view—the view traditionally practiced if not preached. In his *Inferno* Dante describes the divine punishment appropriate to various sinners, such as being buried upside down in hot sand for all eternity; and the point of the punishment has nothing to do with reforming the sinner or changing his will. The punishment is right because it is appropriate, because it accords with divine standards of justice. One who sins deserves a certain penalty; and the punishment is appropriately applied even to incorrigible sinners whose wills cannot be improved. In real life—life on earth—blame and punishment may fulfill an extrinsic purpose of improving our wills (of reforming sinners and deterring potential sinners), but its intrinsic purpose is very different: it is to square moral accounts. In this respect punishment is fundamentally backward looking, to the offense; not forward looking, to better behavior. When St. Paul said "The wages of sin is death," he was expressing the idea that punishment is a form of payment, something morally required for sin, not a mere instrument of improvement. Hell is not a divine reformatory.

As I see it, one of the key reasons for the persistent and seemingly irresoluble controversy between libertarians and reconcilers is that different moral ideals are involved in the two positions. The typical libertarian insists that if the wills of even murderers and rapists are determined by antecedent conditions (no matter what these conditions are, whether they are internal to their psychology or not) then it is *wrong* to hold them responsible for their actions and to blame or punish them—even if the point in doing so is to change their wills. They should be blamed, let alone punished, only if their actions are wholly up to them, not up to motives that we might induce in them. Punishment is moral payment for a wrong, not a mere instrument of moral improvement. Reconcilers reply that such a conception of punishment is morally barbaric, the result of a primitive desire for vengeance. We should punish, they say, only to improve the offender and, incidentally, to deter potential offenders. Rightly understood, punishment is morally allowable only on the assumption that human behavior is subject to laws of cause and effect.

It is entirely possible, as the reconciler Hume pointed out,[19] that one who abhors vengeance may be tempted to reject all forms of punishment by the reflection that, if one's will is determined by antecedent conditions, one cannot ultimately be responsible for it. But this temptation should be resisted, Hume said, by a more realistic attitude toward morals. What people can reasonably be held responsible for cannot be divorced from what they will actually be held responsible for; and people will, in fact, be held responsible for their malicious, antisocial acts regardless of whether those acts have causal antecedents or not. Everything that happens—everything that anyone ever does—may be determined, Hume said, by the will of God. But this possibility, even when universally acknowledged as actual, has not deterred people from blaming and punishing others. It is true that, on grounds of sympathy, people sometimes insist that certain others (the poor, the downtrodden, the victims of bigotry) should not be held responsible for many of their wrongful deeds—their stealing, cheating, or acts of vengeance. Yet those who deny responsibility to such people never, in fact, deny it to others whose ugly behavior is equally determined: the exploiters, the bigots, the smugly selfish and content. A realistic view of moral responsibility must be one that, given the way of the world, we can consistently apply— and this, Hume thought, can only be based on a reformative-deterrent conception of punishment.

According to most reconcilers, any view of responsibility that deserves to be taken seriously must involve a reasonable conception of the world, and the latter can only be a scientific one. By virtue of our reverence for humanity, we may wish to avoid cruel and unusual forms of punishment. Yet if we conceive of morality as a means of social control, we can allow that reformative punishment with a deterrent effect, at least when reasonably humane, is justifiable even if the world is deterministic. The alternative response to a deterministic world— that of holding no one responsible—is not only, in a way, morally visionary, but if (contrary to what is really possible) it were put into effect, an objectionably dehumanized form of life would result. If we are not responsible for anything we do, we are not responsible for the good we do—for our efforts on behalf of others, for our contributions to art or science, for our winning touchdowns or our consumption of midnight oil. In such a world even faint praise would be undeserved, and we could not be rewarded for anything. I doubt that many people would really want to live in such a world; it is perhaps reassuring to know that, human nature being what it is, we shall never have to.

Two Conceptions of Freedom

From my moral and metaphysical point of view, the reconciler has much the stronger case. I cannot deny that we don't really *know* that the behavior of human beings in all its variety is causally determined—as the behavior of trees, cats, and probably even apes no doubt is. Yet the idea that our behavior is so determined, so explainable, fits in far better with the view of the world we have today than the libertarian's idea that we are in some way independent of the causal order. As for the moral significance of our being determined to will (want or choose) what, as it happens, we do will, I think Hobbes and Locke were right to insist that our alleged freedom *to* will (not our freedom *of* will) is ultimately confused.

As Hobbes pointed out, our appetites and aversions are not voluntary:

> Do we desire food and other necessities of nature because we will?
> Are hunger, thirst, and desire voluntary? When desiring, one can,
> in truth, be free to *act*; one cannot, however, be free to *desire*.[20]

I can agree that what we will or choose is not the same as what we merely desire, for we can choose to disregard even a very pressing desire. Still, our choices are not unmotivated; and when we choose not to satisfy a desire, we do so because of some more pressing desire or motive, which we did not "freely" accept. As Aristotle emphasized, our deliberations are carried out against the background of desires and motives that we simply have; and when we choose to do one thing rather than another, we generally act on one desire rather than another, the strongest desire determining our choice. The libertarian idea that, if we are truly free, we can always resist our motives and do other than what we actually want or mean to do, not only seems highly dubious on speculative grounds, but it has little to commend it morally.

It is worth recalling the example of uncaused volitions that I mentioned near the beginning of this chapter. If I actually experienced such volitions—finding myself doing, and meaning to do, certain things without any reason or cause—I might be utterly bewildered by my behavior and begin to worry about what I will mean to do next. Like a kindly old parson who without reason or cause finds himself strangling his loyal housekeeper, I might reasonably fear that I am losing control of myself. My sense of being at the mercy of momentary impulses would no doubt be owing to the lack of connection between the impulses (the intentions or volitions) and the values, aims, and policies that are distinctive of me as a person. Like any normal human being, I can, of course, do things that are, as one says, "out of character," but such deeds are bound to be rare. In the normal case we do what we do because we are the kind of people we are: our actions express values and aims that are characteristic of us. These values and aims are not, for the most part, things we consciously choose or adopt; they take shape in us as our characters develop, and they make us the kind of people we are. The idea that our free actions are not expressions of our characters—not partly determined by values and aims that have simply taken shape as we have grown—is as unconvincing to me as a philosophical idea can be.

I have described the fundamental points of debate between libertarians and reconcilers at such length because the debate seems irreconcilable, reminding me of F. H. Bradley's famous remark that metaphysics is "the finding of bad reasons for what we believe upon instinct."[21] However this may be, the dispute as I have described it, though it may not have convinced the reader one way or the other, does bring out one crucial point that I think is undeniable: It is a serious blunder, naive and wrong, simply to say either that human beings are metaphysically free or that they are not, and "there's an end on it." It is a blunder because the alternatives presuppose different *conceptions* of metaphysical freedom, however vague or cloudy the conceptions may be. If, following Hume, we describe the libertarian's conception as the freedom of indifference and the reconciler's conception as the freedom of spontaneity, then we can say the following:

> If all human behavior is determined or, in principle, causally explainable as social scientists commonly suppose, then (a) there is no freedom of indifference and (b) there is freedom of spontaneity.

Given the soundness of this claim, we might say that the fundamental question concerning metaphysical freedom is really a practical one: "Which conception should we adopt?"

As my remarks thus far have indicated, it seems to me that, all things considered, the reconciler's conception is clearly preferable to that of the libertarian: A metaphysically free human being is best conceived of as one possessing the freedom of spontaneity, and a metaphysically free action is best understood as one that expresses, or is an instance of, such freedom. In the rest of this chapter I shall try to work out a more satisfactory account of the freedom of spontaneity than I have given in preceding pages; what I have said about it thus far requires a number of qualifications.

The Freedom of Spontaneity

The basic idea of the reconciler is that human actions are (can reasonably be said to be) free when they express the will of the agent. Given this basic idea, we might say that the chief contrast between free and unfree actions is that between actions the agent wills or chooses and actions he or she is forced to perform—by circumstances or the will of another. This contrast is difficult to develop, however, as one can easily see if one reflects on actual cases of duress or constraint.

A boxer who is knocked to the canvas by his opponent does not go to the canvas freely, but his going there would not normally be regarded as an action he performs: it is something that happens to him. Yet if I am "forced" at gunpoint to hand over my money to an assailant, I may willingly do so because I fear the consequences of not doing so. Similarly, when an employee donates ten dollars to her employer's favorite charity, she may do so because her employer made it clear to her that her doing so is a condition of keeping her job—in which case she acts intentionally and wills to do what she does for fear of being fired. Both cases are examples of action under duress, and neither seems to be a good case of acting of one's own free will.

Some philosophers have insisted that even in cases of duress, one acts freely if, properly speaking, one acts at all.[22] True, I may be shot by the robber if

I refuse to hand over the money, but I could refuse to comply and take my chances with him. In fact, there are many things I could do instead of handing over the money: for example, I could try to frighten the robber by feigning madness and falling to the ground barking like a dog. Since a particular response is rarely, if ever, required in actual cases of duress, there is clearly some plausibility to the idea in question here. On the other hand, since actions done under duress or constraint are partly owing to the will of another, they should not be considered wholly free. Of course, not all cases of constraint involve another's will. If I am forced to flee my house because the roof is falling in, my action is not wholly free even if I will to leave it. In an obvious sense I leave my house because I am forced by circumstances to do so.

Cases in which people do things, fully intending to do them but doing them only because of duress or constraint, make it natural to say that the freedom of a voluntary action is very often a matter of degree. When an action is constrained by circumstances or the will of another, it is partly nonfree, but it is also partly free because constraint always leaves some room for rational choice. The constraining factors limit one's options and supply motives one does not normally have; they do not fully determine what one will do. To have a fully satisfactory conception of human freedom—of the sort Hume termed the "freedom of spontaneity"—we must have a means of estimating the extent to which an action can be considered free. How can this be done? What considerations are relevant?

One way of gaining light on these questions is to attend to the considerations we appeal to in everyday life when we are concerned to identify the cause (or key explanatory factor) of some phenomenon. Suppose that an explosion occurs in an apartment building. After some investigation the authorities might contend that the cause of the explosion was a leak in a gas pipe. In attributing the explosion to the leaky pipe, the authorities do not suppose that the leak by itself was sufficient to cause the explosion; they know that, without a spark, flame, or other means of ignition, an explosion would not occur even if the building were filled with gas. But sparks and flames are normal occurrences in apartment buildings: cigarette lighters are in frequent use, and gas stoves generally have pilot lights. Since sparks and flames are commonly present in buildings where explosions do not occur, they are not appropriately singled out as the cause of an explosion in such a place. What made the difference in the building that did explode was the leaky gas pipe: the presence of the leak together with things that are normally present in an apartment building is what accounts for the explosion. The leaky pipe is considered the cause because it is the factor we can point to as "responsible" for the explosion—the factor not normally present in apartment buildings and one in the absence of which the explosion would not have occurred. R. G. Collingwood once said that the cause of a phenomenon is the event or condition "with the handle on it," the one that we can or could manipulate to prevent or produce the phenomenon.[23]

Although many causal factors, as they may be called, are generally necessary and sufficient for the occurrence of some phenomenon, the factor termed "the cause" is particularly important. As the example of the leaky pipe shows, the relative importance among causal factors of the one considered "the" cause is largely practical: it is the one that we can get a handle on to produce or prevent the phenomenon. If, with this practical notion of a cause in mind, we reflect on cases of action under duress, we might say that such actions are free in proportion to the importance of the agent's normal state of mind in bringing them about. The idea here, which is admittedly vague and provisional, is that the decisive motivating factor in producing a strongly constrained action is some external threat or danger. The threat or danger, like the leaky gas pipe, is the factor not normally present that led to the effect and that we could hope to get a handle on if, in future cases, we wish to produce or prevent appropriately similar phenomena. If the threat or danger is sufficiently mild so that the agent's normal state of mind may well have led to the action in its absence, then the action is, we might say, maximally free and minimally constrained. Thus, if I wish to leave my gloomy study on a sunny day and would leave it even if the roof were not falling in, my act of leaving my study on such a day when the roof is falling in is only minimally constrained.

The extent to which a particular action is free is closely related to, but must be distinguished from, the extent to which the actor is free when he performs that action. When subject to duress or constraint, I may exercise my freedom in numerous ways: for example, I can freely frown, smile, or clutch my rabbit's foot when I am told to hand over my wallet. Yet in typical conditions of constraint, my possibilities for action are restricted, for there are many things I can normally do but cannot do in the circumstances, even if I willed to do them. Such limitations on my freedom are not peculiar to cases of constraint, however. As I move about in the world, I am constantly changing my circumstances and thereby changing my possibilities for action: things I can do on the playing field I cannot do in my study, and vice versa. As far as the freedom of an action is concerned, the limitation imposed by constraint and duress is that, even when I will to do a certain thing as a means of coping with my circumstances, I am to some extent acting contrary to my will or desires.

When I am told by the robber to hand over my wallet, I may decide to comply, and if I act on this decision, I will to do what I do. Yet in another sense handing over my wallet is contrary to my will: I don't really want to hand it over, and I wouldn't hand it over if I didn't think I had to. Aristotle, groping for a means of describing actions done under constraint, said that they should be considered voluntary, "though in themselves they are perhaps involuntary," since they are not chosen for their own sake.[24] Aristotle's description is not happy, however, for it does not imply that, considered in themselves, they are in some way contrary to the agent's will. Perhaps the best thing to say is that, when we choose under duress, we are commonly required (by our good sense) to do things that are contrary to our normal desires and that, in the absence of duress, we would not do.

Constraint and duress are not the only factors that limit the freedom of an action; other relevant factors may be subsumed under the term "compulsion."

Consider a drug addict. Such a person may reason very carefully about how to get the drug he needs, and he may voluntarily administer it to himself. At the time he takes the drug, he clearly wills to do so, but it is natural to say that his action is not entirely free. If we ask exactly why the addict's action should not be considered free, several answers come to mind. One answer, which Spinoza might have offered, is that the addict's action is motivated entirely by an irrational urge, need, passion, or emotion.[25] But this answer is not satisfactory. As Aristotle pointed out, "the irrational emotions are considered no less a part of human beings than reasoning is, and hence, the actions of a man which spring from passion and appetite [are equally a part of him]."[26] To adapt Aristotle's remark to the case at hand, we might say that if an action motivated by the agent's own reasoning is not unfree, the same should be true, other things being equal, of actions motivated by the man's own passions or emotions.

Another possible answer is that the addict's action is unfree because he could not help doing it, because his condition is such that, even if he didn't want to do it, he would not be able to refrain. This answer is not satisfactory for reasons we explored earlier: the freedom of one *action* cannot depend on the possibility of the agent's doing something else freely, though the extent of the *agent's* freedom might depend on such a possibility. If the agent has no wish to stop taking the drug—if he does not view himself in taking it as acting contrary to his wish, say, to be healthy, wealthy, and wise—then I should say that he exercises his freedom of spontaneity in taking it. In the typical case, where we think of an addict as acting merely from compulsion, we tacitly suppose that his appetite or need for the drug forces him to take it against his best judgment: in an obvious but difficult to clarify sense of the term "want," he does not want to do what he now wills to do. If this is right, the addict's compulsion limits the freedom of his action in a way similar to that in which an action is limited in its freedom by duress or constraint. Emotional compulsion might well be called "inner constraint or duress."

A subtle form of compulsion that deserves some comment here is present when certain people, by the force of their personality, impose their will on others. Morgan la Fay and Svengali are portrayed as imposing their will hypnotically: by mere talk and gestures they induce naive and innocent people to want what they want and to pursue ends that they favor. It is not easy to draw a line between the subtle form of compulsion they exert on others and the influence of a friend's or teacher's efforts to persuade one to do something. Clearly, we are all powerfully influenced by the words of others, but it is only when we are induced to do things against our best judgment, when we seem to lose our power of independent choice, that our freedom of action seems to be limited by the force of another's personality. The fact that a sharp line cannot be drawn between these cases and ordinary cases of persuasion does not show that there is no difference between them. No sharp line can be drawn between dawn and day, but it is absurd to think that there is no real differnce between them.

A final point to be made about spontaneously free actions is that the manner in which they are willed, intended, or chosen is crucial to them. If one does something accidentally, inadvertently, or by mistake, one does not do it of one's own free will because one did not will to do it at all. If I throw a stone and succeed in hitting what I take to be a snake but actually hit the cat's tail, then I did not (it seems reasonable to say) hit the cat of my own free will, for I did not will to hit the cat. On the other hand, I did of my own free will hit what I took to be a snake—even though what I took to be a snake *was* the cat's tail. In recent years philosophers (including myself) have devoted a good deal of attention to unraveling various puzzles that arise when one tries to spell out, in detail, just what an intentional action is, or what it is to do something intentionally.[27] For our purposes here it is enough to say that, when one does something of one's own free will, one does it intentionally; and to do something intentionally one must do what one intends to do: the manner in which one intends one's deed is crucial for its identity as something freely willed.

Although the details of a satisfactory conception of the freedom of spontaneity are difficulty to work out, the general idea is relatively clear. Normal human beings are seen as having a distinctive fund of aims or purposes, and they exercise their freedom of spontaneity when they are able to carry out those aims or purposes without outside interference. People often change their distinctive purposes, sometimes reasoning themselves into new ones; but their fundamental purposes, as Aristotle saw, are not (at least typically) freely adopted: they come to be possessed just as naturally and unreflectively as hunger, thirst, or sexual desire. Particular free actions, as the reconciler insists, may well be causally explained by reference to beliefs, motivating purposes, and the agent's habits of mind (or tendency to reason in certain ways), but the possibility of such causal explanation does not show that the actions so explained do not deserve to be considered free. Doing what we want, wish, or have the purpose of doing seems to be, in fact, the most desirable form of freedom. The contrasting freedom of indifference, which appears to encompass purposeless acts, seems on reflection to be as pointless as it is puzzling. The "freedom of spontaneity" is, of course, a practical notion, and actions may exemplify it only to this or that degree. Nevertheless, it coheres well with a plausible conception of morals as a form of social control, one that views censure or punishment as means of influencing our wills for the better.

NOTES

NOTES

□
□
□
□
□
□
□
□
□

Chapter 1. What Is Metaphysics?

1. See John Passmore, *A Hundred Years of Philosophy*, 2d ed. (Baltimore, 1966), ch. 16.

2. See J. R. Ackrill, *Aristotle the Philosopher* (Oxford, 1981), p. 116.

3. Aristotle, *Metaphysics*, Gamma (bk. 4), 1003a–1003b.

4. Ibid.

5. Ibid.; translation from W. D. Ross, ed., *Aristotle Selections* (New York, 1927), p. 53.

6. Aristotle, *Categories*, 2a11–4b19.

7. W. V. O. Quine, "On What There Is," in Quine, *From a Logical Point of View* (Cambridge, Mass., 1953), p. 3.

8. See David Lewis, *Counterfactuals* (Oxford, 1973), pp. 86–87, and *Philosophical Papers*, vol. 1 (New York, 1983), Pt. 1.

9. For Berkeley's view, see chapter 9 below; for Schopenhauer's view, see *The Philosophy of Schopenhauer*, ed. Irwin Edman (New York, 1928).

10. See Hilary Putnam, *Reason, Truth, and History* (Cambridge, Eng., 1981), and Richard Rorty, *Philosophy and the Mirror of Nature* (Princeton, 1979). Arguments to the contrary can be found in Jay Rosenberg, *One World and Our Knowledge of It* (Dordrecht, Holland, 1980). I discuss Putnam's views below: chapter 6, pp. 126–130.

11. See, for example, Baruch Spinoza, "Thoughts on Metaphysics," in *Earlier Philosophical Writings*, trans. Frank A. Hayes (Indianapolis, 1963), pp. 107–61. See also the note on "Pneumatology" in G. W. von Leibniz, *New Essays on Human Understanding*, trans. Peter Remnant and Jonathan Bennett (Cambridge, Eng., 1981), p. lxiv.

Chapter 2. Existence

1. Bertrand Russell, "The Philosophy of Logical Atomism," in *Logic and Knowledge*, ed. Robert C. Marsh (New York, 1956), p. 268.

2. See Bertrand Russell, "On Denoting," in Marsh, ibid., pp. 41–56.

3. Although I regard Russell's view on this matter as correct, some philosophers dispute it. See notes 6 and 8 below.

4. Bertrand Russell and Alfred North Whitehead, *Principia Mathematica*, 3 vols. (Cambridge, Eng., 1910–13).

5. Russell, in Marsh, *Logic and Knowledge*, p. 238.

6. As I mentioned in note 3 above, not all philosophers agree with Russell's treatment of definite descriptions. Some say, as Frege did, that if a definite description D is satisfied by a thing S, D refers to S. They add that, in cases where a definite description is not satisfied by any existing thing, the description can be assigned an arbitrary referent such as the empty set. This alternative has certain advantages for a systematic semantic theory, but it is less natural than Russell's treatment and less helpful in resolving metaphysical perplexities. I will concede that Russell's theory has some minor blemishes (I point out one in note 11 below), but no theory of descriptions is free of them. For a comparison of Russell's theory with some well-known alternatives, see David Kaplan, "What

is Russell's Theory of Descriptions?'' in *Bertrand Russell: A Collection of Critical Essays*, ed. D. F. Pears (Garden City, N.Y., 1972), pp. 227–44.

7. See "The Philosophy of Logical Atomism," in Marsh, *Logic and Knowledge*, p. 250.

8. Keith Donnellan has pointed out that one may use a definite description to refer to a person who does not satisfy that description, as when, thinking that George is Mary's husband, one refers to George by the words "Mary's husband." As I see it, this observation exposes no defect in Russell's theory. Strictly speaking, if Mary has no husband, one who says that her husband is bald is saying something false, for this statement implies that Mary has a husband. Of course, such a speaker may be saying something true as well—namely, that a certain person is bald. Russell's theory is concerned with the literal import of sentences containing definite descriptions; it is not concerned with the various actions (e.g., referring and characterizing) that may be performed by a person who uses such a sentence, or by the intentions such a person may have. Russell emphasizes this last point in "Mr Strawson on Referring," in Bertrand Russell, *My Philosophical Development* (London, 1959), pp. 238–45. See also Saul Kripke, "Speaker's Reference and Semantic Reference," in Peter French et al., *Contemporary Perspectives in the Philosophy of Language* (Minneapolis, 1979), pp. 6–27; and, in the same volume, Keith Donnellan, "Speaker Reference, Descriptions, and Anaphora," pp. 28–44.

9. Lewis Carroll, *Through the Looking Glass*, ch. 7, "The Lion and the Unicorn."

10. See John M. Robinson, *An Introduction to Early Greek Philosophy* (New York, 1968), p. 110.

11. In speaking of the present king of France as a logical fiction, Russell seems to assimilate definite descriptions to singular terms such as "the average plumber." Although this assimilation is a mistake, Russell does not thereby err in thinking that both kinds of terms are "incomplete symbols." See note 3 above.

12. Bertrand Russell, *Problems of Philosophy* (London, 1912), ch. 9.

13. Bertrand Russell, *Introduction to Mathematical Philosophy* (London, 1919).

14. In a well-known article, "What Numbers Could Not Be," *Philosophical Review* 74 (1965): 47–73, Paul Benacerraf objected to Russell's interpretation of numbers on the ground, roughly, that entities of many different kinds have properties with the abstract structure of the natural numbers and that the classes Russell specified are not better candidates for numbers than these other objects. I think Russell could reply along the lines suggested here: classes do the job and they minimize the mystery. The metaphysical task is to provide a suitable interpretation; it is not necessary to show that no other interpretation—no other way of mimimizing the mystery—is possible.

15. See Rudolf Carnap, *Meaning and Necessity*, 2d ed. (Chicago, 1956), pp. 147–52.

16. For a thorough discussion of ontological reductionism, see Daniel A. Bonevac, *Reduction in the Abstract Sciences* (Indianapolis, 1982).

17. Russell, "Philosophy of Logical Atomism," pp. 232–54.

18. Ibid., p. 241.

19. Ibid., p. 201.

20. Ibid., p. 232.

21. See ibid., pp. 232–33.

22. A model M for a language L is an ordered couple $<D,V>$ where D is a domain of objects and V is a function that assigns semantical values based on D to the expressions of L. A formula "$(\exists x)(Fx)$" is said to be true with respect to M just when, for some V' that assigns to all variables except "x" the same values in D as V does, the value of "Fx" with respect to V' is 1 (or True). See, for example, G. H. Hughes and M. J. Cresswell, *An Introduction to Modal Logic* (London, 1968), pp. 135–36.

23. See Nuel Belnap and J. Michael Dunn, "The Substitution Interpretation of Quantifiers," *Nous* 2 (1968): 177–85.

24. See Bertrand Russell, *Human Knowledge: Its Scope and Limits* (London, 1948), p. 468.

25. For a discussion of such views, see Alvin Plantinga, *The Nature of Necessity* (Oxford, 1974), chs. 7 and 8, and also David Lewis, *Counterfactuals* (Oxford, 1973), pp. 84–91, and *Philosophical*

Papers, vol. 1 (Oxford, 1983), Pt. 1. Both writers believe that *there are* possible though nonactual worlds. Plantinga denies that there are possible but nonactual particular things; Lewis does not.

26. Russell, *Human Knowledge*, p. 468.

27. See W. V. O. Quine, "Existence and Quantification," in Quine, *Ontological Relativity and Other Essays* (New York, 1969), pp. 106–8. A number of philosophers have claimed that substitutional quantification is objectionable on logical grounds; Saul Kripke has effectively refuted such claims in "Is There a Problem about Substitutional Quantification?" in *Truth and Meaning: Essays in Semantics*, ed. Gareth Evans and John McDowell (Oxford, 1976), pp. 325–419.

28. See Saul Kripke, *Naming and Necessity* (Cambridge, Mass., 1980), pp. 91–97.

29. See Immanuel Kant, *Inaugural Dissertation and Other Writings on Space*, trans. John Handyside (London, 1929), pp. 38–42.

30. Russell, "The Philosophy of Logical Atomism," p. 222.

31. See David Hume, *Enquiry Concerning the Human Understanding*, sec. 4, pt. 1.

32. Plato, *Sophist*, 248c; trans. F. M. Cornford in *The Collected Dialogues of Plato*, ed. Edith Hamilton and Huntington Cairns (New York, 1961), p. 993.

33. See Immanuel Kant, *Critique of Pure Reason*, 2d ed., trans. N. K. Smith (London, 1933), B263, B272–74.

34. C. S. Peirce, "What Pragmatism Is," in *Charles S. Peirce: Selected Writings*, ed. Philip P. Weiner (New York, 1966), p. 197.

Chapter 3. Universals and Particulars

1. See Plato, *Phaedo*, 96 and 101, *Theaetetus*, 154c–155c; in *The Collected Dialogues of Plato* ed. Edith Hamilton and Huntington Cairns (New York, 1961), pp. 78, 82, 859–60. Also see G. W. von Leibniz, *The Leibniz-Clarke Correspondence*, ed. H. G. Alexander (Manchester, 1956), p. 71.

2. Ludwig Wittgenstein, *Philosophical Investigations*, trans. G. E. M. Anscombe (Oxford, 1953), pp. 31–35.

3. This view is defended by David Armstrong in *Universals and Scientific Realism*: vol. 1, *Nominalism and Realism*; vol. 2, *A Theory of Universals* (Cambridge, Eng., 1978).

4. Alan Donagan, "Metaphysical Realism," in *Universals and Particulars*, ed. Michael J. Loux (Garden City, N.Y., 1970), pp. 138–39.

5. John Locke, *An Essay Concerning Human Understanding*, ed. A. G. Fraser, vol. I (Oxford, 1984), p. 392.

6. *Encyclopedia Brittanica* (1970), article on "Transubstantiation."

7. Armstrong, *Universals*, vol. 1, pp. 113–15.

8. Ibid., pp. 118–19.

9. Ibid., p. 114.

10. Bertrand Russell, *Human Knowledge: Its Scope and Limits* (London, 1948), p. 312.

11. In fact, the pincushion theory renders *everything* utterly mysterious. If, as subjects of predicates, particulars are mysterious x's in which universals inhere, then universals, since they too are subjects of predicates, are also (by parity of reasoning) mysterious x's in which other x's inhere—and so on without end.

12. See Bertrand Russell, *The Problems of Philosophy* (London, 1912), ch. 12.

13. Bertrand Russell, "The Philosophy of Logical Atomism," in *Logic and Knowledge*, ed. Robert C. Marsh (New York, 1956), p. 220.

14. Ludwig Wittgenstein, *Tractatus Logico-Philosophicus*, trans. C. K. Ogden (London, 1922), p. 31.

15. Wilfrid Sellars, "Naming and Saying" and "Truth and "Correspondence"", in *Sellars, Science, Perception, and Reality* (New York, 1964), pp. 225–46 and 197–24.

16. My remarks are based on the selections in Richard McKeon, ed., *Selections from the Medieval Philosophers*, vol. 1 (New York, 1929), pp. 232–58.

17. For a criticism of the view that concepts are formed by abstraction, see Peter T. Geach, *Mental Acts* (London, 1957), pp. 18–38.

Chapter 4. Linguistic Arguments for Abstracta

1. See D. M. Armstrong, *Universals and Scientific Realism*: vol. 1, *Nominalism and Realism* (Cambridge, 1978), pp. 58–63. See also Michael J. Loux, *Substance and Attribute* (Dordrecht, Holland, 1978).

2. St. Augustine, *The Confessions*, trans. Edward Pusey (New York, 1952), p. 224.

3. The assertion that anyone who is honest is virtuous (or in a way virtuous) has the logical form of a universally quantified conditional. The conditionality involved is not truth-functional, however, since the assertion would not be rendered true if no one happened to be honest. The idea, rather, is that if anyone were honest, he or she would be virtuous (at least in a way). The need for a stronger kind of conditionality can also be seen by the fact that, if every honest person happened to be short, it would not follow that honesty is (or involves) being short. See note 14 below.

4. See A. N. Prior, *Objects of Thought* (Oxford, 1971), ch. 3, and Wilfrid Sellars, *Naturalism and Ontology* (Reseda, Calif., 1979), ch. 2.

5. See above, chapter 2, pp. 30–32

6. W. V. O. Quine, "Existence and Quantification," in Quine, *From a Logical Point of View* (Cambridge, Mass., 1969), pp. 91–113.

7. W. V. O. Quine, "On What There Is," in ibid., pp. 1–19.

8. Ibid.

9. See above, chapter 2, p. 32.

10. See Bertrand Russell, *Human Knowledge: Its Scope and Limits* (London, 1948), p. 468.

11. I take the term "indirect quotation" from Nelson Goodman; see his *Ways of Worldmaking* (Indianapolis, 1978), p. 42.

12. My view on this point is indebted to Wilfrid Sellars; see his *Naturalism and Ontology*, ch. 4.

13. See W. V. O. Quine, *Word and Object* (Cambridge, Mass., 1960), p. 195.

14. I comment on subjunctive conditionals below; see chapter 6, p. 123.

15. See Sellars, *Naturalism and Ontology*, ch. 4.

16. See chapter 7, pp. 141–149, for an extended discussion of meaning and truth-conditions. My remarks here are deliberately oversimplified, though adequate for the task at hand.

17. See W. V. O. Quine, "Ontological Relativity," in *Ontological Relativity and Other Essays* (New York, 1969), pp. 26–68. I offer an interpretation of Quine's argument in "Quine on Translation and Reference," *Philosophical Studies*, 27 (1975): 221–36.

18. I have discussed this at some length in *Reason and Action* (Dordrecht, Holland, 1977), ch. 2. My views on the subject are indebted to Wilfrid Sellars; see his account in *Science and Metaphysics* (New York, 1968), ch. 6.

19. See, for example, John B. Opdycke, *Harper's English Grammar* (New York, 1965), p. 166.

20. Roughly speaking, a possibility *de dicto* is affirmed by a statement of the form "It is possible that *p*"; a possibility *de re* is affirmed by a statement of the form "Thing *S* is possibly *F*." See note 22 below.

21. See Alvin Plantinga, *The Nature of Necessity* (Oxford, 1974), ch. 1, and David Lewis, *Counterfactuals* (Oxford, 1973), ch. 4, or *Philosophical Papers*, vol. 1 (Oxford, 1983), pt. 1. The most important recent discussion of possible worlds can be found in Saul Kripke, *Naming and Necessity* (Cambridge, Mass., 1980).

22. A standard text on modal logic is G. H. Hughes and M. J. Cresswell, *An Introduction to Modal Logic* (London, 1968).

23. Various qualifications are required for these definitions. For example, the notion of formal consistency makes sense only by reference to some system of logic. For my purposes, the relevant system can be understood as any standard first-order quantification theory with identity.

24. My definitions do not show one how to deal with various kinds of *de re* possibilities. The standard strategy for clarifying such possibilities is to refer to possible worlds: a thing *S* is possibly *F* just when *S* is *F* in some possible world *W*. Yet the notion of a possible world presupposes some conception of possibility, for we can conceive of "worlds" as being logically possible, conceptually possible, or physically possible. If a logically possible world is one whose description is formally consistent, then *de re* logical possibilities are to be analyzed in accordance with my definition 1. As for the "metaphysical possibilities" that philosophers sometimes speak of, I should say that they

make sense only as conceptual possibilities. If, for example, we assign the name "Socrates" to a certain *man*, then our definition of "man" assures us that there is no world (or imagined situation) in which Socrates is a squirrel and that Socrates is not, therefore, possibly a squirrel. I discuss this point further in chapter 5, pp. 79–82.

25. For relevant case histories of great interest, see Horace Freeland Judson's remarkable account of the recent revolution in molecular biology, *The Eighth Day of Creation* (New York, 1979).

26. The technical difficulties I allude to are based on Gödel's incompleteness theorems. See Geoffrey Hellman, "How to Gödel a Frege-Russell: Gödel's Incompleteness Theorems and Logicism," *Nous* 15 (1981): 451–68.

27. See Hilary Putnam, "Mathematics without Foundations," in Putnam, *Mathematics, Matter, and Method* (Cambridge, Eng., 1975), pp. 43–59, and Michael Jubien, "Intensional Foundations of Mathematics," *Nous* 15 (1981): 513–29. An interesting alternative approach to mathematics is that of intuitionism; see Michael Dummett, "The Philosophical Basis of Intuitionist Logic,' in Dummett, *Truth and Other Enigmas* (Cambridge, Mass., 1978), pp. 215–47.

Chapter 5. Changing Things

1. Aristotle, *Categories*, 4b15–19.

2. Bertrand Russell, *A History of Western Philosophy* (New York, 1945), pp. 200–201. The view Russell was trying to express here has been nicely put by P. T. Geach: "We may say that the proper name conveys a *nominal essence*; thus, 'cat' expresses the nominal essence of the thing we call 'Jemina', and Jemina's corpse will not be Jemina any more than it will be a cat," *Reference and Generality* (Ithaca, N.Y., 1962), p. 44.

3. Russell, *A History*, pp. 201–2. The quotation in the following paragraph of this text also has this source.

4. See Geach, *Reference and Generality*, p. 39.

5. For a discussion of essential features and possible worlds, see Saul Kripke, *Naming and Necessity* (Cambridge, Mass., 1980), Nathan U. Salmon, *Reference and Essence* (Princeton, 1981), and Hilary Putnam, *Reason, Truth, and History* (Cambridge, Eng., 1981), especially pp. 46–48, where Putnam takes essentially the position I take here.

6. Gottlob Frege, "On Sense and Reference," in *Translations from the Philosophical Writings of Gottlob Frege*, ed. Peter Geach and Max Black (Oxford, 1952), pp. 56–78.

7. My statement of Leibniz's Law runs together two principles known as the Identity of Indiscernibles and Indiscernibility of Identicals.

8. Thomas Hobbes, *Elements of Philosophy*, in *The English Works of Thomas Hobbes*, ed. Sir W. Molesworth (London, 1839–45), vol. 1 (1839), ch. 11, secs. 1–2 and 7.

9. Joseph Butler, *The Analogy of Religion*, First Appendix (1736); his remarks on personal identity are reprinted in John Perry, ed., *Personal Identity* (Berkeley, Calif., 1975), pp. 99–105. My remarks in the text pertain to p. 101.

10. John Locke, *An Essay Concerning Human Understanding*, ed. A. C. Fraser, vol. 1 (Oxford, 1894), p. 448.

11. Ibid., p. 446.

12. Ibid., pp. 445–46.

13. Locke did not, of course, attempt to answer the specific questions I pose here, but the answer I give is in the spirit of Locke's view. See ibid., p. 449.

14. Ibid., pp. 460–61.

15. Corbet H. Thigpen and Hervey M. Cleckley, *The Three Faces of Eve* (New York, 1951).

16. Joseph Butler, in Perry, *Personal Identity*, p. 100.

17. See W. V. O. Quine and J. S. Ulian, *The Web of Belief*, 2d ed. (New York, 1978), chs. 6 and 9. See also ch. 8, n. 37.

18. See René Descartes, *Meditation VI*, in *Philosophical Works of Descartes*, ed. E. S. Haldane and G. R. T. Ross, vol. 1, (Cambridge, Eng., 1911), p. 192.

19. Descartes' arguments occur mainly in *Meditations II* and *VI*; see ibid., vol. 1, pp. 149–57 and 185–99.

20. Descartes, in ibid., vol. 1, p. 190.

21. I give a critical exposition of the most important of Descartes' arguments for the existence of God in my book, *Rationalism, Empiricism, and Pragmatism* (New York, 1970), ch. 1.

22. Descartes, in *Philosophical Works*, vol. 1, pp. 151–52.

23. Ibid., vol. 1, p. 191.

24. Ibid., p. 196.

25. See R. W. Sperry, "Forebrain Commissurotomy and Conscious Awareness," *Journal of Medicine and Philosophy* 2, no. 2 (June 1977): 102.

26. Ibid.

27. Ibid.

28. Plato, *The Republic*, 442c, 580d.

Chapter 6. Worlds, Objects, and Structure

1. See Bertrand Russell, *Human Knowledge: Its Scope and Limits* (London, 1948), pp. 97–98, and Rudolf Carnap, *An Introduction to Symbolic Logic and Its Applications* (New York, 1958), pp. 197–216.

2. Russell, *Human Knowledge*, pp. 284–94, and "On Order in Time," in *Logic and Knowledge*, ed. Robert C. Marsh (New York, 1956), pp. 345–64.

3. See "On Order in Time," ibid.

4. Russell, *Human Knowledge*, pp. 305–9.

5. Although the analysis I offer is my own, I got the idea of using temporal connectives from Wilfrid Sellars's "Time and the World Order," in *Minnesota Studies in the Philosophy of Science*, ed. Herbert Feigl and Grover Maxwell, vol. 3 (Minneapolis, 1962), pp. 527–618. A similar strategy has been suggested, but not developed, by Peter Geach: see his "Some Problems about Time," in Geach, *Logic Matters* (Oxford, 1972), pp. 302–18, and *Truth, Love, and Immortality: An Introduction to McTaggart's Philosophy* (Berkeley, Calif., 1979), p. 96. See also G. E. M. Anscombe, "Before and After," in Anscombe, *Collected Papers*, vol. 2 (Minneapolis, 1981), pp. 180–95.

6. My procedure here requires us to think of action statements as expressible in the awkward form of "*S* does move," "*S* does snap *S*'s fingers," etc. A more natural procedure would be to interpret "*S* does something" by the formula "$(\exists F)(S\,F)$", where the bound variable takes appropriately tensed action predicates as substituends. I have not adopted this more natural procedure (in which the complex expression "does something" does the work of a substitutionally quantified predicate variable) because the core formula "*S F*" will be confusing to most readers. An alternative such as "$(\exists F)(F(S))$" would have been possible, but I wanted my formulas to look as simple and readable as I could make them.

7. The statements resulting from the elimination of expressions apparently referring to times, dates, and motions will be far more complicated than those in the text if one employs the smallest possible primitive vocabulary. In the interests of avoiding such complexity I have not attempted to do this. Conceptual economy is generally a good thing, but it is not always necessary or even desirable in metaphysics, when a less austere vocabulary does not introduce a new category of entity.

8. See P. F. Strawson, *Individuals* (London, 1959), pp. 38–40.

9. See Nelson Goodman, *Ways of Worldmaking* (Indianapolis, 1979), ch. 1. In "Time and the World Order," pp. 593–95, Wilfrid Sellars claims that an ontology of events is not only a legitimate alternative to an ontology of things but may be, for scientific purposes, a preferred alternative.

10. See Alfred North Whitehead, *The Concept of Nature* (London, 1920), pp. 85–86. Russell's analysis of points is given in *Human Knowledge*, pp. 294–304.

11. Donald Davidson, "Causal Relations," *Journal of Philosophy* 64 (1967): 691–703; reprinted in Davidson, *Essays on Actions and Events* (Oxford, 1980), pp. 149–62.

12. In my book *Reason and Action* (Dordrecht, Holland, 1978), p. 105, I develop Davidson's suggestion in a way that accords with the interpretation of *that*-clauses that Davidson develops in his article "On Saying That," which is reprinted in Davidson, *Inquiries into Truth and Interpretation* (Oxford, 1984), pp. 93–108. My idea was that the specimen sentence 3 can be interpreted by the complex formula: "*that*₁ is true & *that*₂ is *true* & *CE*(*that*₁, *that*₂). The bolt gave way so suddenly. The thing in question (the bridge, perhaps) collapsed." The *that*'s in the formula refer,

respectively, to the sentences appearing at the end of the formula. This way of interpreting the specimen sentence is neater and more elegant than the one I adopt in the text, but it involves a controversial treatment of *that*-clauses.

13. In "Causal Relations" Davidson developed an argument against nonevent analyses of singular causal statements that might appear to refute the analysis I offer here. But Davidson's argument is not satisfactory, as I demonstrate in *Reason and Action*, pp. 37–44.

14. See Carl G. Hempel, *Aspects of Scientific Explanation and Other Essays in the Philosophy of Science* (New York, 1965), pp. 488–89.

15. This point has been emphasized by Hempel, ibid., see pp. 463–86. See also my *Reason and Action*, pp. 75, 81–82.

16. See David Hume, *Enquiry Concerning the Human Understanding*, sec. 7.

17. See *The Encyclopedia of Philosophy*, ed. Paul Edwards (New York, 1967), article on "Laws of Science and Lawlike Statements."

18. See C. S. Peirce, "The Laws of Nature and Hume's Argument against Miracles," in *Charles S. Peirce: Selected Writings*, ed. Philip P. Wiener (New York, 1958), pp. 289–321.

19. See C. S. Peirce, "Grounds of Validity of the Laws of Logic: Further Consequences of Four Incapacities," in *Collected Papers of Charles Sanders Peirce*, ed. Charles Hartshorne and Paul Weiss (Cambridge, Mass., 1934), pp. 190–222. (See especially p. 342.)

20. See David Lewis, *Counterfactuals* (Oxford, 1973), pp. 73–75.

21. Aristotle, *Posterior Analytics*, 99b17–100b17.

22. See William Kneale, *Probability and Induction* (Oxford, 1949), p. 80.

23. Hume, *Enquiry*, sec. 7.

24. See C. S. Peirce, "Laws of Nature and Hume's Argument against Miracles." Peirce himself rejected the Occamist conception, however, saying that the lawful behavior of objects could not be an "ultimate fact" about them. As I see it, Peirce was simply mistaken on this point.

25. Our means of confirming natural "laws" supports the Humean contention that the idea of natural necessity is reasonably viewed as a mere expression of our attitude toward natural regularities. The idea that A's are necessarily B's does not warrant any predictions that are not warranted by the simpler idea that A's are invariably B's. Thus, a sound inductive methodology should require one to reject a stronger, or more substantive, interpretation of such necessity.

26. One of the first to defend this view was Gilbert Ryle, who coined the term "inference ticket"; see Ryle, " 'If,' 'So,' and 'Because'," in *Philosophical Analysis*, ed. Max Black (Ithaca, N.Y., 1950), pp. 323–40. Wilfrid Sellars also defended this view in an early essay which, in spite of subsequent developments in his thinking, is still one of my favorites: "Some Reflections on Language Games," reprinted in Sellars, *Science, Perception, and Reality* (New York, 1963), pp. 321–58. Other writers holding some version of the view are cited in Lewis, *Counterfactuals*, p. 65.

27. See Lewis, *Counterfactuals*, ch. 1.

28. See Bas Van Frassen, *The Scientific Image* (Oxford, 1980), ch. 1. For arguments in favor of a qualified scientific realism, see Ian Hacking's highly readable and instructive recent book, *Representing and Intervening: Introductory Topics in the Philosophy of Natural Science* (Cambridge, Eng., 1983).

29. Albert Einstein, "On the Electrodynamics of Moving Bodies," *Annalen der Physik* 17 (1905): 891–93.

30. Strawson, *Individuals*, pp. 38–40.

31. For remarks in support of this claim, see Sellars, "Time and the World Order."

32. See Bertrand Russell, *Analysis of Matter* (London, 1927), p. 287.

33. See Hilary Putnam, *Reason, Truth, and History* (Cambridge, Eng., 1981), especially ch. 3, and *Collected Papers*, vol. 3 (Cambridge, Eng., 1983). My quotations from Putnam are taken from *Reason, Truth, and History*, p. 59.

34. As Peirce emphasized, the word "real" (*realis* or *realitas*) was invented as a philosophical term in the thirteenth century; it was intended to apply to that "which has such and such characters, whether anybody thinks it to have those characters or not." Thus, real things are contrasted with things that are merely imagined or dreamed of. See Peirce, "What Pragmatism Is," in Wiener, *Charles S. Peirce: Selected Writings*, p. 198.

35. G. W. von Leibniz, *New Essays on Human Understanding*, ed. Peter Remnant and Jonathan Bennett (Cambridge, England, 1981), p. 311.

36. Biologically, reptiles make up a highly artificial class. Turtles and snakes are both reptiles while birds are not; yet turtles are genetically much closer to birds than to snakes (as determined by their DNA). See John Gribbin and Jeremy Cherfas, *The Monkey Puzzle* (New York, 1983), p. 93.

37. See chapter 5, pp. 79-82. Putnam argues in favor of substantially the same view in *Reason, Truth, and History*, pp. 51-53.

Chapter 7. Meaning, Truth, and Metaphysics

1. Gottlob Frege, "On Sense and Reference," in *Translations from the Philosophical Writings of Gottlob Frege*, ed. Max Black and Peter Geach (Oxford, 1952), p. 77.

2. See Donald Davidson, "Causal Relations," *Journal of Philosophy* 64 (1967): 691-703; reprinted in Davidson, *Essays on Actions and Events* (Oxford, 1982), pp. 149-62.

3. Rudolf Carnap, "Meaning Postulates," in Carnap, *Meaning and Necessity*, 2nd ed. (Chicago, 1956), pp. 222-29.

4. Donald Davidson, "The Logical Form of Action Sentences," in *The Logic of Decision and Action*, ed. Nicholas Rescher (Pittsburgh, 1967), pp. 81-95. Reprinted with replies to critics in Davidson, *Essays on Action and Events*, pp. 105-48.

5. Romane Clark, "Concerning the Logic of Predicate Modifiers," *Nous* 4 (1970): 311-35.

6. See above, chapter 3, pp. 52-54.

7. See A. C. Ewing, *Idealism: A Critical Survey* (London, 1934), ch. 5.

8. C. S. Peirce, *Collected Papers of Charles Sanders Peirce*, ed. Charles Hartshorne and Paul Weiss (Cambridge, Mass., 1934), 5.494 (pp. 343-44).

9. See Ewing, *Idealism*, ch. 5.

10. This is acknowledged by Nicholas Rescher in his critical study, *The Coherence Theory of Truth* (Oxford, 1973), p. 24.

11. See Donald Davidson, "True to the Facts," *Journal of Philosophy* 66 (1969): 748-64; reprinted in Davidson, *Inquiries into Truth and Interpretation* (Oxford, 1984), pp. 37-54.

12. Alfred Tarski, "The Concept of Truth in Formalized Languages," in *Logic, Semantics, and Metamathematics*, ed. J. H. Woodger, 2d ed. (Indianapolis, 1983), pp. 152-278. A popular exposition of Tarski's theory is given in Tarski's article, "The Semantic Conception of Truth and the Foundations of Semantics," in *Readings in Philosophical Analysis*, ed. Herbert Feigl and Wilfrid Sellars (New York, 1949), pp. 52-84. In later years Tarski defined a more general concept of truth in a model; for an especially clear explanation of his procedure, see the article "Semantics" by Donald Kalish in *The Encyclopedia of Philosophy*, ed. Paul Edwards, vol. 7 (New York, 1967), pp. 351-52.

13. A truth-definition not requiring Tarski's distinction between object language and metalanguage is discussed by Saul Kripke, "Outline of a Theory of Truth," *Journal of Philosophy* 70 (1975): 690-716. Another such discussion can be found in Anil Gupta, "Truth and Paradox," *Journal of Philosophical Logic* 2 (1982): 1-60.

14. As Tarski explains, a recursive definition in which "is true in L1" occurs in the definiens can be converted into an explicit definition in which the truth-predicate occurs only in the definiendum. See Tarski, "The Concept of Truth in Formalized Languages," p. 193. This point is explained in a simpler way by W. V. O. Quine in *Philosophy of Logic* (Englewood Cliffs, N.J., 1970), pp. 42-43.

15. See Tarski, "The Concept of Truth in Formalized Languages," pp. 200-201.

16. Since a true statement is defined by Tarski as a statement satisfying all sequences, the sequence $<a,b>$ is said to satisfy "$(\exists x)(\exists y)(x$ is taller than $y)$" if either a is taller than b or there is another sequence $<d,e>$ such that d is taller than e. In the latter case $<a,b>$ would satisfy the formula because, intuitively speaking, it is such that something is taller than something else. This technicality is nicely explained by Quine in *Philosophy of Logic*, p. 38.

17. See Donald Davidson, "Truth and Meaning," *Synthese* 17 (1967): 304-23; reprinted in

Davidson, *Inquiries, pp. 17–36 (see especially p. 25). For an important qualification to the claims in this paragraph, see note 33 below.*

18. See Davidson, "Belief and the Basis of Meaning," *Inquiries*, p. 150.

19. Ibid.

20. See Davidson, "Radical Interpretation" and "Belief and the Basis of Meaning," in *Inquiries*, pp. 134 and 152 respectively.

21. See Hilary Putnam, *Reason, Truth, and History* (Cambridge, Eng., 1981), Appendix and pp. 32–38.

22. See Davidson, "Belief and the Basis of Meaning," *Inquiries*, p. 150.

23. See Davidson, "On the Very Idea of a Conceptual Scheme," *Inquiries*, p. 197.

24. This can be proved as follows. If Karl is present in a region R where it is raining, then it is true both that it is raining in R if Karl is there and that Karl is there if it is raining there—from which it follows that it is zaining there. The validity of this proof depends on the fact that the relevant *if*'s are to be interpreted (as I intend them to be) truth-functionally.

25. See Michael Dummett, "What Is a Theory of Meaning? (II)," in *Truth and Meaning*, ed. Gareth Evans and J. M. McDowell (Oxford, 1976), pp. 67–137.

26. I clarify this point in the section to follow.

27. Quoted in Davidson, "Reply to Foster," *Inquiries*, p. 174.

28. Peirce, *Collected Papers*, 5.448.

29. Ibid.

30. For more on the relation between meaning and inference, see my paper, "On an Analytic-Synthetic Distinction," *American Philosophical Quarterly* 9 (1972): 235–42. In this paper I argue that the inferences that unpack a statement's meaning should be understood as "immediate" inferences.

31. J. L. Austin, *Sense and Sensibilia* (Oxford, 1963), p. 121.

32. See W. V. O. Quine, *Word and Object* (Cambridge, Mass., 1960), ch. 2.

33. See Davidson, "Reply to Foster," p. 178–79. In this paper Davidson emphasizes that, properly speaking, *T*-sentences provide interpretations for utterances rather than translations. His reason for this is that some *T*-sentences have the complex form of "For all speakers x of L and all times t, S is true spoken by x at t if and only if the object demonstrated by x at t is F." It is obvious that the formula on the right-hand side of such a *T*-sentence is not a "translation" of the sentence mentioned on the left-hand side.

34. See Davidson, "On Saying That," in *Inquiries*, pp. 101–2.

35. I offer an exposition of Quine's argument for translational indeterminacy in "Quine on Translation and Reference," *Philosophical Studies* 27 (1975): 221–36.

36. For a discussion of various "sociobiological" facts about human nature, see Edward O. Wilson, *On Human Nature* (Cambridge, Mass., 1978).

37. See Davidson, "Reply to Foster," *Inquiries*, p. 174.

38. In "Causal Relations," Davidson says that the values of the relevant variables are numbers, but such numbers must be related to temporal intervals by some dating function, $t(y) = x$.

39. Although standard criticisms of analytic truth such as Quine's rely on the premise that the notion of synonymy is too unclear to yield an acceptable account of analyticity, Peirce argued in 1903 that the notion of synonymy (or the meaning of a term) should be "fixed" by reference to what we regard as "necessary reasoning' (or, one might add, primitive analytic truths). He said that "we shall do well to accept Kant's dictum that necessary reasoning is merely explicative of the meaning of the terms of the premisses, only reversing the use he made of it." Instead of adopting a certain conception of meaning and using the dictum to express what necessary reasoning can do, we should use the dictum to "fix our ideas as to what we shall understand by the *meaning* of a term." See Peirce, *Collected Papers*, 5.175. Quine's famous criticism of the analytic-synthetic distinction can be found in his "Two Dogmas of Empiricism," in W. V. O. Quine, *From a Logical Point of View* (Cambridge, Mass., 1953), pp. 20–46. Gottlob Frege's conception of analytic truth is expounded in his book, *The Foundations of Arithmetic*, trans. J. L. Austin (Oxford, 1950), pp. 99–104.

40. I discuss this point in "On An Analytic-Synthetic Distinction."

41. See Michael Dummett, "Realism," *Synthese* 52 (1982): 59.

Chapter 8. Appearance and Reality

1. David Hume, *Enquiry Concerning the Human Understanding*, in *Enquiries Concerning the Human Understanding and Concerning the Principles of Morals*, ed. L. A. Selby-Bigge, 2d ed. (Oxford, 1902), p. 152.

2. See G. A. Paul, "Is There a Problem about Sense Data?" in *Logic and Language: First Series*, ed. A. G. N. Flew (Oxford, 1951), pp. 101–16.

3. John Locke, *An Essay Concerning Human Understanding*, ed. A. C. Fraser, vol. 1 (Oxford, 1894), pp. 169–70.

4. See Maurice Mandelbaum, *Philosophy, Science, and Sense Perception* (Baltimore, 1964), ch. 1.

5. Nicholas Malbranche, *De la recherche de la verite*, bk. 3, pt. 2, ch. 1; English translation in Walter Kaufmann, *Philosophical Classics: Bacon to Kant* (Englewood Cliffs, N.J., 1961), p. 235.

6. George Berkeley, *Principles of Human Knowledge* and *Three Dialogues between Hylas and Philonous*, in *The Empiricists* (Garden City, N.Y., n.d.), pp. 135–216 and 217–306.

7. See Bertrand Russell, *A History of Western Philosophy* (New York, 1945), p. 648.

8. G. E. Moore, "A Refutation of Idealism," in Moore, *Philosophical Studies* (London, 1922), pp. 1–30.

9. Thomas Hobbes, *De Corpore*, *The English Works of Thomas Hobbes*, ed. Sir W. Molesworth (London, 1830–45), vol. 1 (1839), ch. 25.

10. René Descartes, *The Principles of Philosophy*, Principle XVI, in *Philosophical Works of Descartes*, ed. E. S. Haldane and G. R. T. Ross, vol. 1 (Cambridge, Eng., 1911), p. 262.

11. David Hume, *A Treatise of Human Nature*, ed. L. A. Selby-Bigge (Oxford, 1888), bk. 1, pt. 4, sec. 6, 252–53.

12. Hume, *Enquiry*, sec. 7, pp. 149–65.

13. Ibid., p. 32.

14. See Bertrand Russell, *Our Knowledge of the External World* (London, 1914), ch. 3.

15. See A. J. Ayer, "Phenomenalism," in Ayer, *Philosophical Essays* (London, 1954), pp. 125–66.

16. See, for example, Roderick Chisholm, "The Problem of Empiricism," *Journal of Philosophy* 40 (1948); reprinted in *Meaning and Knowledge*, ed. Ernest Nagel and Richard B. Brandt, (New York, 1965), pp. 576–80.

17. See G. W. von Leibniz, *The Monadology*, in Leibniz, *Discourse on Metaphysics, Correspondence with Arnauld, Monadology*, trans. George Montgomery (La Salle, Ill., 1979), pp. 251–72.

18. Immanuel Kant, *Critique of Pure Reason*, 2d ed., trans. N. K. Smith (London, 1933).

19. Kant, *Critique of Pure Reason*, B130–87.

20. Ibid.

21. Ibid., A95.

22. Ibid., B433–599.

23. Ibid., B130–87.

24. Ibid., B176–87.

25. Ibid., B305.

26. Ibid., B275–79.

27. Ibid., B305.

28. G. W. F. Hegel, *Phenomenology of Mind*, trans. J. B. Baille (London, 1931).

29. John Stuart Mill, *Examination of Sir William Hamilton's Philosophy* (London, 1865), chs. 11, 12; reprinted in *British Empirical Philosophers*, ed. A. J. Ayer and Raymond Winch, (London, 1952), pp. 545–60.

30. Karl Marx, "Theses on Feuerbach," in *Ludwig Feuerbach*, ed. Friedrich Engels (New York, 1941), pp. 82–84.

31. Edmund Husserl, *Ideas: General Introduction to Pure Phenomenology*, trans. W. Boyce

Gibson (New York, 1931), secs. 27 and 30; Wilfrid Sellars, "Philosophy and the Scientific Image of Man," in Sellars, *Science, Perception, and Reality* (London, 1963), pp. 1–40.

32. Hume, *Enquiry*, p. 32.

33. Another standard name is "introduction by simple enumeration." See Bertrand Russell, *Human Knowledge: Its Scope and Limits* (London, 1948), pp. 419–24.

34. Hume, *Enquiry*, p. 32.

35. Russell, *Human Knowledge*, p. 422.

36. Nelson Goodman, *Fact, Fiction, and Forecast*, 2d ed. (Cambridge, Mass., 1965), pp. 59–83.

37. I have discussed the method in a general way in my book *Rationalism, Empiricism, and Pragmatism* (New York, 1970), pp. 153–78. For further discussion see (in order of difficulty) Wesley Salmon, *The Foundations of Scientific Inference* (Pittsburgh, 1967), pp. 108–32 and 142–44; Clark Glymour, *Theory and Evidence* (Princeton, 1980), chs. 1–5; and John Earman, ed., *Testing Scientific Theories: Minnesota Studies in the Philosophy of Science*, vol. 10 (Minneapolis, 1983).

38. Leibniz, *The Monadology*, par. 17, in *Discourse on Metaphysics*, p. 254.

39. Descartes, "Discourse on Method," in *Philosophical Works*, vol. 1, p. 116.

40. Ibid.

41. Benedict de Spinoza, *Ethics*, pt. 4, trans. W. H. White (New York, 1949), pp. 187–251.

42. A popular interpretation of mental phenomena that is neither explicitly materialist nor Cartesian is that of "functionalism." This interpretation is discussed critically by Hilary Putnam, who first proposed it, in Putnam, *Reason, Truth, and History* (Cambridge, Eng., 1981), ch. 4.

43. See Paul E. Meehl and Wilfrid Sellars, "The Concept of Emergence," in *Minnesota Studies in the Philosophy of Science*, ed. Herbert Feigl and Michael Scriven, vol. 1 (Minneapolis, 1956), pp. 239–252.

Chapter 9. Metaphysical Freedom

1. The bearing of theological concerns on the subject of free will can be seen in the famous debate between Erasmus and Martin Luther. Excerpts from this debate are printed in J. B. Ross and M. M. McLaughlin, eds., *Renaissance Reader* (New York, 1953), pp. 667–703.

2. I have known this limerick for more than twenty years; I think I learned it from Bertrand Russell, but I cannot locate the source.

3. See Lucretius, *De Rerum Natura*, trans. W. H. D. Rouse (Cambridge, Mass.), pp. 115–19.

4. Sir Arthur Eddington, *The Nature of the Physical World* (London, 1928).

5. See Roderick Chisholm, "Freedom and Action," in *Freedom and Determinism*, ed. Keith Lehrer (New York, 1966), pp. 11–14.

6. Aristotle, *Physics*, 256a, 4–12; in *Aristotle: Selections*, trans. Philip Wheelwright (Indianapolis, 1935), p. 57.

7. See my *Reason and Action* (Dordrecht, Holland, 1978), pp. 1–4.

8. See Aristotle, *Nichomachean Ethics*, 1147a, 25.

9. See pp. 194–196 below.

10. See my *Reason and Action*, pp. 64, 74–84.

11. I cannot find the source for this anecdote.

12. Immanuel Kant, *Groundwork of the Metaphysics of Morals*, trans. H. J. Paton (New York, 1964), ch. 3. I discuss Kant's conception of metaphysical freedom in my book *Kant's Theory of Morals* (Princeton, 1980), ch. 3.

13. David Hume, *A Treatise of Human Nature*, ed. L. A. Selby-Bigge (Oxford, 1888), p. 407.

14. Thomas Hobbes, *De Homine*, trans. Charles T. Wood, T. S. Scott-Craig, and Bernard Gert, in *Man and Citizen*, ed. Bernard Gert (Garden City, N.Y., 1972), p. 46.

15. See G. E. Moore, *Ethics* (London, 1912), ch. 6.

16. According to Harry Frankfort, "Alternative Possibilities and Moral Responsibility," *Journal of Philosophy* 23 (1969): 829–39, this sort of thought-experiment was first conceived by Robert Nozick.

17. John Locke, *An Essay Concerning Human Understanding*, ed. A. C. Fraser, vol. 1 (Oxford, 1894), p. 317.

18. This appears to be the view of Roderick Chisholm in *Person and Object* (London, 1976), pp. 56–57.

19. David Hume, *Enquiry Concerning the Human Understanding*, sec. 8, pt. 2, par. 80; in *Enquiries Concerning the Human Understanding and Concerning the Principles of Morals*, ed. L. A. Selby-Bigge, 2d ed. (Oxford, 1902). See also P. F. Strawson, "Freedom and Resentment," in Strawson, ed., *Studies in the Philosophy of Thought and Action* (London, 1968), pp. 71–96.

20. Hobbes, *De Homine, Man and Citizen*, p. 46.

21. F. H. Bradley, *Appearance and Reality*, 2d ed. (Oxford, 1897), p. xiv.

22. See Jean Paul Sartre, *Being and Nothingness*, trans. Hazel Barnes (New York, 1956), pp. 433–556.

23. R. G. Collingwood, *An Essay in Metaphysics* (Oxford, 1940), p. 296.

24. Aristotle, *Nichomachean Ethics*, 1110a, 18; translation from *Nichomachean Ethics*, trans. Martin Ostwald (Indianapolis, 1962), p. 53.

25. Benedict Spinoza, "Of Human Bondage, or the Strength of the Emotions," in *Ethics*, trans. W. H. White (New York, 1949), pt. 4.

26. Aristotle, *Nichomachean Ethics*, 1111b; in Ostwald, p. 57.

27. See my *Reason and Action*, ch. 2.

REFERENCES

REFERENCES

Ackrill, J. R. *Aristotle the Philosopher*. Oxford, 1981.

Anscombe, G. E. M. "Before and After." In Anscombe, *Collected Papers*, vol. 2, pp. 180–95. Minneapolis, 1981.

Aristotle. *Aristotle Selections*. Edited by W. D. Ross, New York, 1927.

———. *Aristotle: Selections*. Translated by Philip Wheelwright. Indianapolis, 1935.

———. *Nichomachean Ethics*. Translated by Martin Ostwald. Indianapolis, 1962.

Armstrong, David. *Universals and Scientific Realism*. Vol. 1, *Nominalism and Realism*. Vol. 2, *A Theory of Universals*. Cambridge, Eng., 1978.

Augustine, Saint. *The Confessions*. Translated by Edward Pusey. New York, 1952.

Aune, Bruce. *Rationalism, Empiricism, and Pragmatism*. New York, 1970.

———. "On an Analytic-Synthetic Distinction." *American Philosophical Quarterly* 9 (1972): 235–42.

———. "Quine on Translation and Reference." *Philosophical Studies* 27 (1975): 221–36.

———. *Reason and Action*. Dordrecht, Holland, 1978.

———. *Kant's Theory of Morals*. Princeton, 1980.

Austin, J. L. *Sense and Sensibilia*. Oxford, 1963.

Ayer, A. J. "Phenomenalism." In Ayer, *Philosophical Essays*, pp. 125–66. London, 1954.

Belnap, Nuel, and J. Michael Dunn. "The Substitution Interpretation of Quantifiers." *Nous* 2 (1968): 177–85.

Benacerraf, Paul. "What Numbers Could Not Be." *Philosophical Review* 74 (1965): 47–73.

Berkeley, George. *Principles of Human Knowledge and Three Dialogues Between Hylas and Philonous*. In *The Empiricists*. Garden City, N.Y., n.d.

Bonevac, Daniel. *Reduction in the Abstract Sciences*. Indianapolis, 1982.

Bradley, F. H. *Appearance and Reality*. 2d ed. Oxford, 1897.

Butler, Joseph. *The Analogy of Religion*. London, 1736.

Carnap, Rudolf. *Meaning and Necessity*. 2d ed. Chicago, 1956.

———. "Meaning Postulates." In Carnap, *Meaning and Necessity* (1956), pp. 222–29.

———. *An Introduction to Symbolic Logic and Its Applications*. New York, 1958.

Chisholm, Roderick. "The Problem of Empiricism." *Journal of Philosophy* 40 (1948). Reprinted in *Meaning and Knowledge*, edited by Ernest Nagel and Richard B. Brandt, pp. 576–80. New York, 1965.

———. "Freedom and Action." In *Freedom and Determinism*, edited by Keith Lehrer, pp. 11–14. New York, 1966.

———. *Person and Object*. London, 1976.

Clark, Romane. "Concerning the Logic of Predicate Modifiers." *Nous* 4 (1970): 311–35.

Collingwood, R. G. *An Essay in Metaphysics*. Oxford, 1940.

Davidson, Donald. "Causal Relations." *Journal of Philosophy* 64 (1967); 691–703. Reprinted in Davidson, *Essays on Actions and Events* (1982), pp. 149–62.

———. "The Logical Form of Action Sentences." In *The Logic of Decision and Action*, edited by

Nicholas Rescher, pp. 81–95. Pittsburgh, 1967. Reprinted with replies to critics in Davidson, *Essays on Action and Events* (1982), pp. 105–48.

——. "Truth and Meaning." *Synthese* 17 (1967): 304–23. Reprinted in Davidson, *Inquiries into Truth and Interpretation* (1984), pp. 17–36.

——. "On Saying That." *Synthese* 19 (1968–69): 130–46. Reprinted in Davidson, *Inquiries into Truth and Interpretation* (1984), pp. 93–108.

——. "True to the Facts." *Journal of Philosophy* 66 (1969): 748–64. Reprinted in Davidson, *Inquiries into Truth and Interpretation* (1984), pp. 37–54.

——. "Radical Interpretation." *Dialectica* 27 (1973): 313–28. Reprinted in *Inquiries into Truth and Interpretation* (1984), pp. 125–40.

——. "Belief and the Basis of Meaning." *Synthese* 27 (1974): 309–23. Reprinted in *Inquiries into Truth and Interpretation* (1984), pp. 141–54.

——. "On the Very Idea of a Conceptual Scheme." *Proceedings and Addresses of the American Philosophical Association* 47 (1974). Reprinted in *Inquiries into Truth and Interpretation* (1984), pp. 183–98.

——. "Reply to Foster." In *Truth and Meaning*, edited by Gareth Evans and John McDowell. Oxford, 1976. Reprinted in *Inquiries into Truth and Interpretation* (1984), pp. 171–80.

——. *Essays on Actions and Events.* Oxford, 1982.

——. *Inquiries into Truth and Interpretation.* Oxford, 1984.

Descartes, René. *Philosophical Works of Descartes.* Edited by E. S. Haldane and G. T. R. Ross. Cambridge, England, 1911.

Donagan, Alan. "Metaphysical Realism." In *Universals and Particulars*, edited by Michael J. Loux, pp. 128–58. Garden City, N.Y., 1970.

Donnellan, Keith. "Speaker Reference, Descriptions, and Anaphora." In *Contemporary Perspectives in the Philosophy of Language*, edited by Peter French et al., pp. 28–44. Minneapolis, 1979.

Dummett, Michael. "What is a Theory of Meaning? (II)" In *Truth and Meaning*, edited by Gareth Evans and J. M. McDowell, pp. 67–137. Oxford, 1976.

——. "The Philosophical Basis of Intuitionistic Logic." In Dummett, *Truth and Other Enigmas*, pp. 215–47. Cambridge, Mass., 1978.

——. "Realism." *Synthese* 52 (1982):59.

Einstein, Albert. "On the Electrodynamics of Moving Bodies." *Annalen der Physik* 17 (1905): 891–93.

Ewing, A. C. *Idealism: A Critical Survey.* London, 1934.

Frankfort, Harry. "Alternative Possibilities and Moral Responsibility." *Journal of Philosophy* 23 (1969): 829–39.

Frege, Gottlob. *The Foundations of Arithmetic.* Translated by J. L. Austin. Oxford, 1950.

——. "On Sense and Reference." In *Translations from the Philosophical Writings of Gottlob Frege*, edited by Peter Geach and Max Black, pp. 56–78. Oxford, 1952.

Geach, Peter T. *Mental Acts.* London, 1957.

——. *Reference and Generality.* Ithaca, N.Y. 1962.

——. "Some Problems about Time." In Geach, *Logic Matters*, pp. 302–18. Oxford, 1972.

——. *Truth, Love, and Immortality: An Introduction to McTaggart's Philosophy.* Berkeley, 1979.

Glymour, Clark. *Theory and Evidence.* Princeton, 1980.

Goodman, Nelson. *Fact, Fiction, and Forecast.* 2d ed. Cambridge, Mass., 1965.

——. *Ways of Worldmaking.* Indianapolis, 1978.

Gribbin, John, and Jeremy Cherfas. *The Monkey Puzzle.* New York, 1983.

Gupta, Anil. "Truth and Paradox." *Journal of Philosophical Logic* 2 (1982): 1–60.

Hacking, Ian. *Representing and Intervening: Introductory Topics in the Philosophy of Natural Science.* Cambridge, Eng., 1983.

Hegel, G. W. F. *Phenomenology of Mind.* Translated by J. B. Baille. London, 1931.

Hellman, Geoffrey. "How to Gödel a Frege-Russell: Gödel's Incompleteness Theorems and Logicism." *Nous* 15 (1981); 451–68.

Hempel, Carl G. *Aspects of Scientific Explanation and Other Essays in the Philosophy of Science*. New York, 1965.

Hobbes, Thomas. *Elements of Philosophy. In The English Works of Thomas Hobbes*. Vol. 1. Edited by Sir W. Molesworth. London, 1839.

———. *De Corpore*. In *The English Works of Thomas Hobbes. Vol. 1. Edited by Sir W. Molesworth. London, 1939.*

———. *De Homine* In *Man and Citizen*. Edited by Charles T. Wood, T. S. Scott-Craig, and Bernard Gert. Garden City, N.Y., 1972.

Hughes, G. H. and M. J. Cresswell. *An Introduction to Modal Logic*. London, 1968.

Hume, David. *A Treatise of Human Nature*. Edited by L. A. Selby-Bigge. Oxford, 1888.

———. *Enquiry Concerning the Human Understanding*. In *Enquiries Concerning the Human Understanding and Concerning the Principles of Morals. 2d ed. Edited by L. A. Selby-Bigge. Oxford, 1902.*

Husserl, Edmund. *Ideas: General Introduction to Pure Phenomenology*. Translated by W. Boyce Gibson. New York, 1931.

Jubien, Michael. "Intensional Foundations of Mathematics." *Nous* 15 (1981): 513–29.

Judson, Horace Freeland. *The Eighth Day of Creation*. New York, 1979.

Kalish, Donald. "Semantics." In *The Encyclopedia of Philosophy, edited by Paul Edwards, vol. 7, pp. 351–52. New York, 1967.*

Kant, Immanuel. *Inaugural Dissertation and Other Writings on Space*, Translated by John Handyside. London, 1929.

———. *Critique of Pure Reason*. 2d ed. Translated by N. K. Smith. London, 1933.

———. *Groundwork of the Metaphysics of Morals*. Translated by H. J. Paton. New York, 1964.

Kaplan, David. "What Is Russell's Theory of Descriptions?" In *Bertrand Russell: A Collection of Critical Essays*, edited by D. F. Pears, pp. 227–44. Garden City, N.Y., 1972.

Kneale, William. *Probability and Induction*. Oxford, 1949.

Kripke, Saul. "Outline of a Theory of Truth." *Journal of Philosophy* 70 (1975): 690–716.

———. "Is There a Problem about Substitutional Quantification?" In *Truth and Meaning: Essays in Semantics*, edited by Gareth Evans and John McDowell, pp. 325–419. Oxford, 1976.

———. "Speaker's Reference and Semantic Reference." In *Contemporary Perspectives in the Philosophy of Language*, edited by Peter French et al. pp. 6–27. Minneapolis, 1979.

———. *Naming and Necessity*. Cambridge, Mass., 1980.

Leibniz, G. W. von. *The Leibniz-Clarke Correspondence*. Edited by H. G. Alexander. Manchester, 1956.

———. *The Monadology*. In *Leibniz: Discourse on Metaphysics, Correspondence with Arnauld, Monadology*, edited by George Montgomery, pp. 251–72. La Salle, Ill., 1979.

———. *New Essays on Human Understanding*. Edited by Peter Remnant and Jonathan Bennett. Cambridge, Eng., 1981.

Lewis, David. *Counterfactuals*. Oxford, 1973.

———. *Philosophical Papers*. Vol. 1. New York, 1983.

Locke, John. *An Essay Concerning Human Understanding*. Vol. 1, Edited by A. G. Fraser. Oxford, 1984.

Lucretius. *De Rerum Natura*. Translated by W. H. D. Rouse. Cambridge, Mass., 1974.

McKeon, Richard. *Selections from the Medieval Philosophers. Vol. 1. New York, 1929.*

Malebranche, Nicholas. *De la recherche de la verite*, bk. 3, pt. 2, ch. 1. English translation in *Philosophical Classics: Bacon to Kant*, edited by Walter Kaufman. Englewood Cliffs, N.J., 1961.

Mandelbaum, Maurice. *Philosophy, Science, and Sense Perception*. Baltimore, 1964.

Marx, Karl. "Theses on Feuerbach." In *Ludwig Feuerbach*. Edited by Friedrich Engels. New York, 1941.

Meehl, Paul E., and Wilfrid Sellars. "The Concept of Emergence." In *Minnesota Studies in the Philosophy of Science*, edited by Herbert Feigl and Michael Scriven, vol. 1, pp. 239–52. Minneapolis, 1956.

Mill, John Stuart. *Examination of Sir William Hamilton's Philosophy*. London, 1865. Reprinted in

British Empirical Philosophers, edited by A. J. Ayer and Raymond Winch, pp. 545-60. London, 1952.

Moore, G. E. *Ethics*. London, 1912.

——. "A Refutation of Idealism." In Moore, *Philosophical Studies*, pp. 1-30. London, 1922.

O'Connell, M. J. "Transubstantiation." In *Encyclopedia Brittanica*, vol. 22. Chicago, 1970.

Opdycke, John B. *Harper's English Grammar*. New York, 1965.

Passmore, John. *A Hundred Years of Philosophy*. 2d ed. Baltimore, 1966.

Paul, G. A. "Is There a Problem about Sense Data?" In *Logic and Language: First Series*, edited by A. G. N. Flew, pp. 101-16. Oxford, 1951.

Peirce, C. S. "Grounds of Validity of the Laws of Logic: Further Consequences of of Four Incapacities." In *Collected Papers of Charles Sanders Peirce*, edited by Charles Hartshorne and Paul Weiss, pp. 190-222. Cambridge, Mass., 1934.

——. "The Laws of Nature and Hume's Argument against Miracles." In *Charles S. Peirce: Selected Writings*, edited by Philip P. Wiener, pp. 289-321. New York, 1966.

——. "What Pragmatism Is." In Weiner, *Charles S. Peirce: Selected Writings* (1966), pp. 180-202.

Perry, John, ed. *Personal Identity*. Berkeley, 1975.

Plantinga, Alvin. *The Nature of Necessity*. Oxford, 1974.

Plato. *The Collected Dialogues of Plato*. Edited by Edith Hamilton and Huntington Cairns. New York, 1961.

Putnam, Hilary. "Mathematics without Foundations." In Putnam, *Mathematics, Matter, and Method*, pp. 43-59. Cambridge, Eng., 1975.

——. *Reason, Truth, and History*. Cambridge, Eng., 1981.

——. *Collected Papers*. Vol. 3. Cambridge, 1984.

Quine, W. V. O. *From a Logical Point of View*. Cambridge, Mass., 1953.

——. "On What There Is." In Quine, *From a Logical Point of View* (1953), pp. 1-19.

——. "Two Dogmas of Empiricism." In Quine, *From a Logical Point of View* (1953), pp. 20-46.

——. *Word and Object*. Cambridge, Mass., 1960.

——. *Ontological Relativity and Other Essays*. New York, 1969.

——. "Existence and Quantification." In Quine, *Ontological Relativity and Other Essays* (1969), pp. 91-113.

——. "Ontological Relativity." In Quine, *Ontological Relativity and Other Essays* (1969), pp. 26-68.

——. *Philosophy of Logic*. Englewood Cliffs, N.J., 1970.

Quine, W. V. O. and J. S. Ulian. *The Web of Belief*. 2d ed. New York, 1978.

Rescher, Nicholas. *The Coherence Theory of Truth*. Oxford, 1973.

Robinson, John M. *An Introduction to Early Greek Philosophy*. New York, 1968.

Rorty, Richard. *Philosophy and the Mirror of Nature*. Princeton, 1979.

Rosenberg, Jay. *One World and Our Knowledge of It*. Dordrecht, Holland, 1980.

Ross, J. B., and M. M. McLaughlin, eds. *Renaissance Reader*. New York, 1953.

Russell, Bertrand. *Problems of Philosophy*. London, 1912.

——. *Our Knowledge of the External World*. London, 1914.

——. *Introduction to Mathematical Philosophy*. London, 1919.

——. *Analysis of Matter*. London, 1927.

——. *A History of Western Philosophy*. New York, 1945.

——. *Human Knowledge: Its Scope and Limits*. London, 1948.

——. *Logic and Knowledge*. Edited by Robert C. Marsh. New York, 1956.

——. "On Denoting." In Marsh, *Logic and Knowledge* (1956), pp. 41-56.

——. "On Order in Time." In Marsh, *Logic and Knowledge* (1956), pp. 345-64.

——. "The Philosophy of Logical Atomism." In Marsh, *Logic and Knowledge* (1956), pp. 175-281.

——. "Mr Strawson on Referring." In Russell, *My Philosophical Development*, pp. 238-45. London, 1959.

Russell, Bertrand, and Alfred North Whitehead. *Principia Mathematica*. 3 vols. Cambridge, Eng., 1910–13.

Ryle, Gilbert. " 'If,' 'So,' and 'Because.' " In *Philosophical Analysis*, edited by Max Black, pp. 323–40. Ithaca, N.Y., 1950.

Salmon, Nathan U. *Reference and Essence*. Princeton, 1981.

Salmon, Wesley. *The Foundations of Scientific Inference*. Pittsburgh, 1967.

Sartre, Jean Paul. *Being and Nothingness*. Translated by Hazel Barnes. New York, 1956.

Schopenhauer, Arthur. *The Philosophy of Schopenhauer*. Edited by Irwin Edman. New York, 1928.

Sellars, Wilfrid. "Time and the World Order." In *Minnesota Studies in the Philosophy of Science*, edited by Herbert Feigl and Grover Maxwell, vol. 3. pp. 527–618. Minneapolis, 1962.

——. *Science, Perception, and Reality*. London, 1963.

——. "Naming and Saying." In Sellars, *Science, Perception, and Reality* (1963), pp. 225–46.

——. "Philosophy and the Scientific Image of Man." In Sellars, *Science, Perception, and Reality* (1963), pp. 1–40.

——. "Some Reflections on Language Games." In Sellars, *Science, Perception, and Reality* (1963), pp. 321–58.

——. "Truth and 'Correspondence'." In Sellars, *Science, Perception, and Reality* (1963), pp. 197–224.

——. *Science and Metaphysics*. New York, 1968.

——. *Naturalism and Ontology*. Reseda, Calif., 1979.

Sperry, R. W. "Forebrain Commissurotomy and Conscious Awareness." *Journal of Medicine and Philosophy* 2, no.2 (June 1977):102.

Spinoza, Baruch. *Ethics*. Translated by W. H. White. New York, 1949.

——. "Thoughts on Metaphysics." In *Earlier Philosophical Writings*, translated by Frank A. Hayes, pp. 1–40. Indianapolis, 1963.

Strawson, P. F. *Individuals*. London, 1959.

——. "Freedom and Resentment." In Strawson, ed., *Studies in the Philosophy of Thought and Action*, pp. 71–96. London, 1968.

Tarski, Alfred. "The Semantic Conception of Truth and the Foundations of Semantics." In *Readings in Philosophical Analysis, edited by Herbert Feigl and Wilfrid Sellars, pp. 52–84. New York, 1949.*

——. *"The Concept of Truth in Formalized Languages." In Logic, Semantics, and Metamathematics, 2d ed., edited by J. H. Woodger, pp. 152–278. Indianapolis, 1983.*

Thigpen, Corbet H., and Hervey M. Cleckley. *The Three Faces of Eve*. New York, 1951.

Walters, R. S. "Laws of Science and Lawlike Statements." In *The Encyclopedia of Philosophy*, edited by Paul Edwards, vol. 4, pp. 410–14. New York, 1967.

Whitehead, Alfred North. *The Concept of Nature*. London, 1920.

Wilson, Edward O. *On Human Nature*. Cambridge, Mass., 1978.

Wittgenstein, Ludwig. *Tractatus Logico-Philosophicus*. Translated by C. K. Ogden. London, 1922.

——. *Philosophical Investigations*. Translated by G. E. M. Anscombe. Oxford, 1953.

Van Frassen, Bas. *The Scientific Image*. Oxford, 1980.

INDEX

INDEX

Bruce Aune earned his doctorate in philosophy at the University of Minnesota in 1960, taught at Oberlin College and the University of Pittsburgh, and in 1966 became professor of philosophy at the University of Massachusetts at Amherst. In recent years, Aune has also served as a visiting professor at Smith, Amherst, and Mount Holyoke colleges and at the University of California, Riverside. He is the author of *Knowledge, Mind, and Nature* (1967), *Reason and Action* (1978), *Kant's Theory of Morals* (1980), and the textbook *Rationalism, Empiricism, and Pragmatism* (1970).